MANAGING INTERNATIONAL CRISES

Volumes published in this series:

1. THE EMERGING INTERNATIONAL ECONOMIC ORDER: Dynamic Processes, Constraints, and Opportunities (edited by Harold K. Jackobson and Dusan Sidjanski)

2. MANAGING INTERNATIONAL CRISES (edited by Daniel Frei)

Edited by
Daniel Frei

MANAGING INTERNATIONAL CRISES

Published in cooperation with the
International Political Science Association

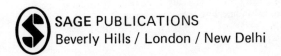

SAGE PUBLICATIONS
Beverly Hills / London / New Delhi

For information address:

SAGE Publications, Inc.
275 South Beverly Drive
Beverly Hills, California 90212

SAGE Publications India Pvt. Ltd.
C-236 Defence Colony
New Delhi 110 024, India

SAGE Publications Ltd
28 Banner Street
London EC1Y 8QE, England

Printed in the United States of America

Library of Congress Cataloging in Publication Data

Main entry under title:

Managing international crises.

(Advances in political science ; 2)
Essays based on papers presented at a Round Table on International Crises and Crisis Management, University of Zürich, in 1981.
"Published in cooperation with the International Political Science Association."
Resumés in French.
Bibliography: p.
Contents: Crisis decision-making, the information approach / Karl W. Deutsch—Managing international conflicts: evidence from field and laboratory experiments / Jean A. Laponce—Patterns of crisis thinking : an analysis of the governing circles in Germany, 1866-1914 / Vadim B. Lukov, Victor M. Sergeev—[etc.]
    1. International relations—Congresses. I. Frei, Daniel. II. Round Table on International Crises and Crisis Management (1981: University of Zürich) III. International Political Science Association.
JX1395.M276   1982   327.1'6   82-5880
ISBN 0-8039-1849-6

FIRST PRINTING

CONTENTS

Acknowledgments   7

From the Series Editor   9

Preface   11

  1. Crisis Decision-Making: The Information Approach
     KARL W. DEUTSCH   15

  2. Managing International Conflicts: Evidence From
     Field and Laboratory Experiments
     JEAN A. LAPONCE   29

  3. Patterns of Crisis Thinking: An Analysis of the
     Governing Circles in Germany, 1866-1914
     VADIM B. LUKOV
     VICTOR M. SERGEEV   47

  4. Communications and Crisis: A Preliminary Mapping
     JOHN MEISEL   61

  5. Improbable Events and Expectable Behavior
     RICHARD L. MERRITT   77

  6. The Middle East Crisis: Theoretical
     Propositions and Examples
     ALI E. HILLAL DESSOUKI   87

  7. Escalation: Assessing the Risk of Unintentional
     Nuclear War
     DANIEL FREI   97

8. Collective Security-Seeking Practices Since 1945
   HAYWARD R. ALKER, Jr.
   FRANK L. SHERMAN   113

9. The UN System: Structural Transformation and Crisis
   KINHIDE MUSHAKOJI   147

10. Nonaligned Countries in Conflict
    RADOVAN VUKADINOVIĆ   173

11. Systemic Crisis: Lessons of Regional Détente
    KARI MÖTTÖLÄ   185

12. Practical Suggestions for Crisis Management:
    An Inventory
    KING-YUH CHANG   199

13. Views from Diplomatic Practice
    ROBERTO de O. CAMPOS
    NIELS HANSEN   211

Abstracts/Résumés   217
Bibliography   227
About the Contributors   237

ACKNOWLEDGMENTS

The contributions published in this volume are based on papers submitted to a Round Table on "International Crises and Crisis Management" held at the University of Zurich, Switzerland, in 1981, under the auspices of the International Political Science Association (IPSA). The editor is most grateful to all participants to this Round Table for their manifold stimulating comments.

The Swiss Association of Humanities and Social Sciences, the University of Zurich, and the German Association for Peace and Conflict Research gave generous financial support for the Round Table.

When preparing this volume, the editor was kindly assisted by Mrs. Aurelia Boermans, Mr. Bruno Rosli, and Dr. Pierre Allan. He also wishes to thank Professor Richard L. Merritt, editor of *Advances in Political Science*, for having agreed to publish this volume in his series, and Sage Publications for their interest in making this book available to a larger audience of social scientists and diplomatic practitioners.

—Daniel Frei

FROM THE SERIES EDITOR

Advances in Political Science: An International Series reflects the aims and intellectual traditions of the International Political Science Association: the generation and dissemination of rigorous political inquiry free of any subdisciplinary or other orthodoxy. Along with its quarterly companion publication, the *International Political Science Review*, this series seeks to present the best work being done today (1) on the central and critical controversial themes of politics and/or (2) in new areas of inquiry where political scientists, alone or in conjunction with other scholars, are shaping innovative concepts and methodologies of political analysis.

Political science as an intellectual discipline has burgeoned in recent decades. With the enormous growth in the number of publications and papers, and their increasing sophistication, however, has also come a tendency toward parochialism along national, subdisciplinary, and other lines. It was to counteract these tendencies that political scientists from a handful of countries created the IPSA in 1949. Through round-tables organized by its research committees and study groups, at its triennial world congresses (the latest of which takes place in August 1982 in Rio de Janeiro), and through its organizational work, IPSA has sought to encourage the creation of both an international-minded science of politics and a body of scholars from many nations (now from more than 40 regional associations) who approach their research and interactions with other scholars from an international perspective.

Managing International Crises, edited by Daniel Frei, is the second volume in *Advances in Political Science: An International Series.* Like its predecessor, it represents well the intent of IPSA in creating the series: it comprises original papers of quality that focus in an integrated manner on a single important topic; and its authors, from various countries and social systems, take differing approaches to the central theme. Like most other volumes to be included in the series, it taps the vast intellectual resource of political scientists linked to the International Political Science Association.

—Richard L. Merritt

PREFACE

The past two decades of international relations research have experienced an unprecedented interest in the study of international crises. In this period, hundreds of books and articles have been published,[1] and in scholarly discussions it has become quite customary to identify several specific schools of thought around which the many-faceted efforts tend to cluster.[2] The problems of international crisis became a paramount focus of interest following the Cuban Missile Crisis of 1962, although the direct confrontation between the two major powers armed with nuclear overkill capabilities may fortunately constitute an exception rather than a typical pattern in contemporary international politics. Irrespective of the definition of a crisis (there are several elaborate and well-defined concepts), it seems obvious that the majority of crises which broke out in the past two decades are confrontations between secondary powers, in many cases serving, however, as proxies to major powers. At any rate, crises constitute a highly salient class of international events and continue to constitute, perhaps increasingly so, a cause for concern for both scholars and practitioners.

It is therefore not surprising to see that the eighties seem to indicate a renewed and more active interest in this subject due to the growing awareness that crisislike international confrontations may escalate into an uncontrolled war. The 1914 analogy has become a topical argument. The question is being asked whether there will be a second Sarajewo and whether the risks today do not increasingly resemble the years and months prior to the triggering of World War I (Kahler, 1979; Der Spiegel, 1980).

After twenty years of smooth crisis management, doubts are being raised as to the allegedly infinite capacity of modern diplomacy to cope with the increasing crises. It is argued that the successful record of two decades of crisis management may breed overconfidence and leave unnoticed the rapidly changing quality and quantity of crisis episodes.

Such reservations seem even more pertinent if one takes into account the trends underlying the average annual incidence of serious international disputes. The frequency of crises has risen more than fourfold between 1960 and 1976 (Cusack and Eberwein, 1980: 4). Projections of the probability of international disputes for the period 1982-2000 also lead to the conclusion that such disputes will continue to occur in the foreseeable future (Eberwein, 1981: 160-176).

On the other hand, scholars and practitioners all agree that for the time being there is virtually no alternative to crisis politics. As former U.S. Secretary of Defense Robert McNamara once stated: "There is no longer any such thing as strategy, only crisis management" (quoted in Segal, 1979: 35-51). Crisis management has become a way of life irrespective of its inherent risk of failure. It constitutes a major "style" of interaction in a world characterized by ideological rivalry, confrontation of major powers armed with nuclear weapons, and increasing regional and local unrest causing increasing instability.

Yet, apart from its present significance, crisis management reflects some deeply rooted properties of the contemporary international system. One main feature is the changing place of force as a political instrument. Facing the risks of escalation, governments in the nuclear age no longer use force or the threat of force in the same way as in the prenuclear age. This does not mean, as some optimists prematurely seemed to assume at the beginning of the nuclear era, that the force option in the conduct of external relations has simply been ruled out as a consequence of the risks of a nuclear holocaust. Nor does it mean that the use of force or the threat to use force has become less frequent in the nuclear age. On the contrary, the major powers are undertaking efforts to develop operative intervention capabilities and to give navies a new role in world politics. Hence, the use of force is obviously becoming increasingly "thinkable" again as it becomes more and more subtle and skillful. It is also more practicable than before. The Clausewitz paradigm of war as a continuation of politics by other means has become fashionable again, although plain "war" has now been replaced by the various techniques of exerting influence and pressure by a refined use of force which is typical for crisis politics in the foreseeable future.

Precisely this fact constitutes a source of uneasiness. The problem is that the states using force are still far from having adopted "rules of the game" or standardized patterns for signalling intentions and capabilities. Therefore, crisis politics implying the use of force necessarily contains an enormous amount of uncertainty. This in turn makes the system of interactions existing between the partners extremely vulnerable to all sorts of breakdowns in communication due to misinterpretation of signals and moves or simply to the inability of governments to convey intentions in a proper way. Additional risks are generated by the change of administrations. Often the new personnel responsible for the crisis decision-making are lacking proper experience and need time to get acquainted with the subtleties of crisis management. Furthermore, the international system has become increasingly complex due to the increasing number of states in the postcolonial era; many more actors are involved in international politics, thus creating a higher degree of incalculability and uncertainty. Also, the possibility must be envisaged that several crises may break out at the same moment. Such a "multi-crisis" would confront the governments concerned with a highly confusing and dangerous situation.

It is one of the major tasks of research on crises to contribute to a reduction in the degree of uncertainty produced in this context by offering insights into and evidence of the inner logic of crises and of the effects of moves made by states in a situation of crisis. Scholarly research has an important practical relevance by making the dynamics of crises more transparent. However, this is a very general aspect only, and more specific contributions are needed. The present volume offers some theoretical thoughts and empirical knowledge in this respect while at the same time developing some policy implications of academic research.

—Daniel Frei

NOTES

1. For an elaborate appraisal of the literature available up to 1978, see Tanter (1978: 340-374), Eberwein (1978: 126-142), and Klimkievicz (1978: 143-154).

2. At least three major schools of thought can be discerned:

(1) The Stanford Project on Crisis, Escalation, and War (main researcher: Prof. Robert C. North, Stanford University);
(2) The Crisis Management Program (main researcher: Prof. Jonathan Wilkenfeld, University of Maryland); and
(3) The International Crisis Behavior Project (main researcher: Prof. Michael Brecher, McGill University, Montreal, and Hebrew University, Jerusalem).

CHAPTER 1

CRISIS DECISION-MAKING

The Information Approach

KARL W. DEUTSCH

In many political science questions, one can often observe a succession of approaches. One first tries to find out what the different manifestations of a phenomenon had in common in different countries and in different times, so that one can establish the general categories of the phenomenon. One then gets a generation of scholars who point out what the differences are. These two approaches consist of stressing the commonalities and the differences.

Four Characteristics of International Crisis

I propose to speak here about what crisis management and crisis decision-making have in common. That does not mean that I pretend that all crises, such as those between England and France at Fashoda and between the United States and the Soviet Union after the October War in 1973, or the Cuba crisis of 1962, or the one in Bangladesh are the same. They obviously are not. Rather, I am stressing what features crisis decision-making has in common in different situations.

By a "crisis" I mean events that have four characteristics: First, they involve a major turning point, a parting of paths in the course of events so that there are strongly different outcomes possible. One may or may not wish to model these after the mathematics of René Thom and the so called "catastrophe theory." But whichever form of the encoding of events one chooses, there is a major difference as to what could happen. These different outcomes involve a wide range of radically different values, so that some outcomes are much more acceptable (or much less unacceptable) to some of the participants than others. The second characteristic is that some decision is inescapable. It *must* be made, since very different outcomes are at stake. Even not deciding in a crisis is making a decision. The third characteristic is that major values of at least one participant are at stake, and that means that strong emotions are likely to be involved. Fourth, I am not dealing with the question of a chronic crisis or an endemic crisis that might drag on over many years. I am speaking instead of a subtype of crisis, an acute crisis where a decision has to be made under time pressure.

Strong emotions imply that the importance of the matter at stake may often be overstated. When the Suez Canal was in dispute between Britain and Egypt in 1954, some British and American writers pointed out that the Suez canal represented "the jugular vein" of the British Empire. This turned out to be nonsense. When the canal was closed for several years, world trade went on; it was not a matter of life and death for England or anybody else. Similarly, when the French fought in Algeria after 1954, the French government tried to pretend that the oil of Algeria was utterly vital to France and that therefore Algeria had to remain French. However, it turned out that the Algerians were perfectly willing to sell their oil at the world price to the French even after they had become independent. Today, crises often involve a wild overrepresentation of the importance of the matters at stake by one or more of the governments concerned.

The Channel Approach

I propose to treat the decision problem in a crisis as a problem of information processing and to explore it with the help of two alternative models of communication processes. The first is a channel approach. Here we are interested in the transmission of messages, and we ask: How many messages can go through a channel? How many messages can be sent or received or otherwise processed in a given time?

In order to make an adequate decision, a certain amount of information is necessary. Without enough information, the likelihood of an adequate decision becomes very small. It would be an accident. We may take as an example a complex medical decision. In order to get a correct diagnosis, one usually needs a medical doctor and the results of a good many tests; one must know many things before one can really decide what has to be done.

Here is a manifest contradiction between the time pressure implicit in crisis decision-making and the information load necessary for making an adequate decision. The information load may clash with the limited channel capacities of the decision-making system, such as the government on one side or both, and with their limited time for a triple search for internal and external information. The decision-makers must search their own memories for relevant precedents. They must search for current domestic political information, and also for outside information from abroad.

We know, for instance, from a study of the American decision to intervene in Korea that of the fifty American officials awakened on June 25, 1950, a large number remembered immediately Japan's invasion of Manchuria in 1931, another group remembered the appeasement of Hitler, and not one of them remembered the sequence of escalations in 1914 that led to World War I. At the time of the Cuba crisis, John Kennedy made sure that at least some members of his staff had read *The Guns of August* by Barbara Tuchman so as to strengthen and refresh their memories of 1914. Time pressure produces *selective* memories, and the wider scanning or searching of memory can suffer a great deal. In addition to searching one's own memories or the memories of an organization, we are also looking for outside information. Again, under time pressure one may get much less relevant information from the outside than one needs.

In general, crises increase the motivation for information search but not the amount of potential search resources. Hence, we can formulate two hypotheses:

Hypothesis 1: So long as there are unused search capacities and resources available, a crisis is likely to increase the information flow and the quality of decisions.

Hypothesis 2: As soon as no further reserve resources are available, crises will tend to reduce information flow and to worsen the quality of decisions.

The latter situations are more frequent than the first. But there are cases as specified by Hypothesis 1 where a crisis might increase the efforts of a government to get relevant information. If they have the resources to assign to this task, their decisions might be better. But this is more likely to be the exception than the rule.

Typical dysfunctional decisions show signs of *information overload*. We know from laboratory experiments, as well as from case studies, the typical responses to information overload. Referring to the work of James Grier Miller, I would mention five typical responses. The first are simply delays. The matters to be decided have to queue up until somebody finally has time to decide. This is most impractical in an acute crisis because of time pressure, but it could happen, as it may have in the crisis of the Iranian Revolution in 1978 when the U.S. government was preoccupied with other matters. Or we may consider the way in which the Carter administration resolved the problem of food relief for Poland in November 1980; they were simply delaying the whole decision until February 1981 and handing it on to its successor, the Reagan administration. What was a crisis for the Poles apparently was less urgent for Washington.

The second response to information overload is skipping, namely, that one omits, more or less randomly, various items of information. For instance, under the pressure of preparing quickly a raid on Teheran to free the hostages, the raid was planned by the U.S. Navy and by an expert on jungle warfare in Vietnam, but obviously somebody skipped the item of information that in desert warfare, sand filters on engine intakes are useful. Hence, the sand filters were removed from the helicopters. There were probably other things omitted in the planning for this particular raid. It seems to have been a typical case of skipping, where some obvious technical problems were not considered.

The third response is error frequency, where outright errors are accepted. One example is the decision by President Nixon in 1970 to invade Cambodia in order to make an "incursion" to destroy the "headquarters of the Vietcong operation." The incursion was made, the place where the headquarters were supposed to be was duly occupied by the American forces, but the headquarters were not there. On the terms stated, this was a flatly erroneous decision.

The fourth response of overbusy governments is chunking and lumping different messages together under stereotypes, whereby they respond to facts by categorizing them into pretested routines. This is a method often used deliberately in emergencies. Irving Janis, in his book *Psychology,* reports how a person in acute danger of drowning off the West Coast of the United States in a region where the tides are tremendously powerful was saved because he had worked out in his own mind beforehand a routine of what to do in case the currents of the tide should become too strong for him. We have boat drills on ships and fire drills in schools for the same purpose. The difficulties and responses are pretested. Such standard procedures for emergency routines, however, are adequate only for the kinds of emergencies one has had in the past. They become less adequate the greater the element of novelty in the crisis. And in the crises of world politics, more and more novelty elements are appearing all the time. The routine response to Arab threats that Israeli military intelligence had worked out over the years, and which had been adequate in the sixties, turned out to be inadequate in 1973. One could no longer consider Arab military threats as empty or ineffective as had been the case earlier.

A fifth response to information overload is the assignment of priorities. One can decide what is most important, but these judgments are also fallible. In 1980, President Carter assigned very heavy priorities to the American prisoners in Iran (where his government could not get very far) and in effect a much lower priority to the ratification of the Strategic Arms Limitation Treaty (SALT II). Erroneous assignment of priorities is another form in which information overload of overbusy governments can reveal itself in the form of inadequate decisions.

Finally, there is inadequate feedback control. When making a decision, one gets some feedback from reality as one begins to carry it out. One finds that when one has a feedback control which is inadequate, subordinate officers tend to take the course of events away from the decision-maker. The classic example in American history is the Southern officer who fired on the Union flag at Fort Sumter in 1861 on the explicit ground, as he later said, that he feared that otherwise the politicians might contrive to make peace and so prevent the war between Southern and Northern states. He wanted to make history and he succeeded. The danger that anywhere, East and West, North and South, one might find officers of this type, is obvious. The other example is the case of the Cuba crisis when the Secretary of Defense, Mr. Robert McNamara, explicitly ordered that while the U.S. Navy should try to stop Soviet vessels approaching Cuba, no attempt should be made to board them. McNamara, perhaps knowing the Navy, then went down into the command room in the basement of the Pentagon and found that the admiral in charge had just sent out an order to board the Soviet vessels, in direct contravention of the order of his superior. This would have led directly to an incident if McNamara had not gone downstairs and found out about it quickly. But McNamara's reflexes were fast. Soon afterward, the admiral became ambassador to Portugal.

One example of where moderation was successful occurred in 1967 when the Johnson administration managed to handle the Pueblo incident against North Korea in such a way so as not to let the crisis escalate—which could have happened very easily. On another level, once the U.S. hostages in Iran had been given top priority, I should count President Carter's performance in the case of the unsuccessful American helicopter raid in Iran in the spring of 1980 on the plus side. President Carter insisted on controlling the effort to liberate the hostages at each stage and to be in touch with what was going on every hour. This may have taken an inordinate amount of his time and attention, but it meant that he could call off the entire operation as soon as it seemed to threaten to escalate into an uncontrollable conflict. Some of the American press said he should not have done it; he should have given the whole thing to a trustworthy general from the marines and ordered him to go ahead, at the risk of learning the consequences later. If one considers some of the things that could have happened, however, it was quite important that the top decision-makers of the government did not renounce control over the events and that they refused to take their foot off the brake.

The Role of Memory Information

There is a second approach to communication analyses: the memory approach. It is interpretive, or hermeneutic. It emphasizes the content in the interpretation of messages. Here one deals with memory information and the matching of incoming messages against certain subassemblies of information stored in and recalled from the memories of the sender and the receiver—memories which may be very different. The first question that is answered in this kind of analysis is that of the *code* or language in which a message is couched: Is it intelligible, and can it be deciphered? The second question deals with its *source*: Who is speaking? What kind of government, what kind of a source has sent the message? And what do we remember about this source?

The third question is that of the *context*: What is the message about? This includes the *intention* of the sender. Is one dealing with a maneuver intended to deceive? With a genuine leak? Into what kind of context is the message to be placed? Are we dealing with a "test of will"? Professor Dieter Senghaas and I were present at a war-game at the University College of the Armed Forces where teams of American officers were representing various countries. One team of American officers was representing Communist China and another was representing the United States. Under the assumptions of the game, Communist China was beginning to create incidents in the Himalayan mountains and at the Indian border. Professor Senghaas and I were observers, and as observers we walked into the "Chinese" situation room, saw the "Chinese" make their decisions, asked them: "Why are you doing this? What is your intention?" They said: "We are planning to show that one cannot keep China out of the United Nations; we would like to show that China must be treated with more consideration as an important country." We then walked across the corridor to the "American" room and asked the "American" team, who just had been notified of the Chinese move: "What is your interpretation of the Chinese move?" They said: "The Chinese are about to conquer India." If American officers from the same culture, with the same background, with identical military training, can misunderstand each other so grossly, one can imagine what could happen with a real American move versus a real Chinese move, or with the real Russians or the real Chinese.

The fourth question is *content*: What does the message actually say?

In addition, there are four dimensions that can be seen as parallel with four basic concepts of Freudian psychology. The first of these corresponds to the fifth question on our list: Is the message pleasant or painful? People have a tendency to dislike unpleasant messages. They also have a tendency to magnify pleasant messages. This *pleasure-pain* aspect (the pleasure principle or the id, as Freud would say) is quite important for the subsequent processing of the message by the receiver.

The second question of these four (our number six), quite distinct from the pleasantness of each message, is: Does it happen to be true? This corresponds to Freud's well-known *reality* principle.

The third "Freudian" question (our number seven) is the question of *morality* or the superego: Is what the message proposes moral or not? Again I must come back to the Cuba crisis. The great majority of the presidential task force in 1962 recommended a massive U.S. bomb-strike of the city of Havana. Secretary of Defense McNamara pointed out that this would cost at least 25,000 dead civilians in Havana. ("Civilians" is a polite expression for what are in the majority women, children, and old people.) John F. Kennedy refused to accept this course of action. The superego of the United States was still in working order, together with a piece of the reality principle.

But one must ask more generally: How effective is the representation of the superego? To what extent is there a common morality, even rudimentary, among the different nations of the world? By "morality" I mean the set of rules that tell us what to do when we do not have perfect information about the consequences of our actions. If we know exactly what our actions will lead to, we don't have to use too much of a moral argument. We know what the consequences are and we know what to do. Morality more or less tells us what to do when in doubt. Should an accused person be considered innocent unless proved guilty or considered guilty unless proved innocent? If in doubt, should one shoot first and ask questions afterward, or should one first ask questions and shoot—if necessary—later?

Fourth among these four (number eight on our list) we have the question of *self-image*: How will our own image of ourselves be affected by this message? For instance, the Iranian demand that the United States should apologize for their role in imposing the Shah on Iran in 1953 was felt by many Americans to be damaging to their self-image, their self-respect. From a cognitive point of view, this was a perfectly reasonable request. The American government agents who had engineered the 1953 coup had taken credit for it on American television. It was not a matter which they denied; they were proud of it, they said so at length, and they were not contradicted by the government. But to say it was wrong in 1980 was probably—perhaps for Freudian reasons of ego and ego strength—not acceptable to a very large number of Americans. And it is important in crisis situations to avoid demands that are perceived by the other side as humiliating.

Together with the first four cognitive questions about code, source, context, and content, these four more psychological questions add up to eight. A ninth question deals with the plans and *intentions of the receiving actor* or system—those parts of its program to which it is already committed but which have not yet been carried out: What difference to these would the message make if it were accepted?

Finally, there is the *pragmatic* aspect of a message: What is to be done about it? What actions does the message imply? Here again, time pressure and emotional tensions are apt to reduce the quantity and quality of information processing. Crucial messages may be misidentified, particularly intelligence reports. The more secretive governments are, the more dependent they become on their own intelligence agents who have claimed to penetrate the secrets of other countries. The more secrets there are between two countries, the more both governments become the prisoners of their intelligence services.

All ten questions imply vulnerabilities. Contexts may be misinterpreted and contents of messages misread. The id and ego aspects of the Freudian quartet will loom relatively larger, while the reality principle and the superego may be weakened. Pragmatics may be erroneous. In the Bay of Pigs crisis of 1961, for instance, the effect that one thought could be accomplished proved to be in error. Similar general problems, vulnerabilities in decision-making, and risks of misjudgment exist on the Soviet side. In the "Prague Spring" of 1968, the Dubcek government was probably much less of a clear and present danger to the Soviet Union than it was perceived to be in Moscow at the time. The cost of Soviet armed intervention in Afghanistan from 1979 onward has been almost certainly higher and the gains smaller than the Soviet leaders expected. More recent spectacular errors were Iraq's attack on Iran in 1980, and Argentina's attempt to occupy the Falkland Islands in 1982.

Large and Small Systems

It is perhaps useful at this point to recall that there are many differences among countries. One country might feel that a conflict-free solution is more important, whereas another country might feel that it can afford to escalate the conflict. That happens at two ends of a scale: The very powerful countries might think that they can afford to escalate the conflict because they feel sure to win. This will become rare in the future. If large countries tried to decide disputes in their favor by brute force, they would create an irresistible pressure to escalate the proliferation of nuclear weapons. In the nineteenth century, the Colt revolver was called the "equalizer" because the big fellow simply became a bigger target. Today nuclear weapons have made small countries unassailable without prohibitive costs for the aggressor. It would seem that the nonproliferation technique depends in part on the studious restraint of the big powers. Otherwise, nonproliferation will become untenable.

At the other end of the scale are countries that feel they have nothing or almost nothing to lose. They may have an objective interest in escalating a conflict in the hope that the cost of a concession to them will be less to the privileged countries than the cost of conflict escalation. Anatol Rapoport and his collaborators have worked out a mathematical game of this type, and it can be mathematically demonstrated that there are situations where it is rational for the underdog to increase the costs of conflict, including even the costs to the underdog himself. In such situations, an escalation of conflict is likely to result.

Finally, we will have differences in the interest in conflict outcomes within countries. Some groups—I cannot say classes, because there are subgroups within social classes—stand to gain more from crises and crisis decisions than do others. Even the richest capitalist usually has a wife and children, and they are no more resistant to radiation than anybody else. Members of the Chamber of Commerce of Hiroshima may have died side by side with the city's unskilled laborers. What Marx, in the Communisto Manifesto, had called the "common perdition of the contending classes" was demonstrated in Japan. On the other hand, there are groups for whom the particular concerns of economics, or class, or ideology, or power are so salient, or who have managed to convince themselves of some life-lie, some saving belief, that what they wish to do can be done at only tolerable risk. They will push for an increase in confrontation and thus increase its risk.

If we believe that no first strike with nuclear weapons can ever be successful, and if we believe that second-strike capacities will be large enough to make any nuclear attack suicidal, we deprive the military profession of a good part of its meaning and existence. Either the military would then have to rethink its own role, or it must convince its members again and again that a first strike is feasible. In this sense, the belief in a first-strike capacity in nuclear warfare plays a role similar to the life-lie for Hjalmar Ekdal in Ibsen's play, "The Wild Duck." It is quite reasonable to predict, therefore, that we shall have first-strike theories every few years, again and again, not because any new reality of physics makes them more plausible or more realistic, but because certain professions and certain sociological milieus will reproduce them spontaneously as an aid to continuing in their cultural and sociological patterns. Groups that have an interest in tension maintenance and crisis enhancement will be with us for many years to come in all countries and in all social systems, and some of their illusions may survive among them.

If these considerations hold, certain inferences follow. The larger and more pressing the problems of a political system, and the smaller its capacities for information search and processing, the more inferior will be its crisis decisions in comparison to its needs for adaptation and survival. Second, the larger such system capacities are, the more adequately and creatively such systems will tend to respond to crisis situations. Third, in most cases capacities will be limited in the short run. There, crisis decisions will most likely be dysfunctional, particularly in foreign policy, for leaders and interest groups pressing for a confrontation crisis will most often represent some action of another nation as a clear and present danger to their own societies. They themselves, therefore, will become one of the most acute dangers to their own societies.

Practical Conclusions

(1) Crises are search operations. It is important to gain time in crisis situations and to increase nonescalatory options as much as possible. It is important to think of a crisis situation not primarily as a question of who prevails but of how not to impose on either side an outcome unacceptable to it, and how to search for a set of possible outcomes acceptable to both.

(2) Second, it is important to disengage emotions and to be careful about threats, direct or indirect. We know from psychological research that the more tired, the more angry, the more frightened people are, the more their decision-making capacity deteriorates. It is typical that a great deal of the deterrence and threat research carried out by the Armed Forces in the United States completely ignored these psychological aspects.

(3) Third, it is important not to overstate the importance of the stakes at dispute. Wars are likely to be the worst threat to the existence of a state, more costly than almost anything at the center of a dispute between two states.

In a crisis situation, it might be important to keep public discussion of the elements of a dispute to a moderate level. A practical way of doing this would be an international agreement, or even an informal agreement, granting the freedom to whisper but not the freedom to shout. Let us assume that Egypt and Israel were once again disputing over an oasis somewhere in the desert, such as years ago regarding the Oasis El Arish, which was then considered to be very important. One could mention such a dispute, but not on the first page, not in headlines larger than 1/4 inch, and not in more space than one column. One might simply agree to place the news so as to keep matters in dispute out of the lead bulletins of the electronic media (radio and television) in order not to inflame public opinion. In English law, there is a rule that the matter before a judge may not be discussed publicly. Both sides might come to an international agreement that what matters in an acute dispute with a foreign country should not be discussed publicly in any prominent way. Such a noninflammation treaty would be the exact opposite of either government trying to drum up passionate patriotic support for its own position.

Perhaps it is too early yet to think of such measures, but they will become inevitable in the future. Inflaming public opinion to the extreme on a matter of international dispute could, in the end, invite a preventive strike from the other side, if that side concludes that the government has inflamed its own public opinion to the point where they will have to go to war sooner or later. For in such a case the question is no longer whether a war will take place, but only *when* it will start, and then the argument for first strike becomes very strong on both sides. The risks of inflaming public opinion are incomparably greater than they used to be, and we must therefore think about ways of keeping this inflammation down.

Let us consider medicine once again. A doctor is not supposed to operate on members of his own family, not because he would not care for them, but because it is known that precisely *because* he cares for them, his judgment cannot be trusted. Where the lives not of individuals but of millions are at stake, we must try to create conditions where the judgment of statesmen becomes somewhat more trustworthy than it has been so far.

Does it Help to Seek Culprits in a Crisis?

My impression is that the major crises in our world today and in the years to come will not be crises of instigation but rather of cumulation. When a glacier moves very slowly to the edge of a cliff in Greenland, the moment comes where the weight of the overhanging ice becomes greater than the cohesion of the ice in the glacier. The iceberg then breaks off with a thunderous crack and floats away. To ask who was the instigator of the break in the glacier would be beside the point. What happened was that the cumulative movement of the glacier went beyond the limits for cohesion of the glacier and the ice broke apart.

I think that we in politics today operate very much in the area of the primitive religions with regard to natural science. When there was thunder or lightning, one asked which god or which devil produced it; animism tried to explain processes in terms of personalized actors. Thus, in the Great Depression of 1932 one wondered who had produced it. Ideologies varied—it was either the Jews or the Bolsheviks or Wall Street bankers—but it was certain that one looked for instigators of the great crisis in the manner of the old animistic religions.

If one looks objectively at the situation of the two superpowers, one can demonstrate that in the last twenty years they have both been losing influence. We could probably compose a sizable list of Third World countries where the United States has lost influence. In 1960, France was a member of NATO; France is not a member of NATO today. In

1960, the situation in Nicaragua was different from what it is now. Also, the Soviet Union's relations with China in 1960 were better than they are today, its influence in Indonesia of Sukarno was greater, and its influence in Egypt was greater. We find that the great superpowers have been steadily losing influence in politics and that their share in the gross national product of the world has been steadily declining. From approximately 55 to 60 percent in 1946, it has gone down to about 49 percent in 1962, and it is now down to about 33 percent (23 percent America, 10 percent Soviet Union). It has been a steady decline, not because some wicked conspirators have sabotaged the American or the Soviet economy, but because the Japanese have been growing faster, the Western Europeans have more or less repaired their damages from World War II, and the Third World has begun to grow and develop, so that the two superpowers are not nearly as "super" as they used to be.

But what counts in the short run are perceptions. The American perception is that every setback to American power must have been caused by the wicked machinations of the Soviet Union, and there may be people in Moscow who think that everytime something goes wrong with Soviet policy, e.g., if Afghan tribesmen oppose the revolutionary government in Kabul, one may assume that their rebellion was mainly created by the United States. To be sure, all superpowers maintain intelligence services and all sorts of clandestine operations, and they all try to cook their soups at the fires that break out in various parts of the world, trying to take advantage of them. But this does not mean that they are creating these situations.

We can forecast an increase in cumulative crises—economic, social, political and cultural—and an increasing temptation of the superpowers to blame it on each other. But if we persist in this political animism, we may end up in an outbreak of collective madness on both sides. Nixon once said that the United States must not tolerate being "nibbled to death" by what he then considered a communist conspiracy. One can imagine very similar moods surfacing on the other side.

We cannot return to normality. We sometimes tend to assume that if crises were instigated, or if they were caused externally, then having coped with them we can go "back to normal," as one does after a traffic accident when the emergency service of the hospital has dealt with the victims. But the world situation will never again be as good or bad—depending on one's values—as it was ten or twenty years ago. We cannot step twice into the same river of history. The cumulative changes will demand from us a new definition of normality. What was normal in

1910 was not normal in 1928, not normal in 1940, not normal in 1981. We will have very different conceptions of normality in the future.

This also means that we will have to ask that the apparent crises should be distinguished from the underlying ones. A seeming crisis can grow very easily from the fact that the Western world depends on imported oil to a large extent, so that anytime some of the ramshackle, social institutions of Near Eastern monarchies totter, we risk getting less oil, and we therefore develop a touchy solicitude for the political stability of Near Eastern countries. We don't really care how many children die there, or about the poverty and child mortality among their common people, but we greatly care that the oil keeps flowing. If the Near Eastern population should have different priorities and different ideologies—Islam or whatever—we are very pained and surprised at this. We might have to ask what the real threats to national security are in different parts of the world.

A Great Crisis To Come

Some of the work that we have done at the Berlin Science Center in our world models suggests that the major threats to national security of all countries will stem from the steady growth of world population and the consequent steady demand for increased food production. In about 2022 or 2032 (50 years from now), we will have twice as many people in the world as now, and we will therefore need to produce twice as much food on fairly much the same number of acres as we have today. The planet will not get bigger, and most of the good farmland is already being tilled. This vast coming crisis will demand intensification of agriculture, and this means more water, more fertilizer, more energy, and more public and/or private capital investment.

This is probably the most important change humanity has ever had to face in its history. In some ways, the crises that are coming are likely to be the most severe since the ice age, which was only survived with the help of such useful discoveries as fire. This time we may have a need within the next few decades for combining several major social improvements and technological improvements to help us to survive. In sum, we have to ask not only how to deal with current crises which emerge on the surface, but how to deal in time with the great tides of human development that are carrying us to a much more serious crisis than anything we have seen so far.

CHAPTER 2

MANAGING INTERNATIONAL CONFLICTS
Evidence from Field and Laboratory Experiments

JEAN A. LAPONCE

It would be unreasonable to assume that all conflicts can or should be managed, whether the object of the conflict is to dominate, assimilate, or exclude (Darwin, 1936; Movikow, 1893; Simmel, 1908/1955; Rapoport, 1974a); but assuming that a conflict, or more specifically an international conflict, is not essentially structural, assuming further that the conflict is manageable within an existing structure, and assuming further that the conflict should be managed rather than left to run its own course, what experimental evidence is there that could guide the actions of politicians, diplomats, and other conflict management practitioners, as well as help the analyst determine the conditions of what Coleman (1957) calls the Gresham law of conflicts, the conditions resulting in the harmful and dangerous elements in a conflict driving out those that would have kept the conflict within bounds?

Less than a generation ago, the experimental evidence that one could muster in support of any interpretation of social behavior was so limited that the experimental social scientist was typically left pleading for more research. That evidence has now become so abundant—the sole prisoner's dilemma game has been used in hundreds of experiments (Rapoport, 1974b)—that one wonders why that evidence is not used more often by political science in its analysis of international conflicts. I have suggested elsewhere that the reason for this failure rests in too constraining a definition of what constitutes the real world (Laponce and Smoker, 1972; Laponce, 1981). Because of that constraint, the political scientist is more likely to use multivariable simulations than parsimonious experiments.[1] I shall depart again from that common course.

What Kind of Experiment? What Kind of "Real" World?

Typically, when we reduce our data to manageable proportions, we proceed either from the whole or from the specific, either from the total landscape or from a given crossroad; our research strategies tend to be shaped either by the image of the box or by that of the cross. The box type of research consists in identifying an event or an institution—NATO or World War I—and then looking into that event or institution for things of interest. The crosstype of research proceeds from a fascination with observed or hypothetical encounters between or among variables: power and aggression, rationality and coalition formation, for example. To put it graphically—since images are more suggestive and better remembered than words—research proceeds usually from either of two major archetypes, (a) or (b):

Applied to the understanding of an international crisis, the (a) strategy leads us from the study of history to the staging of simulations that seek to recreate actors, relationships, and contexts. Whether we give nations and actors real or abstract names, whether we call them Russia or Algo, military commander or Ludendorff, the main purpose of such simulation-theatre is not to establish universal relationships among actors and events, but rather to suggest new historical interpretations, to bring to the fore previously hidden connections.

The (b) strategy, that which dominates in psychology, that expressed in the archetype of the cross, leads more naturally and more frequently to the laboratory and to the use of controlled experiments, because it gives less attention to context. Sometimes it so ignores that context as to focus exclusively on an interaction. Coalition formation or aggression in a laboratory is then seen as being as real as coalition formation or aggression in a parliament or on a battlefield. For the sake of scientific economy, one downgrades the notion of a "real" world (Davies, 1980;

Laponce, 1966, 1981); one argues that subjects do not cease to be real people for having been put behind a one-way mirror or asked to play a game. It follows then that if two variables (stress and aggression, for example) meet in the laboratory at time 2 as they had met in history at time 1, one is justified in comparing the first to the second event and may use both to predict the future. The problem of extrapolating from the laboratory to history is thought to be of the same nature as extrapolating from one laboratory event to another laboratory event, or from one historical event to another historical event.[2]

I have argued elsewhere that political scientists proceed too often from the archetype of the box and that psychologists do not pay enough attention to context (Laponce, 1981). I shall, in this chapter, side—at the risk of sinning—with psychology; I shall be of the cross, downgrading if not ignoring altogether the familiar distinction between the laboratory and the so-called "real world." Some of my examples will come from international simulations, but most will be provided by small group experiments not designed to model interstate relations. My choice of examples will be guided by the similarity of the variables under observation rather than by the similarity of the contexts of their interactions.

LABORATORY EVIDENCE

Political science is too frequently defined as the study of agonistic behavior, too often said to be concerned primarily with the authoritative allocation of values. I prefer to conceive of it as the study of communication, cooperation, competition, and conflict arising from the making, the maintaining, and the unmaking of human hierarchies (CCCCMMUHH); hence my reviewing selected experiments relevant to the management of international crises under the four headings of *communication, cooperation, competition,* and *conflict.*[3]

Communication

THE CAPPELLO EXPERIMENT

Cappello (1972) asked his subjects (Mexican students) to play a standard version of the Inter-Nation Simulation derived by Crow and Raser from Guetzhow et al.'s (1963) basic model. Suffice it to say that seven groups of decision-makers representing seven nations were asked to react to an artificially created crisis arising from internal conflicts within one of the seven "nations." As is usual in such simulations, each "nation" communicated with the others exclusively through formal written messages. The subjects were assigned randomly to either of two experimental conditions. In the first, the nations could exchange as many messages as they wished; in the second, the number of messages was severely restricted. Cappello found that the two groups differed significantly both in their perceptions and in their behavior. The group under restricted communication indicated a much higher level of perceived hostility on the part of others and was far more likely to engage in aggressive behavior. Indeed, all military attacks came from the restricted communication group. The experiment shows that an imposed reduction in the level of desired communication among opponents raises the level of perceived and of actual hostility.

ADDITIONAL EVIDENCE—THE PRISONER'S DILEMMA

The games and experiments using the prisoner's dilemma (PDG) show that lack of communication prevents the players from settling on the solution most advantageous to them (Rapoport and Chammah, 1965). Consider the following typical matrix:

	A2	B2
A1	3,3	1,4
B1	4,1	2,2

If player 1 selects his strategies in the rows and player 2 in the columns, and if the first entry in each cell represents the payoffs of player 1, while the second identifies the payoffs of the second player, the game, as predicted by the theory, will, in the absence of communication, result in a B1 B2 outcome, although A1 A2 would have been preferable.

Of the many experiments that have used this or other versions of the prisoner's dilemma, one most particularly relevant to our subject appears in an early experiment by Rapoport and his colleague, an experiment intended to study the effects of sleeplessness. A key variable (key to the study of the effects of communication) happened to be introduced unwittingly into that experiment. The subjects—who had to play the PDG for about eight hours—had been allowed to have a cup of coffee after four hours.[4] They sat at the same table during the break but were not allowed to exchange information about the game (the coffee break was monitored for compliance to the restriction). The experimenters found to their surprise that the games which had been conflictual during the first four hours became collaborative after the cup of coffee. Apparently, the very limited amount of communication allowed to the players had been enough to shift their behavior from selfishness and distrust to cooperation, enough to shift them from what Rapoport calls individual to collective rationality.[5] Similarly, in a truck experiment that will be described in a subsequent section of this chapter, Morton Deutsch (1973) found that two equally powerful players could not be shifted from nonrewarding conflict to rewarding cooperation by being allowed to communicate at the time of the conflict, but that they could be so shifted by being allowed to communicate before the game, even when the communication was in the form of small talk unrelated to the game and the choice of a strategy.[6] In international relations, the equivalent of Rapoport's cup of coffee is found in the communications unrelated to the conflict that precede and surround that conflict; for example, cultural communication at a time of political isolation (Schelling, 1960).

QUALIFYING EVIDENCE

It should not be assumed, however, that increasing the amount of communication will always lead to tension reduction. Two qualifying factors need be taken into consideration. The first is called by Karl Deutsch (1966) the covariance effect, the second is commonly named "overload."

The covariance effect refers to various combinations of the positive and/or negative effects of contact on those who communicate. If the effect is negative on one or both of two communicators, increasing contact may well increase tension. The Swiss solution to ethnic tensions—reducing contact—offers the simplest solution. But finding that a particular channel of communication is or has become conflictual does not argue against keeping communication open; it argues for closure of the conflictual channel *and* the use of an alternative. If direct contact among heads of state is conflictual, one might prefer contact through ambassadors and, should contact through ambassadors and the bureaucracies to which they report result in negative covariance, one might then prefer contact through economic, social, or cultural rather than through political channels. And, if all direct communications prove to have negative effects, there remains the possibility of contact through third parties.[7] Considering that it is difficult, if not impossible, to forecast before a crisis what channels of communication might become conflictual, one should seek protection against channel closure by maintaining diverse types of communication with a potential opponent—not only diverse political channels but diverse economic, social, and cultural channels as well. In so doing, plural, as distinct from monolithic, societies are at an advantage. Pluralism protects against contamination of one channel by another. Throughout the Algerian war of independence, France maintained very good contact with the "rebels" largely because of her divided polity. The maintenance of such contact facilitated the reestablishment of normal relations after independence.

The second factor to be considered as a qualifier to Cappello's findings is best shown in the experiments reviewed and analyzed by Schroeder et al. (1967), experiments showing that in tactical games of the INS variety, the amount of information received by the players has a **nonlinear relationship to desirable outcomes**. At high as well as low levels of information, the players experienced a decrease in the ability to integrate decisions, a decline in the complexity of these decisions, and a decline in the search for new information. Generally, they were characterized—if compared to those with a medium level of information—by a tendency to make stereotypic decisions when nuances and qualifications were required. The experiments showed a clear curvilinear relationship between quantity of information and quality of information processing. Herman (1976), Holsti (1972), and Suedfeld and Tetlock (1977) have also shown by means of content analysis that the tendency to stereotype, to turn continuums into polarities, and to lose the ability to differentiate and discriminate, is related to stress; typically it characterizes the perceptions of decision-makers before international wars or revolutions. Thus, stereotyping that prevents or hinders conflict management may come from too much as well as from too little information. If Cappello had forced his subjects to receive more information than the optimum, he might have obtained the same results as those born from reduced communication.[8] The danger that there is too much communication among opponents is, however, more theoretical than real. Holsti (1965) and Janis (1972) both noted that prior to the outbreak of World War I, the overload of the channels of communications of the decision-makers they studied resulted from increased communication with one's allies rather than with one's opponents.

Thus, within the boundaries of the covariance and the overload effect, the evidence from Cappello's experiment still stands, and that evidence supports Richelieu's advice to the king: Always negotiate something with every nation.[9] Negotiating (in the political, the business, the social, and the cultural fields) is a means of keeping open the channels of communication.

We have compilations of treaties and contracts. How useful it would be to have worldwide statistics on negotiating densities. How useful it would be to the analysts of international relations to have measures of the intensity of ongoing negotiations. How many man hours per week do the Soviet Union, Poland, the United States, and Canada spend negotiating something with each of the others, and in what field of activity (military, cultural, political, economic)? We would likely find that what Karl Deutsch et al. (1966) call "security communities" are characterized by high negotiating densities in a wide variety of subfields. These societies have many wide open channels of communications, hence almost instantaneous information on one another. Furthermore, they use these channels not only to become informed but to cooperate.

Cooperation

The effects of cooperation will be illustrated by two classic experiments: the Western Electric (Roethlisberger and Dickson, 1939) and the Robber's Cave (Sherif et al., 1961).

The Western Electric Experiment. A team of sociologists was asked by the Western Electric Company to test various ways of improving output at their plant. The group of workers selected for the experiment was separated from its coworkers and submitted to a variety of environmental conditions that were either better or worse than those maintained constant in the rest of the factory (better or worse lighting, and so forth). The experimenters found to their surprise that under adverse as well as under favorable conditions, the output of the experimental group was superior to that of the rest of the factory. The knowledge of participating in an experiment had transformed a set of previously isolated individuals into a community linked by a common collective status and a common task. The experimenters concluded that the level of cooperation and the level of work were positively related. Increasing the level of cooperation increases the level of work; increasing the level of teamwork (within acceptable limits) increases the level of cooperation.

The Sherif Experiment. The experiment conducted by Sherif et al. at Robber's Cave leads to similar conclusions and emphasizes the importance of success as well as the distinctiveness between cooperation and competition.

Sherif and his assistants observed over a period of days the behavior of two groups of young boys left purposely leaderless on what they thought was a normal summer camp holiday. Artificially, the experimenters created tension between the two groups by arranging for one group to cross the territory that the other had staked out for itself. This caused the group boundaries to become more firmly established; each group gave itself a name, a flag, and a more clearly established hierarchy. After a few days, each group behaved as if it were a nation. The experimenters then brought the two groups together under the same roof, made them eat in the same room and compete at similar games. Neither the sleeping, the eating, nor the playing together could break the group boundaries, nor could it lower significantly the dislike flowing across those boundaries. Success in lowering tension was achieved only toward the end of the holiday-experiment when the boys were faced with a common problem (pulling and pushing out of a faked breakdown the truck that was taking all of them to the cinema)—a problem that could only be resolved by the two teams joining forces. Cooperation succeeded where competition and neutral communication had failed.

The Western Electric and Robber's Cave findings, that the total productivity of interdependent units, individuals or groups, is greater when the structure of the game is cooperative than when it is conflictual, are supported by many other experiments, particularly those of Back (1951), Berkowitz (1957), Deutsch (1973), Gerard (1953), Gotthelf (1955), Grossack (1954), Mintz (1951), Mizuhara and Tamai (1952), Raven and Eachus (1963), Thomas (1957), and Workie (1967). The lower performance resulting from a conflictual relationship is due in part to the tendency to overvalue the opinions and recommendations originating within one's own group and to disregard or devalue those of the outgroup (Blake and Mouton, 1962a, 1962b). Adherence to a losing strategy appears more frequent in social than in individual games, probably because of the fear of losing face (Rubin et al., 1980).

Richelieu's statement needs to be completed. It is not sufficient to negotiate; it is essential that the negotiation results in cooperation and success, or at least partial success.

Competition

Useful as it is to distinguish them in theory, competition and conflict are not easy to separate in fact. In its pure state, competition seeks to establish an order among competitors, while conflict, in its extreme form, seeks to eliminate an opponent; but the two typically get mixed at the level of tactics and strategy.

The experimental evidence on competition is large but unfocused. That most relevant to international relations deals with coalition formation. Consider a simple experiment I carried out among schoolchildren and university students in Canada and the United States on the effects of perceived unbalance (Laponce, 1966). I wanted to determine how selected groups of subjects react to variations in the magnitude of the gap separating two competitors. In an artificial multiballot voting experiment, my subjects could either rally to the winner or rescue an underdog. While the children rallied to the winner, the students, whether Canadians or Americans, whether left or right wingers, rallied to the underdog, and the magnitude of the rallying was positively related to the magnitude of the gap. The tendency toward unanimity, inasmuch as it was observed among young children, can be assumed to be a simple, unsophisticated, and primitive mechanism; that toward pluralism and equibalance appears at a higher level of cultural evolution. Altruism and self-interest may well be at the roots of the balance of power, that which maximizes the power of the unit or units that hold the system in balance while precluding that such power be used to form coalitions that would result in the elimination of one of the competitors.

Such rescuing of the underdog appears also, in a different form, in the games played by Caplow (1956, 1959, 1968) and Gamson (1961), where three players move counters on a Pachisi board; any two can form a coalition resulting in a multiplication of the weights by which one determines how far the coalition counter will be moved. The experimenters observed that the coalitions tended to be among the players with the lesser weights rather than with the stronger player. Under conditions of equal cost and benefit, there is strength in weakness.

Adding still to Richelieu's prescription, one must now say that if winning is good, winning too much is counterproductive.

Conflict

Thus far, the prescriptions to be derived from the experimental evidence on communication, cooperation, and competition read like an old-fashioned sermon: Be open and friendly; you may be competitive, but if you win, leave to others almost as much as you get for yourself— Machiavelli is missing. Conflict, the last of our four Cs— and more specifically, the extreme form of conflict that seeks to destroy or reject rather than simply dominate—is the occasion for his coming on stage. Common sense tells us that the meek and the weak, whatever they may inherit in heaven, do not inherit the earth. The experimental evidence lends support to this un-Christian observation, although it is not always easy to interpret that evidence because of its frequent failure to distinguish competition from conflict (competition that seeks to order the competitors while keeping them all within the game, and conflict that seeks to exclude a competitor from effective participation).

To bare the mechanisms of conflict, we need a zero-sum game where the loser loses all. Chess would offer such an example but would not tell us more than what we already know; each player takes effective advantage of the mistakes perceived to have been made by the opponent. Such a game is not particularly well suited to the study of conflicts, for it is too conflictual; the adversaries do not have a choice among cooperative, competitive, and conflictual strategies and the rules are too akin to those of total warfare. To illustrate the mechanics of conflict, I prefer using one of the more interesting games to have originated from political science: Riker's (1967) three-person game, where three players negotiate in a series of bilateral negotiations (one player always being absent from the negotiations) over the way they would split the rewards accruing to their coalition should they decide to coalesce. Inequality is introduced into the game by the rule that each potential coalition has different rewards (for example, the rule that players 1 and 2 can share $4, players 1 and 3 can share $5, while players 2 and 3 have $6 to divide between each other). The game thus has clearly distinguishable cooperative, competitive, and conflictual elements: With whom shall I form a coalition? (*cooperation*); how will the price be shared within that coalition? (*competition,* since the game has a built in logic that leads to unequal sharing); who will be excluded from any reward? (*conflict*). Riker used this game to show that the political analyst need not resort to psychological explanations of political behavior, that he only needs to know the rules of the game to predict behavior. Indeed, once he averaged the final individual claims made by each of his many individual players, Riker found the results to approximate what could have been predicted mathematically ($1.50 for player 1; $2.50 for player 2, and $3.50 for player 3 in our example).

Riker's game shows that in a competitive-conflictual situation, a player maximizes his rewards. Player 3 is stronger than player 2, 2 stronger than 1, and these specific strengths are translated into correspondingly differentiated rewards. That, says Riker, is "rational"; he could also have said that it was "human." But even more interestingly —here I bring forward a finding left by Riker in the background—the experiment showed also that player 3 tended to overplay his hand and get away with it, while player 1 underplayed his game, not daring to be as strong as he really was. We are thus led to note that in a conflict (as in a competition), the strong is in fact stronger than what an objective assessment would predict—and the weak is correspondingly weaker.[10] It is thus advantageous not only to be strong but also to be cunning; to set traps for a weaker opponent by seeming to be weak, or to deter a stronger opponent by seeming to be strong. This un-Christian evidence would not have distressed Cardinal Richelieu. The prescription becomes: Always negotiate something with opponents and friends alike, engage in a variety of successful supranational cooperative endeavours, but always do so from a position of *perceived* strength. Translated into actual behavior, this becomes, again, an argument for the balance of power.

But as indicated in an experiment by Morton Deutsch (1973), balance of power may, under certain common conditions, intensify rather than reduce conflict. In the Riker game, the players had the opportunity to adjust, through negotiations, their own individual rewards to the status hierarchy created by the very rules of the game (player 1 < player 2 < player 3). But in a situation of perfect balance of power between only two competitors, this hierarchy would disappear, and if each of the two players, out of fear of losing rank, thought it necessary to be perceived as being the stronger, a dangerous game of chicken (Schelling, 1960) might turn what could have been a mutually beneficial competition into a less rewarding, if not altogether disastrous, conflict. That is indeed what happened in the classic Morton Deutsch truck experiment.

The basic Deutsch experiment consists of two players who cannot communicate, each moving a truck in opposite directions between point A and point B. Quick delivery is rewarded, slow delivery is costly. Each player has the alternative of selecting either a long road all of his own or a common one-way road where two trucks moving in opposite directions will block each other unless one goes back to its starting base at the cost of losing time and money. The players know ahead of time that the game will be played twenty times. In this basic game, the players are unable to inflict damage on one's opponent without inflicting similar damage on oneself. This equality of power is in effect an equality of powerlessness, since excluding the other from any reward (refusing to back up) excludes the self from the same rewards (assuming the two opponents adopt the same stubborn strategy). In this situation of equality of powerlessness, the players are typically led to adopt, by tacit agreement, collaborative solutions such as: "I will back up this time and assume you will back up next time" or "You take the shortcut this time while I take the long road, assuming reciprocity in the next game."

This basic game (let us call it *balance of powerlessness*) was modified in subsequent versions by the introduction of either of two different conditions. In the first modification, the two players are each given control of a gate located on the one-way road near their starting base. Thus they may, if they so wish, move their truck to that gate, close it, return to their base, and then go to their goal by the long haul. It is an expensive tactic, but one that inflicts greater damage on the opponent who selects the short road.[11] In this situation of balance of power, Deutsch found his players to have great difficulty adopting a collaborative strategy, even when they were allowed to communicate verbally during the game. It was as if each player was prepared to accept economic losses for the sake of having his power and status recognized. Threats and counter-threats, traps and counter-traps, punishments and reprisals led the games away from competition into conflict. A second variation on the original game consisted of giving control of a gate to only one of the players. In that situation where a clear hierarchy was established, where, as in the Riker game, there was a clear *unbalance* of power and status, the experiment showed the games to be, as expected, more conflictual than in the basic version, but more cooperative than in the situation of balance of power. It would thus appear that power leads to conflict, and a perfect balance of power to even greater conflict.

Hierarchy, in human as in animal societies, is a means of reducing conflict, but hierarchies are obviously not nearly as acceptable to humans as they are to animals, maybe for a reason that appears in a variety of prisoner's dilemma experiments, namely, that unilateral cooperation by the weak is rarely rewarded (Shure et al., 1963; Rapoport and Chammah, 1965; Rapoport, 1974b). When a confederate of the experimenter plays a systematically cooperative game, when he uses time after time the turn-the-other-cheek strategy—one that can be answered in either of two ways, cooperation or exploitation—it is the exploitative response that predominates (at least in the Western cultures where the game has been used sufficiently often for the pattern to be clear).[12] It follows from these observations that the strategy of systematic cooperation continued in the absence of reciprocation can be afforded as a means of reducing tensions only if the risk of exploitation is low (cultural exchanges, trade, and so on), but would be dysfunctional in areas of greater risk—the military, for example.

Relating the Experimental Evidence to the Problem of Conflict Management in International Affairs

Durkheim noted the difficulty that modern societies experience in building solid structures of solidarity. Dahrendorf (1979) has returned to that theme in his reflections on the quality of life in industrial societies. Cooperation seems not to come easily to modern industrial man. That modernity is a likely factor appears in a last experiment—one that involves children and marbles. Two children face each other at each end of an elongated table. They each hold a string tied to a magnet; the two magnets meet in the center of the table. Held by the joined magnets, in their very middle, lies a marble, the prize. The children are told that they will play a game of "who gets the marble" ten times. If the two children pull simultaneously on the string the marble will fall to the side and be lost to both of them.

The experimenter, Professor Madsen, has taken the game to countries as diverse as the United States, Canada, Mexico, Israel, Hungary, Australia, and Papua New Guinea. His findings show a remarkable constant. In villages and tribal societies, children are markedly more cooperative than in urban settings. Urban American children are practically unable to win any marble, while the Papuans or Blackfoot Indians win the maximum or near maximum. One could take comfort in the difference I reported earlier between American children and American adults in their willingness to rescue an underdog, but it still remains to be explained why—once we control for age—we find that urban children, whether they be Hungarian, American, Australian, Mexican, or Israeli, have difficulty, indeed find it nearly impossible, to transform a conflict into a simple competition, difficult to establish the communication and adopt the cooperative behavior that would maximize their individual gains while the Mexican villagers, the Australian aborigines, the Papuan tribals, and the kibbutz children have no such difficulty. Very likely the explanation of the difference rests in variations in hierarchical structures (well established in traditional societies, fuzzy in urban industrial settings), and in the presence or absence of clear norms of cooperative behavior. The atomistic, equalitarian modern industrial city is weak on solidarity structures, on structures that favor cooperation. But the world is increasingly shaped and governed from its cities. Hence the danger that competition will irrationally turn into conflict and that conflict will destroy the cooperative structures that would have helped to manage it.

To repeat, I do not assume that all conflicts need to be managed. I do not assume either that cooperation is necessarily preferable to competition or conflict, but I assume that conflict is irrational if the object of the conflict could have been obtained at lesser cost through either competition or cooperation.[13] That assumption is, I realize, culture-bound, as demonstrated in an elegant experiment by Mushakoji (1971), who asked Japanese and American subjects to play a game with a variety of cooperative or conflict options. He observed that while Americans pursued the minimax strategies advocated by American game theorists, the Japanese subjects were willing to suffer losses for the sake of imposing even greater losses on their opponents. Such cultural variations in the ways of relating ends and means would make it irrational to assume that one's opponent would necessarily share one's own view of rational behavior. But for the sake of simplicity, let us assume that two potential opponents agree that conflict is irrational if their objectives can be achieved by other means. Conflict management is then a simple exercise in rationality; specifically, it is an effort to keep the lines of communications open, keep cooperation going, and reduce conflict to competition as soon as it is advantageous to do so. In other words, to satisfy Snyder's simple but often forgotten recommendation: If coercion is your dominant strategy, then coerce, but coerce prudently; if you choose avoidance, then accommodate, but accommodate at least cost. Or, to put it differently: Play a minimax game in the relating of coercion to the avoidance of disaster as in the relating of accommodation to losses. This implied that the instruments of communication, cooperation, competition, and conflict should be treated as autonomous; they should all be played, but should not necessarily play the same tune.

In a primitive system that moves as a bloc—that is all cooperation or all conflict—conflicts are particularly difficult to manage rationally. This is likely to happen when the military, the economic, and the cultural are so intimately tied together that conflicts in one area become conflicts in the others, so intimately linking that the severing of communication in one subsystem means severing of communication in the others. Unfortunately, this has been the trend of national and international politics since the end of the eighteenth century. The cold war represents a culmination in peacetime of this return to primitiveness. One might take some comfort from the evidence presented by Frei and Ruloff (1980), showing that a healthy dissociation between the military, the economic, and the cultural has taken place in the last twenty years in the international system. However, the events of the early 1980s are less than encouraging on the ability of that system not to regress into monolithic behavior.

NOTES

1. By controlled experiment, I mean an experiment in which the experimenter varies and controls the effect of his independent variables. By simulation, I mean a game where the subject is asked to act "as if"—as if he were Bismarck or Nasser or a prime minister, for example. A simulation can of course incorporate the features of a controlled experiment (as in the Cappello study described below), but it need not do so. In contrasting experimentation and simulation, I take the terms as ideal types, well aware of the possible and frequent overlaps. On the distinction between games and simulations, see Seibold and Steinfast (1979).

2. It could be, however, that the choice we make of studying international conflicts either through holistic simulations or through reductionist experiments is born from or at least leads us to different assumptions about the very nature of these conflicts. In a comparison of Leo Tolstoi and L. F. Richardson on the one hand, and of Karl von Clausewitz and Herman Kahn on the other, Anatol Rapoport (1966) contrasts cataclysmic with strategic models of conflict. To the Leo Tolstoi of *War and Peace,* as to the Richardson of *Statistics of Deadly Quarrels,* war (an extreme case of conflict) escapes rational human explanations; it is in the hands of a temperamental and unpredictable history. For Clausewitz as for Kahn, on the contrary, war may, but need not, be irrational. It may thus (and should) be controlled; it is amenable to human management. Could it be that the simulations—at least the man-simulations into which we "throw" a large number of variables—will reinforce an assumption of idiosyncratic unpredictability, while the controlled experiments that relate very few factors, such as those based on parlor games, will reinforce an assumption of rationality and predictability? If such an assumption is a mistake, I take the risk of committing it by taking most of my examples from small group, mixed motive games. That assumption of rationality does not commit me however, any more than it committed Rapoport, to the Clausewitz and Kahn strategic conceptions of conflict resolutions. It may be that conflicts are manageable up to a certain point, the point at which they cease to be rational. Conflict management should thus start before the conflict; like good medicine, it should be preventive.

3. An international crisis is typically defined as a situation that disturbs, gravely and suddenly, the existing equilibrium (Herman, 1972). More specifically, the type of crisis I shall have in mind in this chapter, when reflecting on tactics and strategies of conflict management, is a crisis that modifies or threatens to modify the existing hierarchical ordering of the relevant nations. Wars, new alliances, new technologies, new resources, and the like may occasion such a crisis. The intensity of the crisis is then related to (a) the magnitude of the change and (b) the speed of change. The latter should be measured in terms of the particular decision time span of the decision-makers concerned.

On the notion of crisis in terms of individual psychology, see Bloom (1966) among many others. For the notion of crisis in international relations and a critical evaluation of the literature on conflict management, see Holsti (1979, 1980), Gilbert and Lauren (1980), and Tanter (1975).

4. The game consisted of a three-person version of the PDG where the single "defector" from the cooperative solution got the largest payoff and the single "cooperator" suffered the highest loss.

5. For an assessment of the findings of the beneficial effects of communication among players of the prisoner's dilemma game, see Seibold and Steinfast (1979).

6. A simulation of the INS type by Brody (1963) produced a negative relationship between perception of threat and frequency of interaction with the players perceived to be threatening. Schwartz (1967) found, in a simulation of the same type, that the more one wanted to communicate, the less likely one was to escalate a conflict. True, such negative correlation between communication with one's opponent and conflict escalation does not always appear in the historical and simulation data studied by Zinnes (1966), but it is sufficiently frequent to draw attention to the serious and potentially catastrophic consequences of reducing communication with one's opponent, especially if the reduction results in stereotypic judgment.

Additional evidence supporting the Cappello, Deutsch, and Rapoport findings is in Alger (1965), who notes that the multiplicity of communication channels in an international system results in continual incremental adjustments rather than in confrontation requiring adjustments of greater magnitude. See also Robinson (1962), who finds that a high level of group communication reduces the danger that decisions will be made on the basis of personal values rather than group interests.

7. The importance of third parties for the managing of international tensions is stressed by Boulding (1966), who notes that the escalation of tension and conflict tends to corrupt the learning process and that a reverse of that process is unlikely to come from within the conflictual system. Hence the need for third parties.

In an experiment designed to identify the factors that would induce an opponent to respond in kind to a systematically pacifist strategy (never administer an electric shock when one could, never depart from a collaborative strategy in a mixed motive game), Reychler (1979) found that the following factors were likely to induce cooperation: physical closeness, channels of communication kept open and actually used, the presence of third parties, and the requirement that players justify their moves. He found, however, an unexpected interaction between the presence of neutral third parties and the requirement that the moves be justified. That conjunction caused an increase in violence and aggressive, noncooperative strategies.

8. The relationship between the amount of information received and the ability to make the right decision appears to be an application of the Yerkes-Dodson law (1980), which states that for any task there is an optimal level of arousal such that performance is related to arousal in the form of an inverted U (see discussion in Hockey, 1979).

9. Les Etats reçoivent tant d'avantages des négociations continuelles, lorsqu'elles sont conduites avec prudence, qu'il n'est pas possible de le croire si on ne le sait par expérience.

J'avoue que je n'ai connu cette vérité que cinq ou six ans après que j'ai été employé dans le maniement des affaires. Mais j'en ai maintenant tant de certitude que j'ose dire hardiment que négocier sans cesse ouvertement ou secretement en tous lieux, encore même qu'on n'en reçoive pas un fruit présent, et que celui qu'on en peut attendre à l'avenir ne soit pas apparent, est chose tout a fait nécessaire pour le bien des Etats.

Je puis dire avec vérité avoir vu de mon temps changer tout à fait de face les affaires de la France et de la Chrétienté, pour avoir, sous l'autorité du Roi, fait pratiquer ce principe, jusqu'alors absolument négligé en ce royaume.

Entre les semences, il s'en trouve qui produisent plus tôt leur fruit les unes que **les autres, il y en a qui ne sont pas plutot en terre, qu'elles germent et poussent une** pointe au dehors, et d'autres y demeurent fort longtemps avant que de produire un même effet.

Celui qui négocie toujours trouve enfin un instant propre pour venir à ses fins et, quand même il ne trouverait pas, au moins est-il vrai qu'il ne peut rien perdre et que par le moyen de ses négociations, il est averti de ce qui se passe dans le monde, ce qui n'est pas de petite conséquence pour le bien des Etats [Richelieu, 1929].

10. The Riker effect (it is advantageous to be strong) appears also in the games played by Kahan and Rapoport (1974). The authors find that in a three-person, non-zero-sum game where each player has unequal potential rewards, the stronger players coalesce against the weakest. These findings might seem to contradict the Laponce, Caplan, and Gamson observations on the tendency to rescue an underdog. In the later experiments, however, the problem is one of either winning or losing, being in the game or being out of it; in the case of Riker, Caplan, or Rapoport, the problem is one of sharing rewards and determining the magnitude of those rewards.

The rescuing of an underdog has an obvious limitation, namely, the cost of the rescue (Roth, 1979); for example, the time it takes to operate the necessary moves. Such cost appears in the Apex games where, out of five players, the top player, called Apex, can win by forming a coalition with any one of the remaining four, while a grand coalition of all these four lesser players is required to defeat the Apex. The Apex normally wins (Horowitz, 1973; Horowitz and Rapoport, 1974). Generally, in mixed motive games, the magnitude of the difference in cost and benefits between a cooperative or a defecting move affects the choice of strategies. This appears clearly in an experiment (Vrivohlavy, 1976) that varied the payoff matrices of the PDG.

11. Neither of the two players could see the moves made by the other; an obstacle on the road—truck or gate—could not be known until one's own truck met head-on with it.

12. If cooperative submission leads to exploitation, cooperation, once associated with retaliation, is found to be a most effective strategy, that most likely to produce cooperation and maximize rewards (Axelrod, 1980a, 1980b). The tit-for-tat strategy recommended by Rapoport for playing the PDG (start with cooperation, then answer in kind) proved to be the best overall strategy in a computer game organized by Axelrod among PDG "fans" and theoreticians. There is evidence, however, that an unconditionally benevolent strategy elicits more cooperation than unconditional malevolence (Lave, 1965).

13. For a discussion of individual and collective rationality among Harsanyi, Rapoport, Goffman, Shubik, Schelling, and Lipset, among others, see Archibald (1966: 138-157).

CHAPTER 3

PATTERNS OF CRISIS THINKING
An Analysis of the Governing Circles in Germany, 1866-1914

VADIM B. LUKOV
VICTOR M. SERGEEV

The logic of the development of modern international relations pushes to the forefront more and more insistently the problem of investigating the possibilities of *concerted actions* by states for the aversion and management of international crises. This problem has acquired much greater practical importance in latter years as a series of international crises have reverberated painfully through the process of détente that started to develop in the preceding decade.

A growing number of scientists in different countries, all with different philosophical views, have begun to concentrate their efforts on a solution to the problem. This tendency stood out in bold relief, in our opinion, at the XIth World Congress of Political Sciences (Moscow, 1979), where a number of papers broached the subject of concerted actions by states aimed at managing international conflicts and crises, strengthening the stability of the system of international relations, and consolidating international security (see Arbatov, n.d.; Möttölä, 1979). It is important to note that in many reports presented at the Congress, their authors strove for a comprehensive investigation of the problems of international conflicts and crises, and for utilization of the methods and approaches offered by sociology, psychology, and mathematics, along with the traditional methods of history and international law. A comparative investigation of the *perception of situations* by the leading figures of states involved in the international crises is of great interest, both from theoretical and practical points of view.

The role of an adequate assessment of unfolding events, of a timely decision in a rapidly developing crisis situation, is immensely enhanced as compared to the "usual" run of events. At the same time, it is extremely important in a crisis period to understand the nature of perception of the situation, the tendencies of its development as viewed by opponents and/or leaders of other states. At present there exist several approaches to the analysis of the perception of international situations, and particularly of crisis situations, by their immediate participants (see Axelrod, 1976; Schank and Colby, 1973; Hart, 1976). This space, however does not allow us to discuss the advantages and defects of each approach. Our attention will therefore be concentrated on the exposition of certain preliminary results obtained during the investigation of concrete crisis situations with the aid of a method elaborated by the authors for the analysis of foreign policy thinking.

A Possible Approach to the Analysis
of Foreign Policy Thinking

A preliminary investigation[1] carried out by the authors gives grounds for the supposition that in analyzing an international situation and the course of its probable development, statesmen or politicians think in terms of possibilities. Past events affecting the contemporary arrangement and relationship of political forces, the aims and interests of other participants in the situation, the likes and dislikes of political figures, in effect, all of the elements of the situation are viewed as *actualized* possibilities. Accordingly, the events that did not take place but that may become a reality and change the existing situation can be viewed as *potential* possibilities, with this or that degree of probability assessed by a given politician based on his or her experience and the information available to him or her. The chains of interconnected possibilities ensuing from the actual events and leading to future events or processes constitute the general picture of the situation existing in the politician's mind.

The criterion for an assessment of the existing possibilities is the system of interests represented by a given politician. This system is a complex of class, group, and personal needs that politicians can understand with different degrees of insight. By relating the probable developments of the situation to a system of interests, politicians can classify the events, processes, and aims of the other forces connected with this or that development as desirable, neutral, or undesirable. Hence, the aim of each participant in the situation in its most general form will consist in actualizing the desirable possibilities and preventing the actualization of undesirable possibilities (or in neutralizing them). It stands to reason that each participant strives to attain complete control over the situation, i.e., to gain the power to actualize all desirable possibilities and prevent the actualization of all undesirable possibilities, thereby ensuring the realization of his or her own interests.

In practice, however, this goal can seldom be achieved, since its attainment calls for the overwhelming superiority of one position over the others so that the person is capable of imposing his or her will both on adversaries and partners. Far more frequent in history are situations where none of the participants is in a position to exercise full control over the course of events. In such cases, politicians apply their powers to a limited number of critical possibilities determined by them in accordance with their understanding of their interests and their assessment of the effect on those interests, positive or negative, of the actualization of this or that possibility. The possibilities selected by politicians for application of their material and mental powers are essentially identical with their aims, or, to put it another way, their aims are possibilities which they seek to make good or frustrate by exercising their own or their state's powers.

The first stage in modelling a politician's thinking consists in the "structuralization" of his or her understanding of a situation with a view toward singling out his or her aims and those elements of the situation which are affecting at present or may affect in the future the ways and means of achieving those aims. As a result, the investigator draws up a network of interconnected possibilities in the shape of a complex graph where the apices represent the politician's aims and the environmental elements, and where the arrows indicate the direction and nature of the possible influence of some apices upon others (e.g., the influence of the environment upon the aims and vice versa, some aims on others, and some environmental elements on other elements). The graph also provides for the possibility of taking into account the influence of some elements of the network upon the process of interaction of two or more other elements.

In drawing up the network, the investigator uses the traditional methods of logical and content analysis of historical documents and sources (policy statements of political parties and separate leaders, diplomatic documents, memoirs, and the like). All of the categories and links between them mentioned in the texts are singled out, regrouped, and transformed into the aims of a given participant in the situation and the elements of the situation itself affecting the attainment of those aims. Afterward, using the content analysis, the investigator determines the importance of this or that aim attached to it by a given participant in accordance with his or her assessment of the strength of the links between separate elements of the situation.

It should be pointed out that the proposed procedure of a structural-statistical analysis of information has no analogs among the content analysis procedures employed at present. It has some features in common with cognitive mapping, but the latter method makes no use of content analysis to obtain weighted and functional graphs. This permits us to overcome a serious drawback inherent in practically all currently used procedures which, in comparing the categories singled out of the information, fail to take into account their interaction and the existence of a certain hierarchy among them. This circumstance, however, is of paramount importance for the effectiveness of the traditional procedures, since due regard for the relationship of the categories enables the investigator to use formal characteristics, such as repetition frequency, attributive signs, volume of the text, and so forth for the comparison of those categories that occupy a similar position in the structure of the selected graph and that are connected to the common graph apex (category).

The structural-statistical analysis transforms the information into an aggregate of what may be called formal neurons connected with one another. In this aggregate, the categories characterizing specific features of the environment perform the function of the system "inputs," whereas the main aim pursued by a given politician represents the "output." The significance of any international event that takes place depends on what formal neurons it "triggers" at the input and how it affects the main aim of the politician. Hence, the reproduced model of his or her thinking evaluates, as it were, the event from the viewpoint of the degree of its positive influence on the achievement of certain aims. Since this model permits one at the same time to determine the "weight" of each of the intermediate aims, i.e., its contribution to the attainment of the politician's chief goal, it becomes an instrument for measuring the magnitude of the conflict or cooperation represented by an individual event.

Patterns of Thinking of the Representatives of the German Ruling Circles: 1866-1914

As a concrete historical material for investigation, we have chosen the thinking of representatives of the German leading circles for approximately a 50-year period from 1866 to 1914, i.e., from the Austro-Prussian war to the outbreak of World War I.

This selection can be explained by a number of reasons. First of all, the growth of German capitalism and imperialism during the period mentioned led to a sharp aggravation of interstate contradictions in Europe, and later in all the world, and the policy of the ruling circles of Germany was one of the main causes of a series of acute international crises. Hence, the foreign policy concepts of the ruling circles of Germany at that period offer rich material for the analysis of peculiarities of the perception of acute international crises by the leaders of a large capitalist state. Second, the study of the character of foreign policy thinking by statesmen of the "prenuclear" era and its comparison with the peculiarities of the thinking of modern Western political leaders and statesmen can help in the assessment of the significance of those limitations that the realities of the era of nuclear arms place on the long-term class aspirations of the monopoly bourgeoisie. Third, the testing of any new method of investigation, as is well known, is best made on already well studied empirical material.

The technique of structural-statistical analysis was applied to the analysis of the political thinking of four German statesmen who carried out the foreign policy of that country from the middle of the nineteenth century until the outbreak of World War I: Bismarck, Bülow, Bethmann-Hollweg, and Wilhelm II. The memoirs of these statesmen were used as a source of information for the analysis. It should be stressed that the peculiarities of memoirs quite often hinder their use as a source of totally reliable information, especially as far as descriptions of motives are concerned. However, the use of memoirs in this case was warranted in our view because the aim of the researchers was the analysis of the general thinking patterns of statesmen, which usually seems to be reflected in no small measure in one's memoirs.

Analysis of the memoirs of Otto von Bismarck (1940/1941; Hohenzollern, 1923: 12), who held the post of minister-president of Prussia and Chancellor of the German Empire from 1862 to 1890, leads to the conclusion that this statesman possessed two markedly different models or patterns of thinking. The first of these patterns covers the 1866-70 crisis produced by the foundation during three wars (the Prusso-Danish, Prusso-Austrian, and Prusso-French) of the German Empire. The second pattern is characteristic for roughly the next ten years of the political activity of Bismarck, during which he pursued a line of internal consolidation of the newly formed state and of complicated balancing among the great European states.

The principal feature of the first pattern of thinking, that we call "crisis pattern," is that the attainment of the goal considered vital at the moment is possible only with an extremely favorable combination of exogenous factors, that is, that the perceived environment entropy level is fairly high. Such a pattern of thinking also dictates a *perfectly definite view of the situation structure*. In the goal tree, the branch related to the decisive aim in a given situation will be the most elaborate, right down to the fine tactical details. This is natural, as all the attention and all the efforts of the decision-maker are concentrated precisely on this very aim. The perception of the environment bears a markedly *selective character*; only those of its elements are identified which can influence the achievement of the decisive aim, but such elements are seen in the minutest detail. The state of large blocks of the environment is perceived as unstable. Each factor which can stabilize it in a direction favorable to the decision-maker is usually counterbalanced by a factor acting in the opposite direction.

Crisis thinking is apparently inclined to conceive of a situation from "above downward." Proceeding from a general conviction that the state of an environment is extremely unstable, it forms an image of the environment by selecting factors in pairs, with each pair acting in the opposite direction. This hypothesis permits me to explain the seemingly strange quantitative symmetry in Bismarck's thinking between the positive and negative factors influencing large blocks of the environment.

Strong narrowing of the field of activity is typical of crisis thinking, consisting of the enclosing of all efforts around one or two decisive aims. All other aims are exceedingly dependent on the decisive ones; their advancement either ceases altogether as all resources are concentrated on the decisive area, or else efforts for their realization are undertaken so as not to undermine the decisive aim, which leads to tactics of wait-and-see in areas not directly related to the attainment of the decisive aim. It is apparent that such crisis perception of the situation cannot be persistent. It is bound to change in case of either the realization of or the complete failure to achieve the decisive aim. Such a change in thinking took place with Bismarck after the successful end of the Franco-Prussian war and the founding of the German Empire. Change of the aim structure and of the perception of the environment should be regarded as the main manifestations of change in the character of thinking.

The realization of the decisive aim—the military debacle of France—removed the blocking by the environment of a number of other goals of the second order. As a result, the branches of the goal tree that remained at the embryonic stage during the crisis perception stage now developed into complex, multilevel structures. The *independence of aims* of one and the same order from each other was enhanced; thus, several large aims were being advanced simultaneously. The level of entropy had markedly decreased, and the environment was not blocking any of the decisive aims.

Germany's entry in the 1890s into the monopolistic stage of capitalism and of colonial expansion could not leave unaffected the thinking of the ruling circles about new aims, which the ruling classes of Germany then began to pursue on the international arena. Analysis of the thinking of German leaders paints a picture of a rapid erosion of the principles of "rational" policy formulated by Bismarck, and of the formulation of a new pattern of thinking: *expansionist*. The perception of crisis situations had likewise undergone a radical change.

What is apparently typical of the expansionist pattern of thinking is its confidence in the availability of forces and means, and in their sufficiency to "steer" the outer world in a direction desirable to decision-makers, one that will allow them to force their will on others. "The arrogance of power" deprives the bearer of such a pattern of thinking of the stimuli to even a superficial study of the structure of an international situation; it suffices to have but a superficial idea of the main elements (blocks) of the environment.

This above everything else explains the insignificant degree of attention paid by both Wilhelm II and Bethmann-Hollweg to the action of external factors on the aims of the state. If Bismarck took into account 55-70 factors, Wilhelm II and Bethmann-Hollweg had not more than 10-17 such factors, and yet not a single one from the environment blocks was studied in such detail, as in the reasoning of Bismarck. The international situation of Germany was understood by Bethmann-Hollweg to a somewhat greater extent, his remarks are more integral and developed, but still they are much inferior to Bismarck's comprehensive grasp of the situation.

The peculiarities of the thinking of the German leaders on the eve of World War I also conditioned the *character of perception of the pre-war crisis* in July 1914. The thinking of Bethmann-Hollweg appears to have the character of crisis thinking. We see it "zeroed in" on the critical branch of the graph—the possible development of relations with the Entente powers after the Sarajevo assassination.

From the point of view of the declared aim of Germany, the most favorable variant—the acceptance by Austro-Hungary of repressions against Serbia, along with the localization of the Austro-Serbian conflict—only could be realized if Russia forced Serbia to satisfy the Austro-Hungarian demands, and if England held Russia from declaring war on Austro-Hungary. However, the probability of this favorable concurrence of events, as assessed by Bethmann-Hollweg, was negligent. What was more probable, if not inevitable, was the third variant of the development of events—the outgrowth of the Austro-Serbian conflict into a world war.

More attentive analysis shows that Bethmann-Hollweg's perception of the acute international crisis was qualitatively different from Bismarck's perception of the crisis. What draws our attention here is the teleology, the determinism of Bethmann-Hollweg's thinking. His understanding of the situation left to Germany no other alternative but unconditional support of Austro-Hungary in the conflict with Serbia and Russia.

In contradistinction to Bismarck, who felt acutely not only the crisis character of the situation of Prussia herself in 1866-70, but also that Prussia's actions provoked or could provoke a crisis of the whole international system, neither Bethmann-Hollweg nor Wilhelm II possessed such a complete, all-encompassing perception of the situation. They believed that the crisis situation was inherent only in the foreign aims of Germany due to the actions of the environment, primarily of the Entente powers. The prewar crisis and the war itself appeared therefore to be an inevitable sequel of events initiated by the environment. For this reason, the conception of "crisis," as well as that of "status quo," was interpreted in expansionist thinking in a different manner than in the thinking of the German leaders of the 1860s and 1870s.

Computer Simulation of Crisis Perceptions: Some Results

Computer simulation of the German leaders' perceptions of crises in 1866-1914 was utilized for two purposes: first, to verify the adequacy of the technique for the analysis of political texts (in case of memoirs), and second, to verify and expand the results obtained through the analysis of reasoning graphs. To verify the technique, the reasoning graphs

TABLE 3.1

Period	Actor	Assessment of favorable/ unfavorable courses of events ratio	Environment entropy level assessment
1866-1870	Bismarck	$1 : 4$	2
1871-1878	Bismarck	$5 : 1^X$, $4 : 1^{XX}$	$-2,5$; -2
1914	Bethmann-Hollweg	$1 : 5$	2,5

x — for the goal N 1; xx — for the goal N 5.

obtained by it were computer simulated. Next, memoirs (mainly Bismarck's) were used to derive descriptions of possible effects (states of environment) that could be produced by strategies considered by the German leadership in various periods. These descriptions were coded into combinations of factors of the environment, and corresponding magnitudes of these factors were used as "inputs" of reasoning graphs. The computer then calculated the level of attainment of various statesmen's goals under each of the strategies considered. The results obtained were compared with the actual strategies adopted by a given statesman. This comparison proved that the reasoning graphs construed reflect the logic of statesmen's thinking fairly accurately. Some quantitative results of the reasoning graphs' computer simulation will be discussed below.

First of all, the computer simulation proves the importance of *the assessment of the environment entropy level* by a politician as an indicator of crisis perception.[2] The computer analysis of the reasoning graphs yields data on concrete magnitude of environment entropy levels as perceived by both Bismarck and Bethmann-Hollweg (see Table 3.1). The data show that the assessment of the situation in terms of the environment entropy level perception correlates closely with the intuitive, descriptive assessments contained in Bismarck's and Bethmann-Hollweg's memoirs.

The number of theoretically possible courses of the development of events is yet another essential indicator of crisis perception, as well as of a politician's thinking in general.[3] It is obvious that the greater the number of courses a politician can foresee (within reasonable limits), the greater will be the number of options that the politician can develop out of his or her own strategy. This ability is of the utmost importance for actions in crises. Compare Bismarck's and Bethmann-Hollweg's reasoning graphs in this respect (see Table 3.2).

TABLE 3.2

Period	Actor	The number of theoretically possible courses of the development of events as foreseen in the reasoning graph
1866-1870	Bismarck	10^{17}
1871-1878	Bismarck	10^{23}
1914	Bethmann-Hollweg	10^{8}

Surely this indicator is formal to some degree, for a human brain cannot actually analyze and compare such a great number of possible courses of the development of events. It is obvious, however, that the indicator provides an opportunity to compare possible frameworks of thinking of various politicians and the extent of "elasticity" of their views. In this case, Bismarck's perception of crisis seems to be a great deal more elaborate and rich than that of his successors.

A third essential indicator of crisis perception is a politician's *assessment of the probability of attaining the principal goals*.[4] This assessment impacts directly on an actor's choice of concrete ways and means for his or her actions in a crisis. Bismarck's and Bethmann-Hollweg's assessments of the probability of attaining the principal goals appear in Table 3.3.

Patterns of Political Thinking, 1866-1914: Some Theoretical and Practical Conclusions

Seen from the point of view of analysis of foreign policy thinking, the process of crisis interaction of states includes as an important component the interaction of the logics and patterns of foreign policy thinking of the ruling circles of the states involved in the crisis. With some degree of simplification, this process can be divided into three consecutive stages:

(1) realization in concrete actions of the pattern of foreign policy thinking of the participants in a crisis;
(2) the interaction (conflict) of patterns of two or more participants in the crisis;

TABLE 3.3

Period	Actor	Assessment of the probability of attainment of the principal goals
1866-1870	Bismarck	20%
1871-1878	Bismarck	75-85%
1914	Bethmann-Hollweg	20%

(3) the modification of patterns of foreign policy thinking of the participants in the crisis during the process of interaction.

The results of this study of the thinking of the leading German circles in 1866-1914, as stated in this report, bring us to some conclusions regarding each of the given stages.

REALIZATION OF THE PATTERN OF FOREIGN POLICY THINKING IN A CRISIS

A number of the peculiarities of a crisis can impact strongly on the character of the perception of the situation and consequently on the pattern of the foreign policy thinking in crisis situations. To these belong the abrupt increase of the entropy of the environment, or the threat of such an increase, and also the decrease of time left for making decisions (because the growing probability of an unfavorable outcome of events demands rapid actions to block the increase of the environment entropy). The growing danger of the situation and the lack of time engender stress in the decision-makers. The participants in a crisis develop a tendency to "wind up" the image of the situation; their attention is concentrated on a few fragments of the environment and of their own system of aims.

These factors may result in a *limitation of possible options,* which in turn leads to the hardening of positions and to the acceptance of dangerous courses of actions "as other variants are lacking." All this makes the search for a solution very difficult in the end. Such situations are described by the immediate participants or students of crises of the postwar period.[5] Hence, in crisis situations, the preservation or even extension of the image of the situation that exists in the perception of the decision-maker acquires special importance. This can help to retain tactical pliability and thus to avoid the catastrophic outcome of a crisis by creating conditions for a compromise arrangement.

INTERACTION OF THE PATTERNS OF FOREIGN POLICY THINKING

It is essential to foresee the inception and probable direction of crisis development in order for timely actions to be taken to prevent or control the crisis. Here, a typology of the participants in a crisis situation can help, an example being that offered by the authors of the members of the German leadership in 1866-1914. The level of entropy is seen as the basis of this classification, as can be determined from Table 3.4.

The patterns of thinking identified give grounds to presuppose the existence of another, "puppet," pattern. This pattern of thinking is characterized by the following peculiarities: The environment blocks the main aims of the system, and the "deblocking" of such aims can be achieved only with the support of external forces, the employment of which is linked to the subservience to such forces of a part or all of the aims of the given system. The hypothetical character of the last pattern of thinking must be stressed; the proof of its existence requires empirical testing.

Such patterns of thinking should be regarded as *tendencies* in assessing a situation and in selecting a strategy of behavior stemming from this assessment. As each decision-maker participates simultaneously in a whole complex of situations (intraparty and intrafraction struggles, interparty conflicts, international relations, and so on), the real thinking of a decision-maker can have at one and the same moment the features of different patterns of thinking, depending on the assessment of a concrete situation. Apparently, a decision-maker who is capable of comprehending the situation and rearranging his thinking will be more successful.

The patterns of thinking described above are no more than "carcasses" that require draping with unique specifics of the given historical epoch, and with the social and psychological characteristics of a given decision-maker. However, the identification of a determined invariant base of thinking can be very useful for forecasting the crisis behavior of this or that decision-maker and of the political or social force represented by him, and hence for the elaboration of a course of action directed at the prevention or control of a crisis situation.

TABLE 3.4

Environment entropy level and its dynamics	Perception of the situation by the decision-maker	Preliminary designation of the pattern of thinking
considerable; increasing in future	the environment blocks the main aims, yet through assessment of the decision-maker, resources are available to deblock them; concentration of efforts at 1-2 aims, leaving all others stagnant; possible evolution of the environment is considered to be unfavorable in the immediate future	crisis thinking
considerable; inconsiderable but increasing	at the present moment resources are assessed by the decision-maker as sufficient for complete control of the environment of behavior of the other participants in the situation; possible evolution of situation is assessed as unfavorable	expansionist thinking
moderate; increasing or decreasing in future	situation is assessed as transitory; decision-maker avoids disturbing it by acting, uses the "breathing spell" for rearrangement of thinking (to get a clearer vision of the prospects of development of the situation), also to accumulate resources	status quo thinking

MODIFICATION OF THE PATTERN OF THINKING

Crises can radically change the very pattern of thinking of their participants, as witnessed by the analysis of the evolution of Bismarck's thinking. This leads to the conclusion that an important task in the control of crises is the prevention of the formation of thinking patterns in a partner or partners during a crisis and after it, which can lead to the escalation of a given crisis or to the appearance of new ones. This task can be achieved only if in a crisis situation the communication channels between the participants can be preserved or even widened. Many investigators point to the importance of preserving communications during crises (Neuhold and Herman, 1978). It is important to stress that of special importance during a crisis is the use of communications for a *mutual search of the common or similar elements of perception of the situation,* the identification of common or similar aims, mutually acceptable or nonacceptable variants of the development of events, and so forth. In a wider sense, the "rapprochement" of the images of a situation, or at least of the separate fragments of such images, can be an important step toward the prevention of international crises.

NOTES

1. See the results of this investigation (Lukov and Sergeev, n.d.), see also Pospelov (1980).

2. The environment entropy level can be calculated if the reasoning graph is viewed as a network of interrelated factors, of which one part forms "inputs" that are interdependent within the framework of the graph, while the other part are "outputs," that is, the politician's principal goals. "Inputs" switching on may produce both favorable and unfavorable effects on goal attainment. Each of the "inputs" can be on one of two possible states: "switched on" or "switched off." Proceeding from these assumptions, one can define the environment entropy level as a logarithm of the unfavorable to favorable states of "inputs" ratio.

3. The number of theoretically possible courses of the development of events can be defined in terms of the possible states of the environment. If a reasoning graph has n "inputs," then $N = 2^n$ states of the environment are possible.

4. This indicator can be quantified as the ratio of the number of favorable states of "inputs" to the total number of their possible states.

5. A similar "winding up" of the situation with a consequent limitation of the number of possible actions is described in Schlesinger (1965) and Kennedy (1969).

CHAPTER 4

COMMUNICATIONS AND CRISIS
A Preliminary Mapping

J O H N M E I S E L

The existing literature on our subject is elementary. While discrete case studies of crises and personal memoirs of diplomats and journalists occasionally touch upon communications and crisis, the pickings are, to put it colloquially, exceedingly slim. Under these circumstances, the present chapter has the modest aim of mapping some of the relationships that are observable between crises and contemporary means of communication.

Communications, the transmission of information by speech, signals, writing, or pictures, are affected by crises and other events and circumstances, and they in turn influence the way in which the crises evolve. The latter point can be sketched graphically as in Figure 4.1.

To understand the processes through which crises are influenced by communications, some sort of ordering is needed of the bewildering, virtually unlimited ways in which communications are formed and diffused in the contemporary world. One useful way of distinguishing between prevailing modes of transmitting information is to note two simple dichotomies. Messages can originate with governments or from the private sector. They can, in other words, be either official or unofficial. Each of these modes can at the same time be either public or private. On the one hand, they can be directed at large numbers of

AUTHOR'S NOTE: I should like to acknowledge the help of Johan Sarrazin and of Nicholas Sidor in the preparation of this chapter.

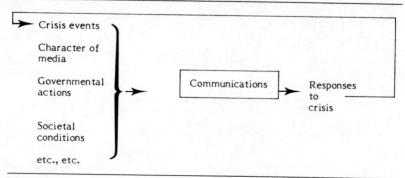

Figure 4.1

individuals indiscriminately and made available to anyone who is interested. But many, and perhaps the most important messages, are intended only for very specific eyes or ears and are shrouded to various degrees in privacy and confidentiality. These distinctions make it possible to identify four kinds of contents in communications (see Figure 4.2). The four types of communications are, of course, occasionally related and so any one may be influenced by one or more of the others.

Because of the magnitude of the subject, the present chapter will focus on only one of them, namely, that identified as consisting of media messages (the shaded area). We are therefore concerned with information which is unofficial and public, beamed not at decision-makers but at general audiences relying primarily on printed and electronic means for perceiving the world around them.

Since for the public the media are the only available means of gaining information about what is taking place during an international crisis, they determine the extent, accuracy, and depth of general knowledge about it. By so doing they may contribute substantially to the course of events. On the one hand, they influence developments with respect to whether an upheaval is contained, exacerbated, or defused. On the other, they may well have a direct hearing on the outcome: who wins, how, and to what extent.

Political scientists, primarily interested in the analyses of crises per se or in a broader context of the state system, or citizens pursuing normative goals need under these conditions to identify and relate to

	Public	Private
Official	Propaganda	Espionage Diplomacy
Unofficial	Media messages	Commercial etc. intelligence, Personal messages

Figure 4.2

one another the factors that determine the nature and scope of media influences on crises. Four sets of conditions stand out as being the chief determinants of "press" performance: (a) the nature of the crisis itself; (b) prevailing sociopolitical conditions; (c) the structure and economic organization of the communications industries; and (d) the technological "state of the art" of the media.[1] With respect to all but the first of these factors, a distinction must be noted between conditions prevailing at the crisis site or sites and those existing in the country where reports are received, but in the present discussion I shall not usually segregate them. A mapping of the factors which enable one to predict how the media will affect an international crisis requires that each of these variables be examined and broken down into its component parts.

THE NATURE OF THE CRISIS

Ideological Direction. Virtually all crises involve challenges to the status quo that pit one ideological position against another. Even the most "materialist"-motivated actions seeking change (hunger riots, for example) are not only symbolically linked by their instigators to broad philosophical arguments, but in fact also intrinsically raise issues related to various value systems. Both domestic and international crises can as a rule be classified as falling into one of two categories: those linked to nationalist or patriotic causes, and those which emanate from issues related to social policy. The two aspects are often related, but it is usually possible to place a crisis predominantly on a nationalist-cosmopolitan axis (which may include ethnic dimensions) or on one reflecting social space—social reform versus entrenchment, socialism versus capitalism, the welfare state versus laissez-faire, and so on. With respect to each of these axes, the crisis will likely compel the participants to opt for the status quo or its abolition.

Since the end of World War II, a great many crises arising from nationalist and/or social causes have been linked to the decline of the old European imperialism and have at the same time often involved issues of modernization and development. More recently they have been linked to challenges to Pax Americana or to the hegemony of the USSR within the so-called socialist camp.

The manner in which the media report the critical events under consideration here inevitably depends to a large extent on the resonance or dissonance between their own dominant ideological orientation and the philosophical content of the crises in question. No aspect, in this context, is as crucial as the relevance of the reported upheaval to the struggle between the great powers. Crises of little concern to the latter will largely go unnoticed and will, when reported, likely receive more accurate treatment than those affecting the Cold War and its aftermath.

The Instigators. Although the origin of crises may be dispersed and complex, they never arise entirely spontaneously. One or more instigators are required to create or ignite the conditions threatening the international order.

The character of the instigators is of the greatest importance in determining media responses, but the latter may alter as circumstances change. Thus, for example, Nasser before the Suez crisis, and Castro before the Cuban missile imbroglio, generally received favorable treatment in the Western press as instruments of reform and "progress." It was only after they "internalized" their cause and became involved in crises affecting the defense and economic interests of the great powers that the coverage they received in the Western media became almost uniformly hostile.

The accuracy and depth of coverage depends, however, not only on the ideological dissonance (or otherwise) of the media and the events covered but also on the location of the instigators. If the latter are scattered (in various countries, in visible or concealed sites, within identifiable organizations, or in obscure private situations), the media may be unable or unwilling to ferret out the necessary facts. It may also be difficult to tell where the instigators really are. Before and during the anti-Allende coup in Chile, few reporters were aware that critical information was to be found not in Chile but in Washington.

Modalities. The means or weapons utilized by the instigators often give a particular crisis its media appeal. Diplomatic exchanges receive very different kinds of attention from reporters than, say, acts of terrorism. The high drama of the latter lends itself to the style favored by the media. This applies especially to television, on whose screens terrorism attracts considerably more resources (and coverage) than more prosaic means of threatening to upset the international order. This fact points to the great importance attached to *drama* in crisis reporting, an emphasis which frequently detracts from attention to the underlying, central issues affecting the events in question.

The particular form a crisis takes also determines whether news about developments can be actively shaped by the parties involved in the crisis through press releases, briefings, and less obvious means of spreading light or obscurity. We shall return to this matter later.

Status. In this context, an important distinction exists between crises that have been formalized into official state actions (possibly culminating in declarations of war) and those consisting merely of growing tensions. The former type is usually accompanied by heavy-handed governmental attempts to control information and to color the reports issued by the media. A difference in this sense is noticeable between totalitarian and pluralist societies, although it is likely to be only a matter of degree. Informal attempts to manipulate the news can be quite as effective as more overt and formal ones. Nevertheless, the fact that the Vietnam war was not officially a *casus belli* recognized by Congress made it possible for its developments to be dealt with much more freely by the American media than might otherwise have been the case.

Scope. A related aspect of the nature of the crisis concerns its scope. If it is essentially a domestic event (which may, however, have significant international implications), the newsgathering agencies will rely on "on site" investigations in which foreign governments are unlikely to be involved. A direct international confrontation, on the other hand, is certain to tempt all participating governments to affect the way in which it is reported. Extensive briefings, at the least, will be used to influence the media; we have also known of more doubtful means, including the fabrication of false documents, staged events by *agents provocateurs,* and the planting of "favorable" stories.

Temporal and Spatial Factors. The duration of a crisis has a bearing on how it is perceived by the media and how it is painted. Even so dramatic an event as the Iranian hostage incident eventually lost its television appeal and was replaced by other events, even when feverish activities were occurring behind the scenes to resolve the impasse. But the length of a crisis nevertheless affects the depth and complexity of coverage: the longer the crisis, obviously, the better informed observers become about it.[2] The nature of media treatment of crises seems, as a rule, to vary depending on whether they are short-lived, long-lasting, or more or less permanent. Although the literature on this subject is woefully inadequate and hence not helpful, it does not contradict the plausible assumption that one can identify certain common patterns in the "lifecycle" of crises and that, *ceteris paribus*, corresponding uniformities are evident in the manner in which the relevant events are communicated to domestic and outside observers. As has already been suggested, media coverage also depends on the stage upon which the crisis action occurs. If events are far-flung, the relevant parts may resist being put together in the available time, and hence developments in only the most obvious and accessible locations may be covered.

SOCIOPOLITICAL CONDITIONS

Nature of the Regime. Nothing has a greater effect on the way in which the media deal with crises than the character of the political regime, particularly in the country in which the news and analyses are reported. The most fundamental distinction here is that between a totalitarian system in which the media are closely controlled and a pluralist one, where they are given a substantial degree of freedom. There are gradations of freedom and constraint, of course, within each of these modal types, but the importance of the quintessential difference between the two cannot be exaggerated. No country has a free press in the absolute sense, and restrictions can take forms other than governmental control. The latter, when thoroughly applied, can to all intents and purposes prevent the majority of the population from knowing what is going on in the world. This is particularly the case in countries not large enough to be reachable by foreign television signals and those protected by the exclusiveness of their language. Short-wave radio can penetrate any defense, of course, but it cannot, against determined opposition, deliver its messages to mass publics. A ruthless government can therefore effectively manage its domestic media and the news made available to the bulk of its population.

In this context it is important to note the difference between various countries, and between diverse circumstances within one country, with respect to the effect of public opinion on decision-making. No government can ignore it completely, of course, but it is particularly in liberal and social democratic regimes that the rulers must pay heed to the moods of the electorate. The latter is subject to manipulation by politicians, the media, and others, but numerous restraints limit the effectiveness of mobilizing or restraining public concerns and support. Thus John F. Kennedy, by the skillful use of television, was able to arouse the United States and much of the world in the Cuban missile crisis to a point where public opinion had a direct effect on the crisis outcome. Lyndon Johnson, on the other hand, failed in his efforts to rally U.S. opinion behind his efforts to deal with the Vietnam war. In these two cases, public opinion responding to media activities had a direct bearing on the outcome of major crises.

Political Culture. Little escapes the net cast by the term "political culture." We shall focus here on only one element of particular relevance to the subject at hand. The level of deference in the receiving society is an important element in the manner in which reports of crises are received. In pluralist countries the press is never unanimous and the population has the choice of accepting anything from official announcements to views which challenge the legitimacy of authorities. The way in which people perceive international events and evaluate them depends to some measure on which end of the spectrum of the news package they choose to accept. If the proportion of those disposed to respect authority and official pronouncements is high, opinions congenial to the establishment will be widespread. Where trust in government is generally low, dissenting views are more likely to gain currency and favor. Tolerance for dissent and conditions facilitating its presence and vitality are, in fact, extremely important aspects of the manner in which the media report world events.

Dissenters normally create and consume written and sometimes spoken information and views at variance with more accepted positions. They therefore facilitate public debate and act as correctives to flaws in the dominant means of communications. The role and influence of *I. F. Stone's Weekly* is an outstanding example, but most liberal democracies manage to support a vast array of journals and weeklies of opinion which act as public watchdogs rectifying many of the oversights and biases of the more widely acceptable voices of the media. The latter in turn correct errors perpetrated by vehicles for minority views.

Locus of Power. In addition to the prevailing laws, customs, and conventions with respect to criticism of government and to the freedom of the press generally, the government structure itself is important. It is well recognized, for instance, that the American system, dispersing power among several branches of the government, and particularly according Congressional committees extraordinary investigative powers, is more encouraging to lively criticism than the more centralized cabinet system found in the British world. Constitutional provisions with respect to freedom of information, civil rights, the role of courts, bureaucratic power, and a host of other factors are relevant here.

At a different level, the respective roles of the public and private sectors may have contrasting effects on the manner in which the media report events of domestic and worldwide significance. Each sphere—the public and the private—possesses immense power over news gathering and dissemination. This power may be applied in tandem or it may conflict. Both those who control the state and the economy tend to be ruthless in defending their interests and to identify their own survival with the public interest. Reasons of state or reasons of universal economic well-being or benefit are therefore often invoked to direct the activities of the media and to restrain the flow of information. This process is related, insofar as the private sector is concerned, to the structure of the news industries—a subject to which we shall turn next.

THE STRUCTURE AND ECONOMICS OF THE INDUSTRY

The Structure of the Industry. In market-oriented societies, much depends on whether the media tend to operate under monopolistic ownership or oligopoly or in competition. If only a small number of powerful owners are dominant, their interests, beliefs, or whims may have serious consequences for the manner in which world events are reported and interpreted. Two forms of concentration are relevant: one *within* the media, where a single owner controls a dominant proportion of the newspapers or of all the media—radio, television, as well as the printed word. But single ownership can go even further when not only the media but other enterprises are embraced by a single corporate structure. Interlocking ownership may lead, for instance, to a television chain being linked to the aircraft industry. Such ties make suspect the broadcaster's disinterested attitude to world events having implications for defense spending.

Some media owners have been known to use their properties to fan international tensions because wars are good for circulation, whereas others have established enviable traditions contributing to peace and humanitarian goals. In other instances, self-perpetuating trusts have been set up to assure long-lasting, beneficent public service.

Other things being equal, it is probably desirable that the media in any country avoid monopolistic ownership and engage in competition with one another. While this is likely to assure variety and hence a fuller coverage of events, it may also have dangers. A variant of Gresham's Law may operate, contributing to the various media competing for larger shares of the market by catering to the lowest audience tastes and thus debasing the value of their product. Efforts to gain a larger segment of a mass market may, as a consequence, reduce the amount and quality of world news analysis.

The presence of numerous owners, on the other hand, is likely to assure the availability of a greater variety of different kinds of publications and programs. The printed press may include not only competing dailies but also a rich offering of weeklies, monthlies, or occasional publications presenting a wide spectrum of views and interests. Having a number of broadcasters, operating individually or in competing chains, assures the availability of various formats of radio and television shows. This provides opportunities for the airing of diverse and perhaps even minority and off-beat reports and analyses. Under these conditions, special efforts may be made to examine critically the assumptions of conventional wisdom and to question the priorities of the media establishment.

Sometimes, in situations where large and wealthy media enterprises play a central role, journalists, particularly those in the field, resent the influence of management. They may then feed smaller organs of opinion or panel programs with articles and spoken contributions challenging mainstream reporting. "Spinoff" journalism of this sort has, on occasion, played an important part in correcting biases which would otherwise have gone unnoticed.

Economic Aspects. Some economic aspects are not directly related to the structure of the industry. Among these the role of advertising, the place of unions, and the costs of serious public affairs coverage are particularly important.

In societies where advertising is an essential media element, program content is often influenced by the need to assure the economic viability of the enterprise. This may result, either unwittingly or through planned action, in the substance of what is presented being influenced by commercial considerations. Furthermore, the location of substantive items may be dictated by considerations related to the revenues expected to accrue from the sale of space or time. Essential items, in terms of the national interest, may thus be relegated to the background so as to make place for less "weighty" or "depressing" content compatible and congruent with mass advertising.

The character of communications-related unions can also be important. In some instances, associations of journalists have won the right to influence editorial content, thereby possibly offsetting the efforts of management to impose *its* views. The character of unions also affects the resources available and the economic viability (and so the quality) of what is being done. In some societies, the unions are as important as management in influencing the quality and character of the final product. They may also determine the extent to which competition exists within the communications industry, since the number of firms or producing organizations may depend on labor-management relations.

Finally, we must note the enormous costs of gathering and delivering world news. One inescapable consequence is that for the most part only a very small number of news agencies and big-media journalists cover important events, thereby greatly increasing the likelihood that certain biases or straight misinformation may be perpetuated and magnified. Consensus among reports from a particular trouble spot may therefore reflect little more than the fact that only one source is relied upon to provide essential information.

Conventions of the Communications World. There is no doubt that the nature of the press—whether it emphasizes education and analysis or entertainment and "escape," whether it pursues sensationalism or profound reflection, whether it expresses concern with internationalism or with isolationism and parochialism, whether it is jingoist or humanitarian—largely reflects the economic context of its activities. Even such seemingly cultural features as the importance of the weekend papers (*Observer, Sunday Times, Sunday New York Times*) are, in the final analysis, dependent not only on the habits of the reading public but on the resources and markets available to the publishers.

Therefore, the treatment accorded crises, whether, for instance, sensationalism and a macabre interest in violence are to be emphasized as distinct from fundamental long-run factors, depends in large part on the economic structure of the relevant industry which, of course, in turn reflects the economic order of the whole society. The quality of crisis coverage cannot be divorced from the resources and general place that a society is prepared to allocate to its media and their coverage of world events. While the factor is critical, it is not, however, the only determinant of media response to crises.

THE STATE OF THE ART

The media are composed of an integrated complex of human and technological resources. On the human side, four distinct groups can be identified. First, the people who gather news in the field, the journalists, must be noted. They cover events and prepare raw news and information which, in the case of the printed word, is forwarded to members of the second group, the editors, or as is an increasingly appropriate designation, the media managers. This group makes news judgments, deciding what is of interest, what will attract readers or viewers, how much play a story should get, and most importantly, how the story should be rewritten or edited in part, usually so as to conform to the biases of the third group, the people who own the specific newspapers, magazine, network, or other media outlet. The fourth group operates the technology that transmits the news. It includes the personnel who, for instance, operate the television cameras—a job that by its very nature allows a lot of latitude for journalistic and editorial functions which are all the more influential because they are subtle.

All of the above functions are performed under the umbrella of a variety of organizational forms. There is a certain division of labor which permits the subcontracting of various necessary jobs. Among the most important of these is that performed by the news agencies (Reuters, *Agence France Presse*, UP, and so on) mentioned above, who sell their products to a wide range of subscribers. Each of the four components is critical. But the overall performance depends not only on the contribution of each but on the manner in which the whole is brought together, particularly under the extraordinary conditions associated with international crises.

General Conditions. Much depends on the supporting infrastructure in both the crisis site (or sites) and the country in which news is being received. Here such matters as the level of industrialization, technological development, and the literacy and sophistication of the population play a major role in facilitating or impeding the gathering and transmission of news by local and foreign operatives. To some extent the question becomes one of matching the available resources to the terrain and conditions in which a crisis unfolds, especially those concerning the independence of the industry and of its professionals. Governments are particularly anxious to influence crisis coverage, but owners, as we have seen, may also wish to interfere with accurate reporting. There are also unwitting and unperceived forces at play that may color what is reported about a particular event. One example must suffice: Graduates from American schools of journalism, now beginning to occupy key positions in much of the press of the English-speaking world, unwittingly bestow on their work the values and priorities of their training institutions, thus giving widespread currency to a somewhat idiosyncratic and particular point of view (Tunstall, 1977: ch. 12).

In this connection it is useful to note some of the consequences that follow from the dominance in the world of the English language. Journalists frequently suffer from the so-called "jackal syndrome," also known as the "boys on the bus disease," which reflects the degree to which they infect one another with what they perceive as reality. There is a tendency for the press corps, or a particular group of reporters, to form a collective impression of a given situation that is then imposed on the world as if it were the result of a series of independent observations. It may, in fact, result from the findings of only one or two reports that are then adopted by the rest of the pack.

Since English-speaking reporters share a language and culture and tend to chum together, they and their audiences are susceptible to being misled by this phenomenon. A salutary corrective occurs when British and American media diverge in the interpretation they accord the events of their beat. Thus, during the Suez crisis, when serious differences were evident between observers on each side of the Atlantic, English-speaking readers (and to some extent listeners) were able to benefit from somewhat divergent accounts of what was going on.

At heart, it is the professionalism of the media that determines the quality of crisis reporting. Journalism of some kind or other is one of the oldest occupations, and like the oldest profession of them all, it attracts a motley crew of practitioners motivated by a wide variety of goals. Many are passionate professionals imbuing their work with a tenacious concern for the highest standards, but as well as the less well-motivated pros there are also many transients and part-time operatives who are more seriously interested in political, bellelettristic, or other careers. While the latter group may add significant insights from time to time, on the whole it probably detracts from the efforts of fully committed life-long practitioners to bestow the highest levels of professionalism on their trade.

It is probably both an advantage and a drawback that many individuals attracted to journalism are those with strong ideological commitments who wish to help change the world. These individuals bring to their work a vitality and fervor that the more jaundiced outlook of a mere journeyman may lack. But they also, of course, may contribute to the ideological or partisan orientation of reporting. It is difficult enough, notably in periods of crises, to maintain objectivity and to contain patriotic loyalties without being aided and abetted by those wishing to influence events rather than merely striving to report them. This brings us to a nearly fatal impediment to accurate crisis journalism.

Reporters and editorialists are social beings and citizens like everyone else, and it is not easy for them to insulate themselves against the values and passions surrounding them. They therefore bring to the tasks before them the same prejudices, loyalties, and preconceived ideas as those held by most of their countrymen. When a crisis is related to events that challenge some comfortable national assumptions (as in the case of American relations with Iran, culminating in the hostage crisis), the mainstream of the media is likely to perform inadequately, and the small minority of dissenting interpreters, if any, is viewed with deep suspicion and disbelief. At this point, not an unusual one in periods of deep-seated international tensions, the public in even the most open and tolerant of liberal democratic regimes may be ill served by the mass media and generally also by the more specialized organs of information.

CONCLUSION

The foregoing catalogue of some of the principal factors influencing media performance in crises indicates how extremely complex, far-ranging, and subtle are the conditions that impinge on how crises are reported and interpreted. And our list is clearly far from complete and structured to respond to criteria and priorities not shared by all observers. How is one to respond to this bewildering array of variables?

Within the context of the present chapter, two quite distinct approaches seem inescapable: that of the political scientist wishing to sharpen his tools, and that of the citizen concerned about the well-being of mankind. For the political scientist, two exercises may prove rewarding. Both call for empirical studies of current and past international crises. The first would seek to establish whether some master variables can be identified that subsume or correlate with a number of others, and that therefore reduce the complexity of the problem. For theoretical as well as practical reasons, I am not giddily optimistic about the success of this enterprise. Such searches in other domains have all too often resulted in the emergence of variables which only *seemed* homogeneous and independent. On careful examination, and when applied to specific problems, they have tended to be too crude and to lack both consistency and autonomy. Still, the effort might be successful, and it would in any event shed additional light on the problem before us.

The other approach is to subject the relevant factors (as identified above or in some other way) to systematic scrutiny in a number of international crises. Each might be scored (high, medium, low; positive, negative) on various dimensions, among which three seem particularly relevant. In the first place, their impact on the *accuracy* of the coverage could be measured. More shall be said about this below. Second, the *speed* of the reports and analyses might be gauged. And finally, *media performance with respect to the nature of the crisis* would be identified and measured. Here, the *partisanship* with respect to the issues would have to be established (pro- or anti-status quo, pro- or anti-nationalist, pro- or anti-Western, and so on; intermediate positions might also be allowed). Media performance should also be examined with respect to the question of whether it tends to *exacerbate or attenuate the crisis*. The latter aspect in fact points to a question that is of critical importance to a particular crisis: the conditions under which diverse forms of media behavior can be expected to affect the outcome.

This dimension points to an intriguing aspect of this kind of inquiry: characteristics of media coverage that might commend themselves to the observer from one vantage point may be rejected when seen from a different perspective. Take accuracy, for example. This is a term which, in the present context, probably ranks with motherhood as an absolute good. But is it? There can be little doubt that in some situations—when a crisis can only be contained, for instance, if public opinion is restrained so as to permit the leaders to resist precipitous retaliatory action—full and truthful disclosure of events may seriously exacerbate conditions. In the event that ghastly atrocities were committed, detailed knowledge in the "victim" country might prevent the leaders from cooling the crisis so as to achieve a peaceful outcome.

This aspect of the matter directs our attention to what might be termed the "nondisciplinary" or "citizen" approach to media coverage of crises, namely, the question of when or under what condition the latter *should* be contained or escalated. The answer depends on the issues involved and the normative reaction to them. Many people of good will argue that in an era of nuclear and worse weapons, the avoidance of war is so high a good that all other considerations must be made subservient to it. But others, equally worthy individuals, believe that some actions of states (with respect to nationalities, for instance) are so heinous that nothing justifies their being tolerated.

There is, of course, no absolute, objective way of resolving this dilemma. Everything depends on one's assumptions. And in this sense the citizen is as well placed as the political scientist for reaching the ethically appropriate conclusion. This perspective allows us to rank the necessary characteristics of media performance with greater confidence than was possible within the framework of the political scientist. For to make ethical judgments adequately requires that the facts creating crises be known and understood. If this is to happen, accurate and full reporting is absolutely essential, regardless of whether it deepens potential conflict.

This discussion of the factors that influence the quality of crisis reporting by the media makes it clear that a great deal is left to be desired and that the task of assuring satisfactory coverage is awesomely difficult. No one has recognized this better than the media themselves. National and international associations of journalists have repeatedly expressed concerns about the condition of their craft, partly because of internal obstacles to high performance and partly because of the interventions of governments. The latter have, in some instances, sought to protect the freedom of the press, but the history of these efforts throughout the world is discouraging.

UNESCO has made this subject one of its major concerns. The heated controversy over the recommendations of its McBride Report reflects the complexity of the issues covered and the ethical relativity that dominates the way in which they are perceived. These problems can perhaps best be tackled by the maximization of contacts among journalists from different countries and between those who subscribe to different ideologies. It would also help to facilitate regular interaction between journalists and scholars. Such contacts might enhance the work of both without raising the spectre of government interference or of domination by multinational or other vested interests.

NOTES

1. For the sake of simplicity, the word "press" is occasionally used to include the electronic media.

2. For decision-makers, the result may not always be salutary. For a suggestive discussion of this phenomenon with respect to the nature of the response, drawing on psychological literature and a number of studies of crises, see Suedfeld and Tetlock (1977).

CHAPTER 5

IMPROBABLE EVENTS AND
EXPECTABLE BEHAVIOR

RICHARD L. MERRITT

Crises are frequently defined as decision-making situations characterized by (a) a threat to a system's central values, (b) a high probability of violence, and (c) the shortness of time within which a decision must be reached. Accordingly, crises require decision-making under conditions of severe stress for the system concerned.

Such a definition, although intuitively satisfying, contains a number of problems if applied to national decision-making. One of these is the well-known difficulty of delineating a national system's core values (or, if you will, national interest). Attempts by national leaders and scholars to define their own country's value priorities have not been notoriously successful, and the propensity of any country's leaders to view values from different perspectives merely compounds this problem by proliferating value rankings. They may not even agree on the centrality of survival as a systemic value—as we have seen in the intellectual debates of the 1950s as to the relative merits of being "red or dead," and in the behavior of some states such as Yugoslavia, which in 1941 considered autonomy more important than mere survival as a puppet state in the hands of Nazi Germany.

A second problem centers on ascertaining the probability of violence inherent in a decision-making situation. Some situations, such as the collapse of a country's export market, may contain little direct threat of violence but nonetheless pose a severe crisis for that country. Others may entail a self-fulfilling prophecy as far as violence is concerned. Soviet leaders agreed that their intervention into Afghanistan in the last days of 1979 was a matter internal to the socialist system and that it was the U.S. definition of the situation as a crisis requiring American sanctions that produced the real threat of violence. More generally, these and similar situations suggest that the possibility of violence is actually a subclass of the first variable: core values that may be destroyed or disequilibrated by violence.

Third, determining what time frame characterizes a crisis has proved to be problematic. In the case of an ultimatum, the amount of time available to a national system to meet a crisis is determined by another national actor, that is, the country giving the ultimatum. In other cases, however, the national system in question sets its own time frame. In October 1962, American decision-makers decided that action was required before Soviet missiles en route to Cuba were landed. After creating a blockade, they then imposed on the Soviet Union their own definition of the amount of time available to resolve the crisis they saw. Almost nineteen years later, American decision-makers, facing what they surely defined as a crisis, refused to impose on Iran time limits within which the U. S. embassy officials held hostage had to be returned.

Above all, defining a crisis in terms of a decision-making unit's stress poses a severe analytic problem. For one thing, stress on the national decision-making system may or may not coincide with stress on the individuals who are making decisions on behalf of the national system. Evidence from the Cuban missile crisis of October 1962 indicates that individual decision-makers behaved as though they themselves were under stress, as though any national loss would be a personal loss (Janis, 1972; Wiegele, 1978), and an aide to President Jimmy Carter reports that the president, when informed that the mission to rescue the American hostages in Teheran had collapsed because of technological breakdowns and a fatal accident, "looked as though someone had stabbed him; pain was evident all over his face" (Brzezinski, 1982: 78). In an extreme case we might speak of "true believers" (Hoffer, 1951) who identify their personalities completely with the organization of which they are a part.

Such complete identification, however, is doubtless rare at high governmental levels, since most decision-making situations are multivalent for their participants. Being in the middle of the storm when the outcomes of battle or the destinies of great nations (or even of small firms) are in the balance gives some participants a sense of exhilaration (if the biographies and autobiographies of great leaders are to be credited).[1] Personal depression and even mental deterioration may follow upon the happy warrior's removal from the arena of battle. Similarly, a severe blow to the organization for which one is responsible may enhance the individual's position with respect to other values. Thus, President Carter's failure to deal adequately with the Iranian hostage situation actually brought him short-run advantages in the form of a strategy that could be used to defeat his opponents for the Democratic party's presidential nomination. In all these situations, organizational crisis may relieve the personal, psychological stress felt by individual participants.

For another thing, there is an important gap in our knowledge about the effects of individual and organizational stress in decision-making. Numerous studies at the level of the individual reveal that performance varies directly with the amount of stress up to a point, after which increasing stress causes a sharp drop in performance (McGrath, 1976). Many writers have suggested an isomorphic pattern at the level of the group. Perhaps the most important of these in modern times was Arnold J. Toynbee, who spoke of civilizations' responses to challenges, but the metaphor is found elsewhere as well. Even if we grant this assumption of isomorphism, we must face the fact that we know little or nothing about the effects of systemic stress on the performance of individuals acting on behalf of national systems.

A Probabilistic Approach to Crises

It is less dramatic but more productive to focus not so much on "crises" as situations sui generis than on varying dimensions and magnitudes of problems to be resolved. In this view, the concern with crises as somehow abnormal may actually hinder us in our study of international politics. In delineating problems with varying characteristics that face national decision systems, of course, the centrality of the values affected (including the probable effects of violence) and the time available for decision-making—however problematic these concepts may be as variables—play key roles. Just as there is a difference between a man's selection of the tie he will wear that day and the same man's choice when confronting a life and death situation (such as choosing to save the life of the child or the mother in the case of a difficult birth), so too is there a difference between a country's response to the death of a leader in a stable foreign country and its response to a missile attack. Perceptions, whether imposed from within or without, of the amount of time available for decision-making are also important.

A third variable plays a role as well: the probability that a particular class of problem will actually arise. By this I mean two things. The first is the probability that any particular event (or closely tied set of events) will occur. At one end of the continuum are problems arising with such frequency that we have developed standard operating procedures for dealing with them. Every tourist who loses a passport does not cause an international incident. And industrial countries are learning to cope with periodic increases in the price of crude oil by OPEC members. At the other end of the continuum are highly improbable problems—not unimaginable problems such as an invasion by creatures from outer space, but rather those that are quite imaginable (such as an exchange of nuclear-tipped missiles) but that have either never occurred or else have occurred with such infrequency that we have little experience in dealing with them. It is our bafflement in dealing with the occurrence of a highly improbable situation that is at the nub of crisis decision-making as discussed at the outset of this section (see Close, 1979).

The other aspect of our third variable is the probability of occurrence of a concatenation of individual events, none of which, viewed by itself, would normally be significant but all of which, taken together, constitute an important change in the country's decision-making environment. Scholars systematically analyzing international events on a continuum ranging from extreme conflict (e.g., extensive war acts causing deaths, dislocation, and high strategic cost) to extreme cooperation (e.g., voluntary unification into one nation) have developed the notion of *normal relations* between any pair of states (Azar and Cohen, 1979). The weighted sum of events, each recorded separately, for a given time period between two states yields an average interaction intensity score for that period, and changes in the index over several time periods produce a curve of average interaction intensities. By examining such curves, one can establish the "normal" range of relationships for the pair of states. It follows that any time period in which the average interaction intensity between them goes beyond the thresholds of "normal" conflict or "normal" cooperation is one to which analysts should be alert for potential sources of instability that could lead to precipitate action.

The following pages deal with strategic considerations in responding to highly improbable problems in the international arena. Although communications and communications procedures are at the center of attention, the chapter will not deal with their technical aspects, including modes of overseas representation, technological innovations such as the "hotline" between the White House and the Kremlin, or specific bargaining techniques. It looks rather at a national decision system's means for improving its standard operating procedures, responding to unexpected contingencies, changing behavioral patterns, and developing stable expectations about behavior. A main concern throughout the chapter is the possibility of preventing little problems from becoming big ones, and transforming major "crises" into their component parts which then can be dealt with routinely, at least to some measure.

IMPROVING STANDARD OPERATING PROCEDURES

The probabilistic view of crises outlined above contains some clues to decision-making at the national level. First of all, most international problems facing national decision-makers occur frequently and regularly. Their probability of occurrence is sufficiently great that, irrespective of their seriousness (as indicated by affected values and decision time), national governments develop routine ways of handling them (Inbar, 1979). This is true in the United States, for instance, whether we are speaking of the apprehension of an illegal alien or the receipt of information indicating that Soviet missiles may have penetrated the country's northern defense perimeter.

The task of the government in such circumstances is to ascertain what is possible and how probable it is, and then to act accordingly. It says to *expect the expected.* Note that this does not imply acceptance of such maxims as "If you would have peace, prepare for war"—which, by assuming the ubiquity of violence, contributes to the very conditions that foster it. It is, rather, the model of an emergency ward at a major municipal hospital. Knowing the pattern of reported injuries over a long period of time tells administrators how many doctors with what specializations to have on hand on a given evening, how many splints they should stock, and so forth. In most cases, most of the time, the staff will be able to treat patients adequately with available supplies. For the exceptional situation emergency procedures (such as plans for transporting patients by helicopter to a nearby hospital) can be arranged in advance.

Improving a country's capacity to address highly probable problems coming its way requires attention to its information system, that is, its ability to assemble, process, and evaluate information (see Deutsch, 1963). Relevant information about foreign countries and the international environment as a whole is gathered through traditional diplomatic channels, overt methods such as analyzing press reports or surveying areas via satellite photography, and espionage and other covert forms of intelligence operations. Such streams of information are combined with others stemming from the domestic environment. The development of electronic computers and appropriate computational programs has greatly improved a country's capacity to sort through this information, store the data in readily accessible form, and retrieve them in ways that enhance their proper evaluation.

Such "normal" procedures for foreign policy decision-making are not without their attendant problems. They are very expensive to begin with, and even though cost efficiency may decline with increases in the extent to which the information system is elaborated, poor states are put at a disadvantage vis-à-vis their wealthier neighbors. They are also subject to information overloads and inherent biases that may lead information processers to ignore entire categories of relevant data (see Whiting, 1960). Excessive pressure for efficient communications may render the system even more fragile, reliant on each actor or component functioning at peak levels of efficiency (Cioffi-Revilla, 1979). And, of course, there is no guarantee that very human decision-makers will in fact be able to evaluate and use the information effectively in formulating policy. There are occasional breakdowns and "noise" in even the best of communications systems.

RESPONDING TO UNEXPECTED CONTINGENCIES

A second implication of a probabilistic notion of decision-making is that some problems will arise too infrequently for national decision systems to develop stores of experience and routinized procedures for dealing with them. The lack of attention to conceivable but highly improbable phenomena (or to events or behaviors, some aspects of which are highly improbable) can severely test the adaptability and even survival of a national system, should such an event of a serious nature actually occur. Yet most national decision-making systems are so wrapped up in routine problems that they fail to take seriously the concrete need for contingency planning.

Modeling and simulation are recently developed techniques that can help governments to plan for the unexpected. The first task is to identify the range of possible but improbable events that could impinge on the national decision system. Traditionally, members of policy planning staffs or consultants at private or quasi-official think-tanks have performed this vital service, or decision-makers themselves have sat around tables dreaming up possible scenarios of future events. Such procedures, frequently very insightful, are usually limited by their nonsystematic quality. Important scenarios may be ignored because of their low probability of actually occurring. Global modeling programs such as that currently being developed by Karl W. Deutsch and his colleagues at the Science Center Berlin will eventually be able to spin out more systematically a still broader set of alternative futures for decision-makers to consider (Bremer, 1981).

The next step is to determine an appropriate course of action—or at least ascertain what the decision-makers need to know—for the possibility that any one or a combination of these alternative futures should occur. The purpose of such an exercise is to train decision-makers to respond to unfamiliar situations with both an openness born of confidence in handling similar situations and a modicum of learned behavior, such as how to go about finding innovative solutions (see Deutsch, 1975). The model here is in part like that of an aircraft simulator, in which experienced pilots "flying" a simulated airplane learn to respond instantaneously and without panic to untoward malfunctions that they have never encountered in their real-life experience. This approach has been used extensively in military planning. In another part, however, the model goes beyond learning responses to preprogrammed emergencies. It must simulate situations in which decision-makers *learn how to learn*, and do so in a way that can mitigate any tendency for stress at the national and individual levels to coincide (see Phillips et al., 1974, 1977).

CHANGING BEHAVIORAL PATTERNS

A third implication of this view of national decision-making is that participants in this process should encourage the development of long-term behavioral patterns that minimize any risk of deflecting effective decision-making. One important aspect—one in which modern democracies are having difficulty—focuses on public presentation of international problems. Although few if any liberal democrats would argue for press censorship or news management by the government, a danger lies at the other end of the spectrum we call freedom of information, the end at which the media have abrogated any sense of public responsibility. To a great measure, President Carter permitted the American media to define the country's stake in the Iranian hostage issue. By emphasizing the personal tragedy of the 52 U.S. embassy personnel, the media effectively constrained the president's freedom to handle the crisis in accord with his concept of national interests (Brzezinski, 1982). The line between investigative reporting of the kind that uncovered the nature of the American intervention in Vietnam and the Watergate scandal on the one hand and, on the other, irresponsible intrusions into the legitimate foreign policy making functions of the government is clearly a fine one. To deal effectively with foreign policy problems, it is nevertheless imperative that the government avoid getting trapped in someone else's definition of the situation, regardless of whether that someone else is a foreign government or its own citizens.

Another requirement, easily noted but in fact extraordinarily difficult to accomplish, is to destroy the shibboleths of the past that constrain a national decision system's handling of a foreign policy problem. Years gone by saw many countries initiate bizarre schemes in the name of national honor. Almost two centuries ago, Americans rallied to the cry, "Millions for defense, but not a cent for tribute!" And smirches on a country's honor, such as a foreign mob trampling on that country's flag, led many a patriot to demand satisfaction and even led some countries to take punitive action to restore their "lost" honor. The world since 1945 has seen leaders of the major countries toning down this concept. The risk of wider repercussions or even mutual destruction is great enough that these leaders have sought to reeducate their populations to accept a moe tolerant view of foreign behavior. (Some in the United States during the presidential campaign of 1980 insisted that Carter, by refusing to retaliate for such outrages as the seizure of the U.S. embassy personnel in Teheran and the burning of the U.S. embassy in Pakistan, had pushed the pendulum of sensitivity to national honor too far in the opposite direction, and had even made such incidents more likely in the future.)

It is also possible to redirect national behavior so as to avoid foreseeable or even possible problems. In the 1920s and 1930s debts remaining from World War I and reparations payments imposed on defeated Germany contributed to a series of international confrontations, including an Anglo-French occupation of the Rhineland, and more generally to frictions that poisoned the international atmosphere. American leaders in World War II worked out lend-lease agreements to avoid postwar conflict over debt settlement, and the Western allies chose to seize captured German property rather than demand that postwar Germans be placed for a long time in a position similar to that of the 1920s. Some contemporary leaders of industrialized countries, faced with certain knowledge of future shortages of oil and rising oil prices, are now trying to develop policies that will reduce their countries' dependency on foreign oil. In short, it is not necessary to repeat the errors of the past, nor is it necessary to blunder into new ones if they can be seen in advance and national behavior directed away from them.

A more difficult task of learning is to change national approaches to the international arena. It took two decades and major conflagrations in Europe and Asia to persuade the United States to back away from the isolationist stance it adopted in 1919, and the American propensity to intervene in defense of liberal democracies throughout the world endured more than two decades before President Richard M. Nixon repudiated the Truman Doctrine of 1947. The British Empire, too, and British behavior commensurate with its claims, were not destroyed in a day, as the Falkland Islands crisis recently demonstrated once again. While the process of developing a West European community based on cooperation and reciprocity, under way for well over three decades now, still has a long way to go, other voices are calling for their countries (or others) to pursue the path of autocentric development. Available evidence indicates that none of this learning proceeds smoothly and monotonically but rather has the ups and downs of typical learning curves of individuals.

DEVELOPING STABLE EXPECTATIONS ABOUT BEHAVIOR

In a world beset by major conflicts among nations, very few seize the headlines and hold on tenaciously to the world's attention. The attention given to these issues hides the fact that most such conflicts, whether potential or actual, are prevented from emerging as contentious issues, mitigated or even resolved quietly before coming under public scrutiny. The latter do not excite the interests of the media, for "news" of this kind (or, in Johan Galtung's term, "olds") makes dull reading indeed. For analysts of international politics, it is nonetheless important to remember that the *norm* is peaceful resolution of disputes. To the extent that foreign policy-makers act in ways that enhance this norm, they contribute measurably to stabilizing expectations about the behavior of national actors in the international arena (see Boyle, 1980).

A related aspect is the expectation that national actors have a propensity toward escalating or deescalating disputes that arise. The fact that the behavior of any single country may change as one government replaces another is a destabilizing element, since it forces the decision-makers of other countries to revise their estimates of what that country might do should an international incident occur. Some writers, such as Herman Kahn (1965), have offered "ladders" of escalation designed to provide guidelines for those seeking *quids* for *quos.* An innovative suggestion in the opposite direction is Charles E. Osgood's Graduated Reciprocal Initiatives in Tension-reduction (GRIT)—a strategy that seems to have been attempted with some success during the presidency of John F. Kennedy (Osgood, 1962). To the extent that such guidelines become fixed as norms of international behavior, they approach the status of what is sometimes called normative international law.

Upon occasion, however, national states have turned such norms of stable behavior into rigid guidelines that dictate unthought-through action. The effect is to render brittle any expectations of behavior. Responses to specific events are so well prescribed that national decision-makers have no latitude in deciding what to do. Such policies, akin to knee jerk reactions, may end in tragedy, as occurred in 1914 after the Russian military mobilization, or they may be ignored, as happened with the American doctrine of massive retaliation outlined in the early 1950s. The prospect that the United States might unleash its military might on the Soviet Union—that is, strike at places and with means of its own choosing—in the event of a Soviet incursion anywhere in the world was not viewed by most observers as being especially credible.

Stabilizing expectations about the behavior of nation-states aims at making patterns of international interaction more predictable. It is ultimately this predictability—to a high degree and over a wide range of behaviors—that forms the basis of international community. It does not eliminate conflicts, nor does it preclude totally the possibility of surprises. It does, however, give national decision systems the security of knowing what the international norms of behavior are, estimating the costs of violating these norms, and developing means to prevent or mitigate the consequences of major crises.

NOTE

1. Pertinent here is President Harry S Truman's remark: "If you can't stand the heat, get out of the kitchen."

CHAPTER 6

THE MIDDLE EAST CRISIS
Theoretical Propositions and Examples

ALI E. HILLAL DESSOUKI

Issues of crisis management and crisis diplomacy attracted a great deal of attention in the 1970s.[1] Topics such as crisis avoidance, crisis escalation, and crisis deescalation have become legitimate areas of academic investigation. Most of the research on crisis analysis, however, seems to emphasize the superpowers' and nuclear states' interactions and take the management of the Cuban missile crisis as a model. Little research has been done on crises in developing countries. Whether crisis management in these countries differs from that in developed countries remains an open question. Putting it differently, how do the societal, systemic, and behavioral characteristics of developing countries manifest themselves in a crisis situation?

There is one methodological remark which must be made at the outset. Crisis management research should not assume that crisis avoidance or deescalation is necessarily a desirable goal of all participants in a crisis situation. Neither the assumption that international crises take place as a result of events over which no one has control nor the notion of "the crisis that nobody wanted" can be accepted uncritically across the board. Though crises usually contain some elements of the unexpected, they can be and are in fact planned, engineering, and steered by some states to achieve their national interests. Indeed, "crisis

AUTHOR'S NOTE: I would like to thank the Center of International Studies of Princeton University for its financial help, allowing me to attend the Zurich IPSA Round Table, and Professors Henry Bienen and Cyril Black of Princeton for reading an earlier draft and suggesting modifications.

as a policy" can be observed in the external conduct of a number of states.

Also, crisis management does not necessarily mean the avoidance of the use of force. Limited use of force can be a successful instrument of foreign policy, as the 1973 war demonstrated. Finally, there are certain crises, I believe, that should not be prevented or avoided, such as those related to national liberation and the right to self-determination. These are often the prerequisities for a stable and just world peace.

It follows that managing a crisis does not always mean deescalating it. Crisis management is not crisis resolution. The concept of "management" refers to a way of handling or success in accomplishing one's objectives. Different parties to a crisis situation employ different strategies of management depending upon their interests, objectives, and capabilities. Implied here is the view that the management of a crisis means different things to different actors at different stages of the crisis. Crisis participants tend to steer the crisis in a way conducive to the achievement of their goals. From the nonparticipants' perspective, that objective is often likely, but not always since some nonparticipants may also have an interest in the prolongation of the crisis, to prevent the crisis from developing into armed hostilities, and if it does, to limit the level of hostilities and to prevent their spread to other countries. Thus, there exist no general rules on the "proper" management of crisis. Rules and guidelines differ according to type of actor (size and level of development), nature of threat (economic and political threats as opposed to identity threats or to the survival of the political community), objectives of the actor, and the global system.

This chapter deals with one aspect of crisis management. It analyzes certain types of foreign policy behavior that should be avoided in crisis situations. The chapter addresses itself to a number of foreign policy behaviors and draws on the experience of the Middle East crises of 1967 and 1973.

The analysis is predicated on the assumption that the management of a crisis by one actor ought to take into consideration the situation of its adversary. A two-actors crisis situation, for instance, is therefore viewed as one of a deadlock in which the two are tied together. Perhaps with the exception of the cases of total defeat and surrender (Germany and Japan in World War II), or when the prolongation of a crisis situation is obviously beneficial to a particular actor, crisis managers ought to help their adversaries find a tolerable exit from the deadlock. In the language of bargaining analysis, crisis behavior, as Snyder and Diesing (1977) argue, is a combination of coercion and accommodation. Thus, what seems at the surface a zero-sum game is also a situation that both parties have a common interest of ending. Perhaps no crisis in the 1970s exemplified this more than the 1973 War in the Middle East, which is celebrated by its two major protagonists, Egypt and Israel, as a victory. It is in this context that the chapter deals with four aspects of foreign policy behavior in a crisis situation.

Dealing with the Adversary's Perception of Threat

Decision-makers act upon their perception of the environment, and in a crisis situation the role of individuals, and therefore of their psychological environment, tends to increase. This is even more crucial in developing countries where foreign policy output is more a function of individuals than institutions.

An actor in a crisis is ill advised to create a situation that would unwarrantedly increase his adversary's sense of threat. A leadership ought to refrain from enhancing its adversary's fears, and thus leading to a further escalation of the crisis, unless of course it perceives its interests to lie in such an escalation. In particular, one must not threaten the basic values of one's adversary. When a leadership perceives great threats to the basic values of its political regimes, or worse, the political community, the greater the risks it is ready to take.

The enhancement of an adversary's threat perception can take place in a number of ways. A leadership may get carried away by its initial successes in a crisis and start to change and expand its objectives. The same can take place due to elite factionalization and domestic political cleavages. Another issue is the clarity of signals between adversaries. When the objectives of one actor in a crisis are ambiguous, the adversary tends to perceive them in their most extreme sense. In both cases— expansion of goals and ambiguity of objectives and signals—the adversary's perception of threat is promoted and intensified. This is more likely to take place in developing countries where there is a tendency to perceive threats as directed toward the survival of the regime. Such a tendency may be explained by the newness of the statehood, the low level of political institutionalization, and the prevailing sense of leadership insecurity.

Egypt's handling of the 1967 and 1973 crises is strikingly different in this regard.[2] In 1967 Egypt moved from the modest request to redeploy

UNEF (United Nations Emergency Forces) along a part of its frontiers with Israel, to the request for their withdrawal altogether and ultimately to the takeover of Sharm El-Sheikh and the subsequent closure of the Straits of Tiran to Israeli navigation. Egypt moved from one position to another under the push of events contributing to the escalation of the crisis. The signals that came from Egypt before June 5th, the beginning of military hostilities, were confusing. For instance, after the closure of the Straits of Tiran, Nasser stated that this act terminated Israel's gains from the 1956 tripartite aggression and opened the way to look into "the 1948 aggression and the Palestine question." Egyptian ambiguity and confusion played well into the hands of the Israeli leadership, which was ready for war. Israeli leadership employed this ambiguity to invoke a perception of a concerted Arab assault to "destroy the Jewish state."

By contrast, in 1973 the Egyptian leadership had a much narrower objective, and the initial military victory in the war did not entice it to change its position. It was a war to liberate one's occupied lands. In fact, the objective was even narrower. Sadat never entertained the probability of liberating the whole of the Sinai peninsula through military action. In his view it was a war intended to prove the falseness of Israel's theory of secure borders, to demonstrate that the unlawful occupation of Arab territories was no guarantee of Israeli security. It was also intended to focus international attention on the seriousness of the situation in the Middle East. Thus it was a limited war in terms of its objectives.

Egypt's mass media displayed similar restraint and discipline in reporting the war and Egypt's objectives. In particular, *Kol Kahir* (Egypt's Hebrew-language broadcasting service) deliberately made a point of not exacerbating Jewish fears during the war. It decided, for instance, that no emphasis would be placed on Israel's international isolation (which was a fact) so as not to revive the images of the lonely Jew, the eternal hostility of the gentiles, and ultimately the image of Massada.

Proposition I: In crisis situations, each side must avoid challenging the basic values of its adversary or intensifying the adversary's threat perception. It may even attempt to justify its actions in terms of the adversary's cultural tradition.

The Importance of Communication: With Whom?

A customary argument in research in crisis management stresses the importance of maintaining open communication channels with one's adversary. The argument is that during a crisis situation, the need for adequate communication between adversaries increases. Adequate communication channels, direct or indirect, have two beneficial functions: to permit proper judgment of the adversary's objectives and to convey one's own. A further argument is that the transmission of signals in a crisis situation depends on the existence and effectiveness of the communication channels between the adversaries.

This thesis, which carries the imprint of the Cuban missile crisis, has been uncritically incorporated into most of the literature on crisis management. The validity and relevance of such a proposition can be challenged in the analysis of international crises between developing countries. In most of these cases, a crisis usually involves a breakdown of diplomatic relations; termination or freeze of economic, educational, and cultural interactions; closure of borders; dismissal of the adversary's nationals (private citizens) from the country; hostile mass media campaigns; and even the halting of one's commercial air company traveling to the adversary's airports. These practices, and others, suggest that developing countries' elites act in a way contrary to the "maintenance-of-communication-with-the-adversary" thesis. Thus, the need for adequate communication channels, logical as it may be, does not seem to be very useful in understanding crisis management in developing countries. It is interesting to recall, however, that until World War I, all states tended to close their communications with adversaries in crisis situations. This behavior can be related to the stage of socioeconomic development, prolonged stable statehood, and the nature and intensity of threats. Finally, there are the facts that developing countries have few communications to be closed, that such an action, in most cases, will not have much of an impact on either state, and yet that it has a great domestic political value.

Communication channels remain vital, however, from a different perspective. Crisis management in developing countries requires communication with one's regional friends and more importantly with one's superpower patron. In a global system characterized by power hierarchy and unequal status, developing countries are basically dependent acctors. They depend on the developed countries in almost every respect, from food to armaments. In a crisis situation, the need for political support in international councils and military supplies is paramount, thus requiring increased coordination and communication with the friendly or patron power.

In the 1967 crisis, for instance, Israel received a green light from the United States to resort to war while Egypt misinterpreted the signals of its ally, the Soviet Union. The handling of the crisis by the Egyptian leadership was so poor that it did not have proper consultation with the Soviet Union. The Minister of War, Shams Badran, returned from Moscow with a misinterpretation of the Soviet stand: that the Soviets were solidly behind Egypt in a war situation.[3] Nasser expressed this understanding in his public speeches, giving the impression of Soviet support to Egypt in the case of war. When the war ended miserably, there were a number of anti-Soviet demonstrations in Cairo because of the Soviet Union's failure to come to the rescue of Egypt.

In 1973 the link with the superpowers was no less vital. Both superpowers resupplied the military machine of their respective allied states during the hostilities. American aid to Israel was crucial for regaining the initiative and changing the course of the battle. Lack of proper communication existed between Sadat and the Soviet leadership. Sadat refused to accept a Soviet-sponsored proposal for a cease-fire on October 13 at the height of Egypt's victory and before the Israeli penetration into the western side of the Suez Canal became serious. The Soviets probably found out or anticipated the Israeli plan but could not bring Sadat to agree on the cease-fire. If a cease-fire had been enforced at the time, a different end of the war and its subsequent diplomatic negotiations might well have been recorded.

Proposition II: In a crisis situation, developing countries are in need of the political and military support of their superpower ally, and therefore successful management of the crisis depends to a large extent on the effectiveness of communication and the proper understanding of signals between the two.

Options in Crisis Situations

The essence of political decision is the choice between different alternatives and courses of action. This is more important in a crisis situation where options are usually perceived as limited. A leadership ought to resist the temptation, strong in crisis times, to view its options as limited. Decision-makers are in a better bargaining position when they recognize that their adversary is in a situation similar to their own and that in the worst of situations different options, or variations of the same option, exist. When a leadership perceives its options as narrow, its behavior tends to become extreme and one-sided, resulting in an unwarranted increase of its demands at the time of victory or unnecessary concessions at the time of setback. Thus, in a crisis situation, decision-makers ought to retain their options for probable escalation or deescalation. Equally important is that decision-makers have an understanding of the adversary's situation and keep a certain amount of options open to the other side.

A clear example of leadership's perception of the narrowing of its options was the case of Egypt in 1967. In the perception and practice of its leadership, the mobilization of the army into the Sinai and the withdrawal of UNEF were linked to the takeover of Sharm El-Sheikh and then to the closure of the Straits of Tiran to Israeli navigation. Whether these successive events were really the only options to Egypt remains an open question.

Similarly, Sadat's diplomatic negotiation after the cease-fire of October 22 displayed a perception of narrow options. By the closing days of the war, Israel managed to penetrate west of the Canal and encircled Egypt's third army. Sadat seemed to have believed that Egypt would not be allowed by the United States to handle the "Israeli military pocket" by force. According to him, Henry Kissinger gave Egypt what amounted to an ultimatum: The United States would not allow American arms to be defeated again by Soviet ones.

Proposition III: Successful management of crisis situation depends on keeping one's options open and not acting under the belief that there is only one choice.

Proposition IV: In crisis situations, the existence of a consultation process is crucial so that each side can neutralize the other's "closure of options" and investigate the various alternatives present in the situation.

Dangers of Past Experience

All human beings are prisoners of their past experiences in one way or another. Decision-makers naturally tend to be influenced by their successful behavior in previous crises. They are likely to repeat those strategies which proved effective without seriously considering the changing domestic or external milieu.

In 1967 Nasser was heavily influenced by his successful management of the 1956 crisis. In the latter, he managed to transform a military defeat into a definite political victory. As a result, he emerged as the uncontested ruler of Egypt, a Pan-Arab hero, and a rising star of the anticolonial movement in the Third World. In May-June 1967 he attempted to repeat what had happened eleven years earlier. For instance, after closing the Straits of Tiran, he showed his readiness to negotiate, and one of his Vice-Presidents, Mr. Zakaria Muhi-El-Din, was to travel to the United States on June 5th. Militarily, the Egyptian leadership employed the same tactic of 1956—withdrawal from Sinai—albeit under radically different circumstances. Nasser and his colleagues must have misperceived their environment. The United States, for instance, was no longer impartial or responsive to Egypt as it was in 1956 but rather intent on teaching Nasser a lesson and putting a limit on Egypt's active foreign policy. In particular, Egypt's military presence in Yemen had to be terminated. Another difference was Israel's success in the battle of public opinion in the West. Israel managed to project the situation in 1967 in the images of David and Goliath.

Similarly, in the 1973 crisis, the Israeli leadership was a prisoner of past experience and conceptions. Throughout the period from 1970 to 1973, it developed two major concepts in relation to the Arabs: one, that Egypt was not to start a war given definite Israeli air superiority as displayed in the 1969-1970 war of attrition; the other, that due to Arab fragmentation and the lack of trust among Arab governments, no war on two fronts was likely to occur. Stated differently, the Israeli leadership believed that the Arabs had neither the political will nor the administrative military skills to coordinate a simultaneous attack on two fronts. The prevalence of this "conception" was to a great extent responsible for Israel's failure to predict the war. In particular, it failed to predict the effectiveness of Egypt's armed forces.

Proposition V: In crisis situations, decision-makers ought to shy away from the natural inclination to repeat past strategies that were once proved successful. They are advised to look into each crisis in its own right and within its own specific context.

Though this chapter ventured into the area of what decision-makers should and should not do at times of crisis, it must be noted in the end that crisis management depends to a great extent on the personalities of the decision-makers in each particular case. The successful management of a crisis therefore relies on their shrewd, perceptive analysis of the situation, correct evaluation of alternatives, and their ability to make decisions and take risks at the right time. The successful management of a crisis is undoubtedly related to the firmness and robustness of the leadership. Thus it cannot be totally reduced to a set of rules and regulations on how to manage a crisis. Though the existence of such a code may be useful, a significant part of the successful management of international crises is, and is likely to remain, an expression of individual genius and leadership qualities under stress. Crisis management is partially an art, notwithstanding social scientists' efforts to systemize and thematize it.

NOTES

1. Examples of this attention are Holsti (1971), Bell (1971), Herman (1972), Williams (1976), Nomikos and North (1976), *International Studies Quarterly* (1977), Snyder and Diesig (1977), Frei (1978), Brecher (1979), and Cohen (1979).

2. On the 1967 and 1973 wars, see for example: Laquer (1968), Safran (1979), Abu-Lughot (1970), Sharabi (1970), Evron (1973), and The Sunday *Times* (1974).

3. Recognizing the dangerous implications of such an understanding, the Egyptian Ambassador to Moscow, Dr. Murad Ghaleb, dispatched a more sober analysis of the Soviet position. Unfortunately, the report reached Nasser only after the beginning of hostilities.

CHAPTER 7

ESCALATION
Assessing the Risk of
Unintentional Nuclear War

D A N I E L   F R E I

The Crisis as a Catalytic Trigger

International crises are usually examined with a view to their defusion or settlement. Research generally tries to discuss ways and means for ending dangerous international confrontations. In this chapter, the focus will be on the other end of the crisis, i.e., on crisis escalation and ultimately on the generation of an unintentional nuclear war by crisis situations. The possibility of a nuclear holocaust triggered unintentionally in fact constitutes a matter of growing concern. Large segments of the public are increasingly alarmed by the traumatic horror fiction of a system of strategic deterrence getting out of control and confronting mankind suddenly with a doomsday nightmare.

Ever since the movie *Dr. Strangelove* presented such a fiction, it has become quite popular to worry about insane colonels ordering an unauthorized missile launch, unfortunate officers pushing the wrong button, the self-activation of an electric guidance system, signals on a

AUTHOR'S NOTE: This chapter is based on a comprehensive study on the *Risks of Unintentional Nuclear War,* which the author wrote on behalf of the United Nations Institute for Disarmament Research (UNIDIR) and which has been published in Fall 1982. As this publication is fully documented (listing about 500 references), no references are given here. I am indebted to Christian Catrina, Research Associate, for his kind assistance in preparing the study. The views expressed in this chapter are those of the author and not necessarily those of UNIDIR.

radar screen reflecting a flock of geese mistaken for attacking missiles, and so on. Yet the popularity of these and other nuclear-war-by-accident scenarios does not necessarily imply the appropriate relevance of such scenarios.

Although one certainly must not underestimate the dangers emanating from the possibility of nuclear accidents and incidents, one cannot avoid the conclusion that the focus on the risk of nuclear war by accident may misrepresent the problem and misdirect attention from more serious risks. While redundant and efficient safeguard systems practically preclude any grave consequences of human and technical failure, a far greater danger is looming in the nature of international crises. As the following analysis will demonstrate, it is quite conceivable that an acute international crisis may act as a catalytic trigger to start a nuclear war which in fact was not intended by the governments concerned.

What is envisaged here, therefore, has nothing to do with accidental nuclear war; the proper denomination, rather, is nuclear war based on false assumptions, i.e., on misjudgment or miscalculation by the persons legitimately authorized to decide on the use of nuclear weapons. Crisis situations are particularly prone to many types of suboptimal performance by decision-makers. More than two decades of crisis research have provided ample evidence of all kinds of individual and organizational failures, such as misperception, erratic behavior under stress, improper handling of information, escalation of hostility by mirror image mechanisms, the hazards of "groupthink," failure to implement decisions due to overwhelming complexity, confusion due to organizational bottlenecks, inflexibility of standard operating procedures, and the like. This creates a multitude of opportunities for making fatally wrong decisions. Some authors have recently pointed at the 1914 analogy, which in fact continues to constitute a frightening model event of the cumulative effect of such mistakes in an acute crisis confrontation. Today, similar situations might involve states armed with nuclear weapons and hence would very likely mean nothing less than the beginning of a nuclear holocaust.

Why Unintentional Nuclear War?
The Anatomy of the Danger

When examining international crises as possible catalysts of an unintentional nuclear war, it would be quite simplistic to claim that any crisis creates a trigger-prone situation implying the risk of nuclear war. The risks do not originate in the crisis situation alone; they are generated by the crisis if and only if the strategic system has a certain propensity to become destabilized. Strategic instability and a crisis as a catalytic cause are necessary and sufficient conditions for triggering an unintentional war. It is their combination which creates the synergistic effect that may lead to nuclear war.

Strategic instability can be said to exist if the governments facing an international crisis feel a high degree of urgency to decide on the use of nuclear weapons. This urgency in turn depends on the vulnerability of both the strategic weapons and the C^3 (command, control, and communication) systems. If the strategic forces and/or the command channels that carry the threat of retaliation are vulnerable to sudden destruction, this threat can be removed by a preemptive attack aimed at those forces. On the other hand, strategic stability exists if the overall relation of forces leads potential opponents to conclude that any attempt to settle their conflict by using nuclear weapons entails a clearly unacceptable risk. Related to this is the concept of Mutual Assured Destruction (MAD), which implies that neither country's strategic nuclear deterrent force should be vulnerable to a first strike by the other; therefore, neither country has any incentive whatsoever to strike first. Some authors very pertinently prefer to substitute for the term "strategic stability" that of "crisis stability," meaning a configuration of strategic forces that, in a situation of international crisis, allows each side to wait without incurring great disadvantage in case the other side attacks. By contrast, crisis *in*stability is conducive to preemption by generating an urge for timely action and first use of nuclear weapons.

Strategic or crisis stability constitutes a central concept in strategic thinking in both the East and the West. Although Soviet sources do not use this term as explicitly as is the case in offical American sources, the issue of strategic stability can be justly said to be a matter of common concern. The two major powers formally acknowledged its importance in the *Joint Statement of Principles and Basic Guidelines for Subsequent Negotiations on the Limitation of Strategic Arms*, signed on June 18, 1979 in the context of the SALT II negotiations. In this statement, the two signatories reaffirmed that "the strengthening of strategic stability meets the interests of the Parties and the interest of international security." They agreed to "continue for the purpose of reducing and averting the risk of outbreak of nuclear war to seek measures to strengthen strategic stability."

The nature of crisis stability can be further represented and illustrated by two familiar paradigms offered by games theory. Under conditions of strategic stability, both opponents recognize that the use of nuclear weapons would inevitably entail destruction and death on both sides and possibly mutual annihilation. Therefore, both sides have an interest in choosing a cooperative strategy, i.e., avoiding the use of nuclear weapons. Thus, the situation tends to stabilize itself. This is the typical outcome of so-called "chicken" game situations.

If, on the other hand, there is a premium on preemptive attack, i.e., if by a preventive first strike the opponent's capability to retaliate can be successfully knocked out, and if both sides perceive the situation this way, they may feel a strong urge to launch a disarming first strike. Under these circumstances, common to the so-called "prisoner's dilemma" game, the strategic system is highly unstable. In such a situation, a crisis confrontation is liable to trigger a nuclear war even if the governments concerned may not intend to do so. It is the simple fear that the opponent might strike first that creates a powerful incentive for each side to keep at least one step ahead on the escalation ladder.

In order to assess the risk of unintentional nuclear war, two main questions have to be asked:

(1) What factors tend to affect crisis stability in the contemporary international system?
(2) What are the prospects of the use of force as a "continuation of policy by other means," generating acute international crises?

In addition, one might inquire into the institutions set up and the multilateral and bilateral agreements signed in view of mitigating the risks of both crisis instability and crisis avoidance and/or crisis management:

(3) What is the contribution of existing agreements to counter the risk of unintentional nuclear war?

Factors Affecting Crisis Stability

When trying to assess the probability of averting crisis instability, three aspects of the current evolution of the strategic system have to be envisaged: (1) the arms race, (2) the development of strategic doctrines, and (3) nuclear proliferation. These three issues imply serious challenges to future crisis stability.

The Risk of Nuclear War   101

ARMS RACE INSTABILITY VERSUS CRISIS STABILITY

The current arms race implies the danger that the vulnerability of the strategic systems deployed by the two major powers is constantly being increased by technological improvements. Hence, qualitative changes play a more important role than the quantitative arms race. The retaliatory forces of the other side are being threatened, and a preemptive first strike made potentially feasible, by way of developments such as the introduction of multiple independently targetable reentry vehicles (MIRVs), the greater yield of warheads, higher accuracy of delivery systems, and the improved certainty with which the location of targets can be determined. At the same time, the invulnerability of potential targets is also being challenged by the development of antisatellites capable of interfering with early warning and C^3, and even more so by potential breakthroughs in antisubmarine warfare jeopardizing the relative invulnerability of sea-based deterrent forces. Furthermore, the feasibility of launching a disarming surprise attack is supported by the ability to fire missiles whose time of flight is just a few minutes, due to either increased speed or close stationing of the launchers. Thus, a grave threat is also posed to the invulnerability of C^3 systems, thereby giving rise to fears of a "decapitation" surprise attack against command centers and communication facilities. These prospects may in turn offer temptations to adopt launch-on-warning policies or predelegation measures giving subordinate commanders the competence to decide about the release of nuclear weapons. Finally, new technologies contribute to developing defensive protection of strategic forces, especially the land-based intercontinental ballistic missiles (ICBMs), as well as civilian targets. If it were possible to establish an operational antimissile defense system, the first power having such a system might be tempted to launch a disarming strike against its opponent, which in this case would be deprived of the capability to punish the attacker by a retaliatory second strike.

Recent official U.S. and Soviet publications offer ample proof that both sides are afraid that their respective opponent is acquiring or intends to acquire first-strike capability. They tend to think with precision along the same lines of fear, suspicion, and nervousness. Their expectations and allegations tend to fuel the arms race independently of whether they are correct or not. They preclude the arms race from becoming stabilized; arms race stability can be said to exist as long as there does not appear to be any way for one side to achieve an over-whelming advantage over the other side by quickly acquiring a feasible quantity of some weapon, and so there exists no really strong inducement to do so.

Much has been written about the causal factors determining the dynamics of the arms race. The armaments process seems to be largely governed by an intrinsic inertia having its own momentum independently of conscious decisions taken by policy-makers. There is also a tendency toward mirror imaging; scientists and engineers often do not wait for a potential enemy to react, but operating on "worst case" assumptions, themselves react against their own brain children by designing counter-weapons designed to neutralize the weapons developed previously. The arms race is progressing on an incremental, step-by-step basis lacking proper national (let alone international) control. Whatever the causes of the arms race, it cannot be denied that the instability prevailing in the contemporary international system undermines any crisis stability.

This does not mean that the arms race has already succeeded in overthrowing crisis stability. One must not ignore the fact that there are some mitigating factors. The nuclear powers are extremely sensitive and attentive to the potential vulnerability of their retaliatory capacity and C^3 systems. As a consequence, they undertake huge efforts to forestall potential "windows of vulnerability." Also, new weapon technologies require testing because no sane decision-maker would be inclined to launch a preemptive attack with a new weapon without having first determined its reliability. In addition, testing mitigates the danger of being surprised by a technological breakthrough achieved by one's opponent. For the foreseeable future at least, the MAD relationship continues to prevail. Hence, the risks originating in arms race instability are not yet liable to overthrowing crisis stability. Still, they are alarming in the long run.

DESTABILIZING EFFECTS OF DOCTRINAL DEVELOPMENTS

The international strategic system is determined by (as Soviet authors call it) "objective factors"—arms—and "subjective factors"—doctrines. Strategic doctrines are sets of operational beliefs, values, and assertions that guide official behavior with respect to strategic research and development, weapons choice, acquisition policy, force deployment, operational plans, force employment, arms control, and so forth. Notwithstanding their high degree of sophistication, they ultimately rest on complex and insoluble political judgments and are thus subject to all kinds of fallacies, distortions, and misjudgments. This has particularly dangerous consequences in U.S.-Soviet strategic relations, because U.S. strategic doctrine is characterized by a bewildering amount, and sometimes inflation, of partly contradictory conceptions, while Soviet strategic doctrine is surrounded by a high degree of secrecy. There are therefore reasons to assume a mismatch of strategic doctrine between East and West.

This mismatch ultimately lies in differences deeply embedded in philosophical and national traditions. Assumptions like the perenniality of conflict, the "ultimate triumph of socialism," the emphasis on surprise in war fighting, and so forth can hardly be said to be conducive to finding an easy way to mutual understanding and harmony in matters of strategic doctrines. Linguistic problems contribute to the problem. For instance, the English word "stability" cannot be adequately translated into the Russian language by "stabilnost"; while "stability" in the Western sense corresponds to crisis stability as defined above, the Russian term "stabilnost" seems to be synonymous with "balance" or "parity," in general. In the American context, the debate about "parity," "superiority," and "sufficiency" constitutes a particularly confusing aspect of strategic thinking, since the practical implications of these terms are rather doubtful. Mismatch and confusion in the field of strategic doctrine challenges crisis stability in two ways: by leading to either underestimating or overestimating an adversary's intentions in a situation of acute international crisis.

Underestimating an adversary's intentions means that deterrence ceases to be credible. A may assume that B is bluffing, and thus underestimate B's resolve to honor its commitment, or A may assume that it would be irrational for B to carry out its threat to retaliate. Hence, deterrence fails and a crisis may easily escalate into a nuclear war in which the attacker may realize too late that his action was based on miscalculation. On the other hand, overestimating one's opponent's intentions is a result of "worse case" assumptions common to a strategic relationship dominated by ambiguity and a lack of proper mutual comprehension of each other's strategic doctrines. "Worst case" thinking may lead A to infer from everything he sees and hears that B is engaged in preparations for launching a disarming first strike. Hence A feels a strong urge to prevent the impending disaster by quickly attacking B by surprise according to the logic of "use it or lose it." Again, this kind of reasoning would have disastrous consequences if it prevailed in decision-making during an acute international crisis.

The dilemma generated by the asymmetric and fuzzy nature of the strategic doctrines of East and West is particularly grave with respect to the strategic situation in Europe. The governments of the NATO countries realize that the strategic situation in Europe is characterized by a marked conventional imbalance favoring the Warsaw Treaty Organization (WTO). As the NATO countries, for various reasons, do not feel in a position to redraw this imbalance by an appropriate build-up of conventional armaments, NATO strategy basicaliy refuses to exclude the use of nuclear weapons (mainly tactical nuclear weapons) to counter a WTO attack carried out by conventional or nuclear means against the territory of a NATO ally should NATO's conventional defenses be overrun. This doctrine renders highly uncertain the profitability of an attempt to exploit conventional superiority by launching a tank "Blitzkrieg," for example.

NATO's strategy implies a twofold credibility problem: first, the Soviet Union outrightly rejects the idea that a nuclear war, once started by NATO's first use of nuclear weapons, could be kept limited or controlled. Second, Soviet sources threaten to launch a "full-scale devastating and annihilating" retaliation strike against the homeland of the United States, thus shedding doubts on the credibility of an extended deterrence and implying nothing less than the incineration of Chicago and New York for the sake of Hamburg and Hanover. On the other hand, NATO tries to enhance the credibility of its concept of extended deterrence and nuclear deterrence against any kind of attack by introducing a land-based intermediate-range nuclear force (INF) in Western Europe. However, this policy is promptly denounced by the WTO as an attempt to achieve first-strike capability and even the capability of surprise attack against Soviet strategic forces and C^3 installations by launching highly accurate INF missiles with extremely short flight time (6-8 minutes).

By putting the emphasis on such prospects and uncertainties, the West's deterrence is in turn being deterred, thus eroding the credibility of the American "nuclear umbrella" for Europe and at the same time accusing the West of preparing a disarming first strike. Both aspects give clear indications of casting doubt on the crisis stability of nuclear armament and strategic doctrines in and for Europe. It would be naive to assume that the problem can be solved and stability redressed by negotiating a common understanding of strategic doctrines. On the contrary, it seems that the mutual rejection of strategic concepts is part of a deliberate and conscious effort to manipulate each side's deterrence postures and in particular their doctrinal underpinnings.

When assessing the risks originating in the problem of strategic doctrines, one should, however, avoid neglecting the mitigating factors. One also should not confuse tendencies and potential dangers with the actual state of affairs. Doubts about credibility do not automatically lead to a complete breakdown of credible deterrence. For the time being, the threat of retaliation and thus the expectation of uncalculable damage is still efficient and credible. No nuclear power could expect to escape retaliation if it launched a preemptive strike against its opponents unless its government were guided by insane, risk-taking behavior. Therefore, the nature of strategic doctrines, although far from being satisfactory, does not destroy crisis stability. Yet this situation of relative stability is not safe for an indefinite future. It should also be borne in mind that the doubts and erosions of credibility of deterrence by the evolution of strategic doctrines result in a propensity to generate low-key crises and limited probes which in turn imply a risk of escalation.

PRECARIOUS STABILITY IN A WORLD OF MANY NUCLEAR POWERS

In the very near future, a considerable number of countries will acquire nuclear weapons. Efforts so far undertaken to halt nuclear proliferation will eventually prove to be insufficient. In the context of this contribution, the question has to be raised whether more nuclear powers will mean more nuclear wars or a greater risk of international crises triggering nuclear conflagration. In trying to answer this question one has to specify the problem with respect to the likelihood of the outbreak of nuclear war between countries newly emerging as nuclear powers, on the one hand, and the likelihood of a new nuclear power triggering an all-out nuclear war among other nuclear powers, and in particular the United States and the Soviet Union, on the other hand.

As far as the first problem is concerned, the respective arguments put forward in the rapidly growing literature on nuclear proliferation are very controversial. Some specialists argue that the increase in the number of nuclear powers should reduce the probability of war by providing an additional restraining force and increasing the uncertainty about the reaction by the others. Other authors, however, point at the delicate situation of regional crisis instability existing on the eve of a nation becoming a nuclear power: As a state develops nuclear capability, there will be a temptation for its potential enemies to attack it before its nuclear delivery system is operational. That was the rationale underlying the "surgical strike" executed by Israel agaisnt Iraq's "Osirak" research reactor. A similar incentive to preempt may also be generated after two regional rival countries have acquired nuclear weapons, which in the initial stage will be characterized by a high degree of vulnerability, creating the temptation to launch a preemptive strike. Hence, there is a certain probability of local crises escalating into local nuclear wars.

The second problem refers to the chance that such a local nuclear war might ignite a general nuclear war. One might assume the two major powers to behave with utmost care and circumspection in any such conflict. They may even be tempted to exert pressure on their respective clients not to use nuclear weapons. Nevertheless, any generalized conclusion would be misleading. The outcome of a conflagration of this type would probably be determined by the nature of involvement and commitment incurred by the two major powers. Hence, the evolution of a crisis would be different in different regions.

The Future of International Crises

As unintended nuclear war may result from a cumulative effect of inherent crisis instability and acute crisis confrontation, one has to examine the prospects of future crises. In particular, two aspects have to be analyzed: (1) the impact of nuclear armaments and nuclear strategy on the nature of crises and (2) the propensity of the international system to generate crises.

THE NATURE OF CRISES IN THE NUCLEAR AGE

According to a familiar definition, crises are an outcome of a threat to basic values, a high probability of involvement in military hostility, and the awareness of finite time for response to the external threat. It hardly needs any further explanation to conclude that the existence of nuclear weapons and the evolution of nuclear strategic doctrines inevitably amplifies both the gravity and the urgency of crisis situations. The nature of nuclear threat establishes a completely new order of magnitude and of a danger never heard of before, one virtually leading to terror. (It should be noted in this context that the term "terror" shares the same etymological roots with "deterrence.") At worst, terror tends to shock firmly established role structures and traditional patterns of perception and behavior, thus making it improbable or extremely difficult for one to think soberly and to decide properly. In other words, the element of terror inherent in any nuclear threat may lead to maladaptive behavior on the part of both individuals and organizations faced with an international crisis.

Furthermore, any tendency of nuclear weapon systems to create urgency as a result of vulnerability in turn contributes to aggravating a crisis. The more serious a crisis, however, the more the decision-makers' capability of making an appropriate, rational analysis of the situation is reduced. This is highly unfortunate in a time when strategic doctrines have become increasingly complex, based on a variety of arms with different performance characteristics. The question must be raised, therefore, whether the political leaders of the countries concerned, in the hectic situation of a crisis emergency, will still be capable of deciding and acting in full accordance with the requirements of the complex and infinitely subtle logic of nuclear crisis strategy. Decision-makers may become victims of urgency and commit all kinds of mistakes, miscalculations, and misperceptions.

In other words, the propensity of the strategic system to become unstable has additional consequences aggravating the risk of unintended war by increasing the probability of making inappropriate decisions. Thus, crises in the nuclear age are far more dangerous than in the prenuclear age. Of course, contemporary political leaders still have the view of Hiroshima, and therefore they have a very careful attitude toward the use of nuclear weapons. Yet the general trend may offset these restraints in the long run.

THE USE OF FORCE: TENDENCIES AND PROSPECTS

Despite the threat of nuclear disaster, the frequency of international crises has not declined in the nuclear age. "Coercive bargaining" still constitutes and will continue to constitute a dominant pattern in international politics. The symbolic use of force is a general practice in the international system. The use of force for the purpose of conveying signals to an opponent in a situation of coercive bargaining may easily produce incidents of all kinds that have a propensity to escalate. This risk is even more serious if nuclear weapons serve for demonstations of resolve; there are reports about such measures as calling for various levels of alert status for missiles, deploying strategic bombers, putting more bombers in the air on airborne alert, deploying tactical nuclear weapons near crisis areas, sending more nuclear submarines on patrol, and so forth.

The danger inherent in this type of manipulation of the risks of nuclear war of course leads statesmen to behave with much more caution whenever nuclear weapons are involved. Both the United States and the USSR are known to put more emphasis on the central control of their systems. Also, as soon as a crisis escalates, the political leaders of the countries concerned tend to devote much more attention to minute, tactical details than in periods of "normalcy." Nevertheless, one must not disregard the great difficulty of conveying messages credibly by using this kind of manipulation of force in a situation dominated by distrust. The likelihood of misunderstanding, and hence, miscalculation, looms larger in every step made in this delicate field.

There are many reasons to expect a continuing and maybe even increasing frequency of cases of coercive bargaining. Whenever a situation of rivalry between two nuclear powers is characterized by a high degree of ambiguity, it invites provocation, i.e., all kinds of "limited probes" and "controlled pressure." Ambiguity is presently growing in Third World regions where the two major powers are increasingly inclined to engage in all kinds of poorly defined commitments. In contrast to "classical" alliance commitments, this new type of commitment implies a large scope of uncertainty and unpredictability. This fact multiplies the number of opportunities available to the two major powers to "test" each other by means of crisis confrontation and coercive bargaining. Hence, the risk of unintentional consequences of such behavior is multiplied correspondingly.

Existing Agreements to Counter the
Risk of Unintentional Nuclear War

Confronted with the risk of unintentional nuclear war, the powers (and especially the two major powers) undertook efforts to mitigate this risk by arms control agreements and related other agreements. The general evaluation of the measure agreed upon so far tends to lead to rather gloomy, if not sarcastic, conclusions. Some authors do not hesitate to call them "futile, ineffective and outside the main thrust of great power military effort." There are two main groups of agreements: those open to adherence by all states, and bilateral agreements (or agreements with limited membership). From the first group, the following are relevant for the prevention of unintentional nuclear war:

Antarctic Treaty (1959)

Limited Test Ban Treaty (LTBT) (1963)

Outer Space Treaty (1967)

Treaty of Tlatelolco (1967)

Nuclear Non-Proliferation Treaty (NPT) (1968)

Seabed Treaty (1971)

Confidence-Building Measures (CBMs) of the CSCE Final Act (1975)

Among the bilateral agreements, the following have an immediate bearing upon the problems discussed in this chapter:

Hot Line Agreement (1963)

Agreement to Reduce the Risk of Nuclear War (1971)

Agreement on the Prevention of Incidents on the High Seas (1972)

Basic Principles (1972)

SALT I (Interim Agreement) (1972)

Anti-Ballistic Missile Treaty (ABM) (1972)

Prevention of Nuclear War Agreement (1973)

SALT II (1979)

Although it is not possible, in the present context, to offer a detailed evaluation of these agreements and treaties, a summary assessment may lead to some tentative conclusions. In the following table, each agreement is examined in view of its contribution to strengthening crisis stability and to containing future international crises. The symbols used are:

+ The provisions of the agreement or treaty are capable of *fully* coping with the risk concerned.
(+) The provisions *partly* cope with the risk concerned or *mitigate* it.
(-) There are *doubts* about the utility of the provisions; they may even slightly *mar* the efforts to contain the risk concerned.
- The provisions are completely *counterproductive*.

The results of the analysis presented in Table 7.1 are quite revealing despite their tentative and somewhat impressionistic basis. The

TABLE 7.1

The Agreements	The Risks			Future Crises	
	Crisis Instability				
	Arms Race Instability	Destabilizing Doctrines	Nuclear Proliferation	Gravity of Crises	Frequency of Crises
Antarctic Treaty	(+)				
LTBT	(+)		(+)		
Outer Space Treaty	(+)				
Tlatelolco Treaty	(+)		(+)		
NPT			(+)		
Seabed Treaty	(+)				
CBMs		(+)		(+)	
Hot Line		(+)		(+)	
Risk of Nuclear War Agreement				(+)	
Naval Incidents Agreement				(+)	
Basic Principles					(+)
SALT I (Interim)	(−)	(+)			
ABM	(+)	(+)			
Prevention of Nuclear War Agreement		(+)		(+)	
SALT II	(+)	(+)			

conclusion cannot be avoided that the existing agreements cope with a small fraction of the risks only, and they do so in a very incomplete and hence unsatisfactory way. Nevertheless, it would be misleading to conclude that the existing provisions are simply worthless. They are in fact capable of controlling some of the risks. More importantly, their existence reflects at least a widespread awareness of the risks looming in contemporary crisis politics.

Practical Conclusions

The risk of an international crisis escalating into an unintentional nuclear war requires energetic efforts on the unilateral, bilateral, and multilateral levels. The foregoing analysis may lead to the following practical conclusions:

With regard to coping with arms race instability:

(1) inclusion of additional issues in the agenda of international arms control negotiations, e.g., prevention and prohibition of antisatellite and anti-submarine developments;
(2) increased emphasis on the qualitative aspects of the arms race and the development of appropriate verification and inspection procedures;
(3) efforts to achieve strategic stability at the lowest possible level.

With regard to destabilizing consequences of strategic doctrine:

(4) talks among military experts of the major powers on strategic doctrines with a view toward finding areas of common understanding;
(5) negotiations on possible solutions of the dilemma of extended deterrence, e.g., of an agreement on no first offensive use of nuclear weapons.

With regard to the destabilizing consequences of nuclear proliferation:

(6) satisfaction of legitimate security needs of threshold countries by non-nuclear means;
(7) priority for regional arms control measures as compared with universal approaches.

With regard to the aggravation of crises by nuclear strategy:

(8) improvement of quick and efficient communication between opponents in case of crisis;
(9) restraint in using nuclear alerts and deployments for demonstrations of resolve.

With regard to the future frequency of crises:

(10) avoiding additional and reducing existing commitments of major powers to the Third World;

(11) bilateral and multilateral restraints on arms transfers to the Third World that may cause new commitments;

(12) discussions about "conventions of crisis," with a view toward agreeing on minimum standards of behavior when using force.

It goes without saying that the lasting and proper answer to the problem can only be general and complete disarmament coupled with the creation of a peaceful international order, i.e., a working system of international conflict resolution. In the absence of these two ultimate goals, however, these and other concrete short-range measures deserve further examination.

CHAPTER 8

COLLECTIVE SECURITY-SEEKING PRACTICES SINCE 1945

HAYWARD R. ALKER, Jr.
FRANK L. SHERMAN

Determined to save succeeding generations from the scourge of war, the leaders of the victorious states in World War II set up a system for the avoidance or speedy termination of future wars. Centered in the Security Council of the new United Nations Organization, this system had two, often contradictory, bases: (1) Wilsonian universal moral obligations "to provide [collective] security *for* all states, *by* the action of all states, *against* all states which might challenge the existing order by the arbitrary [aggressive] unleashing of their power"; and (2) the even older primary reliance on the "Concert of the Great Powers" for the effective management of such a system.

The new version of a collective security system actualized its contradictory bases when major differences among the great powers themselves arose.[1] Not only was the reality of "collective security of the Great Powers, for the Small Powers, when the Great Powers could agree" less

AUTHORS' NOTE: We gratefully acknowledge the availability of Robert Butterworth's original data set (which he has recoded and extended with the help of the U.S. Defense Advanced Research Projects Agency), the computational and coding assistance of Patricia Lee Farris, Renee Marlin, and Marilyn Webster, plus our principal source of financial support, grant 7806707 of the National Science Foundation to the Center for International Studies at MIT. The views expressed here are our responsibility alone. Earlier versions of this chapter were presented and discussed at IPSA Round Tables in Bucharest and Zurich.

glowing a path to world peace than many had hitherto supposed, but collective security as a world order concept "halfway . . . between the terminal points of international anarchy and world government" became a rationale for Cold War "collective self-defense" organizations like NATO and the Warsaw Pact, in part legitimated in such purposes by the United Nations' ambiguous charter language endorsing these and other "regional arrangements."[2]

Since the smaller, ex-colonial, and often nonaligned powers themselves have taken increasing control over their own destinies, a process in which UN decolonization efforts and the great powers played a significant role, the Secretary-General and the General Assembly have enhanced and qualitatively changed their security-seeking efforts. Preventive diplomacy designed to keep the great powers out of Third World conflicts coincided with the "balancing" role of nonaligned states on Cold War issues and the growth in importance of regional organizations among the Arab, African, and American states performing crisis management, dispute settlement, collective security, and collective defense functions. Great power security concerns have led to greater reliance on unilateral actions, buttressed by alliance relationships and moderated by changing patterns of mutual recognition, détente, and competitive coexistence. Recently, we can detect the partial reappearance of a multipolar balancing process associated with both recognized and contested spheres of influence, and controversial regional doctrines of asymmetric collective security responsibilities.

Ironically, the "new and more wholesome diplomacy" of the Wilsonian "collective" security system has led to the incomplete but real return of competitive, loosely bihegemonial, power balancing practices rather like those that it was designed to supplant. Pessimistic political realists could easily attribute such a return to self-help security politics grounded in external, dismal truths of human nature. Marxian global systems theorists might see the continued reproduction, as well as the self-contradictory development, of world capitalism through the adaptive restructuring of its global economic markets and its multipolar political parts. While inter-estested in such large issues, as peace researchers of operational collective security systems—those both politically real and scientifically analyzable—we wish primarily in the program of research outlined and illustrated here to find practical lessons about war avoidance.

The plethora of recent empirical studies, almost entirely by North American scholars, of collective management practices of postwar international organizations (Butterworth, 1978a, 1978b; Ruggie, 1974; Holsti, 1966, 1972; Bloomfield and Leiss, 1969; James, 1969; Alker and

Greenberg, 1971) makes us worry whether significant new knowledge can be gained and widely shared on this important subject. We do not want such studies to enter an era of diminishing returns associated with mechanical replications using the same change-insensitive research designs extended to a few new cases by North American graduate students.[3] We wish instead to reinvigorate the scientific study of collective security systems by redirecting its focus toward *more or less collective* security-*seeking* systems, by trying to conceptualize these phenomena of concern in a more dialectical fashion, and by furthering the more universal participation of peace researchers in such investigations. We wish to do this without giving up the hard insights gained, and the regularities ascertained, by those working in primarily positivistic, North American empirical traditions.

Because for us Istvan Kende's (1971, 1979) episodically organized *empirical* studies of international conflicts represent exemplary (but rare) contributions from an East European, Marxist peace research perspective, we shall depend heavily on them, even though they only indirectly address collective efforts to avoid or resolve such conflicts.[4] We shall also rely on previous epistemological discussions of dialectical-hermeneutical and Marxist-Leninist social science research, especially as they are sympathetically understood in Western Europe and North America (Alker, 1979, 1981), in order to correct certain limitations we see (and have in part already indicated) in the empirical literature we have cited. Our hope, stated technically in the language of Alker's (1979) study, is that there is enough common ground politically, epistemologically, and substantively to define one or several cross-paradigm, empirically oriented research programs with a view toward convergent practical learning about war avoidance. Our concerns to be explicit about the need for, and the components of, an internationally sharable conception of scientific knowledge accumulation derives from the realistic concern that such standards be communicable to the national political leaders who decisively influence war and peace processes and research thereon, as well as the national citizenry bearing the financial burdens and sharing the consequences of such activities.

A reasonable breakdown of the topics of subsequent discussion in this chapter can now be given. Our next concern will be to contribute to the operational reconceptualization of key terms in the collective security-seeking, crisis management, and war avoidance literature: "order," "security," "crisis," "aggression," "peace," and "war." We shall then discuss operational ways in which richer, less state-centric, contextually sensitive, yet still scientifically operational characterizations of international disputes might be undertaken. After this follow some practical considerations of conflict and crisis management practices. Our concern to be more dialectically sensitive about security-seeking practices goes beyond the need to be sensitive to the narrowing effects and the different boundaries of relevant experience associated with different research paradigms; it leads us to a more general interest in ways in which more or less collective security-seeking practices themselves should be studied and understood. Some important comparative case studies not focused on the UN collective security system suggest numerous insights about war avoidance. In particular, we have some specific ideas on how collective security-seeking agenda processes might be better understood. Finally, our concern for less static, less episodic, and more suggestive "natural histories" of security-seeking practices brings us to some rather dialectical ideas about the transformative development and decay of collective security-seeking systems.

On the "Collectivization" of Relevant Research Concepts

Within the "pure" Wilsonian collective security system, it assumed that the world is essentially made up of sovereign, territorially integrated nation-states widely recognized by each other as legitimate international system members. (Historically, colonial territories had something of an anomalous status, but were assumed eventually in the League system to become self-determining, at least those that had belonged to the states defeated in World War I; World War II led to a similar provision in the UN Charter.) Moreover, a democratically enforced, consensually legitimated normative world "order" exists which has as its key deterrent component the illegitimacy of interstate "aggression." A state's "international peace and security" means at least that it is not faced with the imminent threat or actuality of cross-border military intervention from another state. If deterrence fails, all such substantial, recognizable, and nonaccidental interstate intervention are to be considered "aggressive," requiring an appropriately punitive collective response.

Politically, the Wilsonian collective security ideal failed, at least in large part. The popular democratic forces that were necessary to energize such a system turned (or were turned) sufficiently against its normative universalism so that the United States never joined the

League. Wilson himself was at least partially competing in his liberal-internationalist world order design with Lenin's own stirring (and for many, frightening) revolutionary pronouncements about the birth of a socialist world order (Levin, 1970). The universalism of the League system to which an isolated, cautious Soviet state was eventually admitted, suffered mortal blows from Japanese, Italian, German, and Soviet "aggressions," against which League members were unable or unwilling to retaliate effectively. Only World War II and its decisive but costly victory over the Axis powers could be said sufficiently to have "collectivized" or "concerted" political wills so that a revised collective security system was reborn.

JUST WARS AND AGGRESSOR STATES

We add this brief account of the League system to our equally brief overview of the UN system in order to highlight key political and conceptual issues in the scientific study of collective security-seeking systems. For it is our belief that the major problems in developing a more universal, more valid empirical research program on this topic are at least in part derivative from the recent political past. Do not League history and the failure of UN diplomats (until a few years ago) to define in general and apply in particular such a perjorative label as "the aggressor" (before or during the Cold War) give us pause? Even today, Americans believing the American-Vietnamese war was a "noble cause" would not consider the United States as the "aggressor" pictured in either wartime NLF, Soviet and Chinese statements, or new Vietnamese history books. Neither will many Soviet scholars allow the current Soviet military intervention into Afghanistan to be labeled "aggressive," as most Americans now think.

Can scholars who maintain their political allegiances, one would hope with some critical detachment, do significantly better?[5] Kende and Zacher take rather different, but not completely opposed, positions. As a liberal/Wilsonian positivist, Zacher does not debate the justifications people give for wars; rather (1979: 6), he takes an objectivist, empirically operational stance defining "aggression" descriptively, but in a way that corresponds quite clearly to the pure Wilson/liberal world order conception sketched above. An "aggressor" is a state that threatens to employ or does employ military personnel against the citizens of another country.

Kende (1971: 6f, note 9) thinks, at least concerning internal political wars fought with foreign participation, that "who the immediate initiator is, who fires the first shot . . . seems besides the point, and in addition, can often not be determined." He takes an explicit Marxian position, arguing in terms of a preferred distinction between just and unjust wars, roughly as follows. Most, but not all internal wars since 1945 have been antiregime wars, typically of the anticolonial or class war sort. The Marxian position is less ambiguous about anticolonialism than Wilsonian liberalism. In both such cases and in class wars, an aggressor and an oppressed party can be identified and revolt is, in general, justified. Whether the oppressed (in revolt) or the oppressor (as a deterrent) initiates the conflict may vary. But the difference between the 1946 Indochina war (initiated by the French in a recolonization effort) and the Algerian-initiated anticolonial war of 1954 is not very important because even the latter "initiative was brought about by colonialist oppression. It would be hard to dispute that these two wars were very similar in character even if the circumstances of their being were dissimilar."

Are we at a point of scholarly deadlock when Zacher and Kende must talk completely past each other? Surely Kende must recognize some antiregime wars other than class wars and colonial conflicts. Which wars have been class wars, and which parties deserve the label of certified "oppressor" are questions requiring a much longer debate. So does the issue of antidependency revolts affecting nominally sovereign states in both the so-called Second and Third Worlds.

Kende takes an important tack that preserves a meaningful universe of scientific argument and analysis. From a definite political viewpoint (his own, or that of different parties to a conflict), he admits it is frequently difficult (as in the Biafran war) to decide whether a war is just or unjust. When such differences are the case, "no reliable results can be achieved in a scientific survey," so he shifts to a causally and historically sensitive substantive classification. Although pre-1945 studies of wars (like Quincy Wright's and L. F. Richardson's) emphasized (like Zacher's and Wilson's views already noted) the prevalence of interstate "frontier wars," often without the participation of nonbordering parties, times have changed. Internal wars fought on the territory of one country are much more frequent; internally oriented tribal, religious, and related border adjustment disputes, as well as antiregime wars, should be distinguished from classical cross-frontier wars. His resulting typology (for which reasonably clear operational definitions are suggested) distinguishes six types of war by determining whether the two internal and one international (frontier) wars occur with or without the actual large-scale participation of foreign military personnel in advisory and/or combat roles. Delivery of arms, harboring or training guerrillas, and other lesser forms of support are not deemed sufficient grounds for his positive "foreign participation" label.

Although Zacher (1979: 211) sticks to an elaboration of an aggressor/victim and alignment-nonalignment classification for his basic analyses, and does not address the decolonization issue very directly, he does recognize in a deviant case analysis that the "response to the Rhodesian interventions into Mozambique in 1976 and 1977 actually indicates a consensual element in the global system—opposition to the White-dominated regimes of southern Africa and their attempts to retaliate against nationalist rebels operating from outside their borders." Furthermore, in this elaboration of his definition of an aggressor, Zacher looks beyond what Kende would call an international/frontier war perspective to include antiregime rebellions. He labels as an aggressor any foreign government militarily supporting (or opposing) an incumbent regime. Thus,

> while an aggressive state will generally use its forces against the official forces of another country, it may alternatively use its forces to fight on behalf of another official government against a rebel group seeking to overthrow or secede from it. Such participation in a civil war is often not viewed as aggression, but it is included in this study's definition of the term [1979: 6f].

Thus we find a real basis for further discussion, and the likelihood of significant (but not total) convergence between Zacher's "aggressors" and "unjust" parties, were Kende to elaborate upon his judgments in these matters and Zacher to entertain the reasonable possibility that in some internal wars (dare we ask about the American Civil War?) the aggressor/victim distinction is difficult to defend in a deep, meaningful way.

THE SEARCH FOR CORRESPONDING CLASSIFICATIONS OF CRISES AND WARS

Cross-paradigm communication is a form of dialectical hermeneutics with empirical consequences. At least three types of empirical studies are opened up by the above remarks. First, taking definitional issues into account, do the different, empirically oriented perspectives see and agree on the same universe of wars, crises, or disputes threatening international peace and security? Second, how much agreement exists con-

TABLE 8.1   A Comparison of Crisis, War, and Dispute Universes in Published Kende, Zacher, and Butterworth/Scranton Studies

	Crises*	Wars**	Disputes***	Total
Revised Kende list (1945-1976)	Not applicable	126	Not applicable	126
Zacher list	23	93 (70 wars; 23 military interventions)	Not applicable	116
Revised Butterworth/ Scranton list (1945-1977)	80	180	38	298

*Crises have been defined in two ways: (1) those cases listed by Zacher as having been coded as crises, and (2) those cases in the Butterworth/Scranton MIC study that entered Phase II but did not intensify into Phase III (Hostilities).

**Wars were defined as (1) Kende coding category; (2) Zacher's coding categories of wars and military interventions; and (3) a Butterworth/Scranton MIC case that intensified into Phase III (Hostilities).

***A dispute was defined as a Butterworth/Scranton case that did not intensify past Phase I (Dispute). To Kende's (1978) list we have added three wars starting in 1977 that are mentioned in his latest text (1979). Butterworth and Scranton (1976) list 247 separate interstate conflicts. For this (and most subsequent purposes) we have included new cases from Butterworth (unpublished), as well as four additional cases we split off from his original list: Indian Independence, Mongolian UN membership, Chinese UN representation, and the Naga uprisings in India.

cerning substantive typologies of types of wars, like Kende's sixfold distinction mentioned above? Are differences arguably reconcilable? Third, if we can get enough agreement on a common universe of relevant cases to justify the testing of competing hypotheses, what might we ascertain about conflict causes, or about the effectiveness of collective security "managers" of such conflicts? Are there practical "lessons" to be derived from their record of successes and failures? Briefly, Tables 8.1 and 8.2 give us some clues to the first kind of inquiry which might take place.

Partly due to definitional differences, there are large quantitative differences in the "war universes" of these studies: Zacher's international organization focus sees only about 74 percent of Kende's wars and not much more than half of the hostile conflicts on Butterworth's lists. If conceptually different hostility thresholds are taken into account, and definitions and time periods matched as closely as possible, quite high

TABLE 8.2 A Comparison of 114 Cases Found in Both Kende and Butterworth Lists

| | Merged Butterworth/Scranton Issue Categories | | | | | |
Kende's Categories	Colonial	Interstate Cold War	Internal Cold War	Interstate Non-Cold War	Internal Non-Cold War	Totals
A/1 Antiregime wars with foreign participation	25]	4]	7]	9?	11?	55
B/1 Tribal wars with foreign participation	4]	1X	0/	4]	4]	13
C/1 Frontier wars with foreign participation	1X	2]	0/	5]	0/	8
A/2 Antiregime wars without foreign participation	1X	1X	4]	3X	5]	14
B/2 Tribal wars without foreign participation	0/	1X	0/	0/	12]	13
C/2 Frontier wars without foreign participation	0/	0]	0/	8]	2X	10
Totals:	31	9	11	29	34	114

+Our own expectations concerning how Kende's categories should fit into Butterworth/Scranton categories are as follows: "]" means "cases expected"; "/" means "cases not expected and not found"; "X" means "cases found contrary to expectations"; "?" means "Deviations possibly due to differences in definitions."

overlaps may nonetheless be found. Liberally matching corresponding or overlapping cases in lists from each author, we find only 63 percent of Butterworth's wars in Kende's data set, but 88 percent of Kende's and 94 percent of Zacher's wars and crises in our augmented Butterworth list. Although its own conceptualizations of "international conflict management" could as easily be problematized, Butterworth's is clearly the more inclusive data set.

Our preliminary quantitative comparisons also suggest some qualitative commentary. Because he is not limited to internationally "recognized" or "relevant" conflicts, Kende's list of wars catches a number of early colonial conflicts missed by Zacher, and even by Butterworth and Scranton. On the other hand, Kende does noticeably worse in picking up hostilities among Communist states. The former result shows how colonial allegiances or biases in the early postwar era supported the treatment of such conflicts as "domestic" or "trusteeship" rather than "international" concerns. The latter indicates a difficulty in Communist abilities to recognize certain kinds of political controversies in terms that most other non-Communist commentators would employ. What constitutes a genuine "breach of the peace" is not a trivial, technical issue! In arenas where dissensus exists on whether human rights, cultural identities, or oppressed classes are being suppressed, we agree with Mushakoji (1978) that there are many meanings to "peace" or its denial that deserve further study.

Turning to Table 8.2, we see a matched comparison concerning Kende's six categories of war and the Butterworth classification (with mixed cases assigned to the more relevant pure type). Of the 114 mutually recognized cases, only ten appear inconsistently classified; 27 of Kende's "anti-regime wars with foreign participation" are hard to assign exclusive Butterworth categories, but 76 other cases fit into reasonable correspondences. Given this reassuring degree of overlay, we are encouraged further to check Kende's very provocative generalizations about postwar trends in wars—in particular, his claims that U.S. France-, U.K.-, and Portugal-involved antiregime wars have dominated the post-1945 era, rising in frequency and length until about 1967 (later in Asia) and then significantly diminishing during an era (1967-1976) of real, worldwide détente. Depending on how "internal cold war" and antiregime wars are further rationalized, we may or may not sustain such summary historical accounts.

Kende's claims that internal antiregime wars with foreign participation are the most prevalent wars since 1945 should also be further investigated. To put it more graphically, is not the anticolonial "revolt against the West" (in Barraclough's terms) a key alternative explanation of conflict manager's involvement records? Could it not do as well as Zacher's alignment categories in explaining management involvements, noninvolvements, successes, and failures? Alker and Greenberg (1971) and Ruggie (1974) have found multivariate explanations to account for significantly more variance in manager involvement and success than any single variable explanation. Historically grounded conclusions about the fundamental explanatory power of colonial past and political-economic dependency require stiff, competitive research testing if scholars are to go beyond diplomatic arguments.

Beyond Ahistorical, State-Centric Positivism in Coding Security-Seeking Practices

What our discussion has least adequately addressed is the meaning of individual and collective security-seeking practices. These include the actions of participants in a dispute and the activities of what are now usually called crisis managers, which of course include collective security organizations of which participants may be members. We include within the practices of such actors (participants or parties and agents) the *actions* they take, their interpretive *perspectives*, the *phasing* or sequencing of actions *cum* perspectives, the historical/institutional *contents or arenas* in which they occur, the *outcomes* of these actions for relevant participants, and their longer-run *systems*-maintaining or -transforming *effects*.

ACTORS

In situations involving threats to international peace and security, it is false to locate all responsible actions in the hands of governments of nation-states. Even traditionally, governments have been able on occasion to disown responsibility for actions from their territories or by their nationals when these were undertaken without governmental knowledge and approval. In the post-1945 era, anticolonial actions, new state-building conflicts, and the existence of important transnational, transgovernmental, international, and supranational actors all suggest broader definitions of both dispute participants and management agents. (The variety of managers, often simultaneously at work on just those disputes that reach the United Nations, is evident from Table 8.3.) Our own recent research practice has been to go beyond Kende, Zacher,

TABLE 8.3 Hostile Disputes Managed by the United Nations, 1945-1979

Case Number, Name & Dates	Complete and Managed Phase Sequence	Manager Sequence
4 Moroccan Independence, 1944-56	12(3434)56	(UNGA)[4]
9 Chinese Civil War, 1945-49	12(34)	(UNGA)[2]
10 Indonesian Independence, 1945-49	12(3434356)	(UNSC)[7]
13 Azerbaijan, 1946-47	23(4)345	(UNSC)
15 Israeli Independence, 1946-49	(1223344)	(UNGA)(UNGA,UNSC)[3]
16 Status of Eritrea, 1946-53	(123456)	(UNGA)[5]
21 Greek Civil War, 1946-51	(35)	(UNSC)(UNGA)
29 Kashmir Accession, 1947-48	12(34)	(UNSC)[2]
43 Hyderabad, 1948	1(234)	(UNSC)[3]
53 Chinese Troops in Burma, 1949-61	2(3)4	(UNGA)
62 Tunisian Independence, 1950-56	2(34)56	(UNGA)[2]
63 Indonesian Post-Independence Conflicts, 1950-62	(3)5	(UNSC)
67 Korean Invasion, 1950-53	(33)	(UNSC)(UNGA)
69 Status of Puerto Rico, 1950-52	(235)	(UNGA)[3]
83 Guatemalan Intervention, 1953-54	1(23346)	(OAS)(UNSC)(OAS)[3]
86 Guyanese Independence, 1953-66	2(3)5	(UNGA)
87 Temple of Preah Vihear, 1953-75	23(44343434)	(UNSC)(ICJ)(UNSC)[6]
92 Cypriot Independence, 1954-58	2(334)	(NATO)(UNGA)(NATO)
95 Chinese Offshore Islands, 1954-55	2(3)4	(UNSC)
97 Algerian Independence, 1954-62	12(334)6	(UNSC)(UNGA)[2]
100 Camerouni Independence, 1955-61	2(356)	(UNTC)(UNGA)[2]
103 Goa, 1955-61	12(24433)56	(ICJ)[2] (UNGA)[3]
110 Cambodian Border, 1956-70	2(33)	(ICC)(UNGA)
113 Tibetan Autonomy #1, 1956-58	2(3)	(UNGA)

118 Hungarian Intervention, 1956	12(3345)	(UNSC)(UNGA)³
119 Suez War, 1956-57	1(2233446)	(USA,UNSC)(USA,UNGA)² (UNGA)
130 Lebanese/Jordanian Civil War, 1958	12(333456)	(LAS)(UNSC)(UNGA)(UNSC)³
132 Sakiet, 1958	2(335)	(UNSC)(USA)(UK)²
139 Laotian Civil War #1, 1958-62	1(2233344)	(UNSC)(ICC)(UNSC)(ICC, Cambodia)²
143 Rwandan-Burundian Independence, 1958-62	2(3456)	(UNGA)⁴
154 Tibetan Autonomy #2, 1959-65	2(335)	(IComJ)(UNGA)²
157 Dominican Tyranny, 1959-62	(334)	(OAS)(UNSC)(OAS)
161 Repressions in S. Africa, 1960-76	2(33)	(UNSC)(UNGA)
167 Zaire Independence, 1960-64	(122345)	(UNSC)² (UNGA)(UNSC)³
175 West Irian #2, 1961-69	(33456)	(UNSG)(UNSC)⁴
178 Bay of Pigs, 1961	12(355)	(UNSC)(UNGA)(UNSC)
179 Port. Territories in Africa, 1961-74	1(2334)56	(UNGA)(UNSC, UNGA)(UNSC)
190 Bizerte, 1961-63	12(34)6	(UNSC)(UNGA)
194 American-Vietnamese War, 1962-73	3334	(ICC)(UNSC)² (ICC)
207 Yemeni Civil War, 1962-70	12(334434)5	(UNSC, LAS)² (Sudan)²
212 Sarawak/Sabah, 1963	12(246)	(UNSC)³
213 Malaysian Confrontation, 1963-66	12(33345)6	(UNSC, USA, Thailand)(Thailand)²
216 South Yemeni Independence, 1963-67	1(2334)6	(UNGA)² (UNSC)(UNGA)
217 Port. Guinean Border Security, 1963-74	2(35)	(UNSC)²
220 Vietnamese Buddhists, 1963	2(3)5	(UNSC)
221 Intervention in Haiti, 1963	2(344)	(OAS)(UNSC)(OAS)
223 Angolan Border Security, 1963-74	3(3)	(UNSC)
224 TFDADI, 1963	(2344)	(OAU, UNSC)²
228 Southern Rhodesia, 1963-80	1(22333444)56	(UNGA, UNSC)(UNGA, UNSC, US/UK)² (US/UK)²
230 Tutsi Restoration Attempt, 1963-64	12(334)	(UNSC)(OAU)(UNSC)
231 Cypriot Civil War, 1963-74	12(334434)	(UNSC)(NATO)(UNSC, UNGA)(UNSC)²
234 Panama Canal #1, 1964-67	12(334)	(UNSC)(OAS)²
239 Zaire Civil War, 1964-65	(33)5	(OAU, UNSC)
242 Spanish Sahara, 1964-76	(1233443)	(UNGA)² (UNGA,ICJ)² (UNGA)
245 Kashmir War, 1965-70	(344)	(UNSC)(USSR, UNSC)

(continued on next page)

Table 3 (continued)

Case Number, Name & Dates	Complete and Managed Phase Sequence	Manager Sequence
250 Dominican Intervention, 1965-66	12(3334445346)	(OAS,Nuncio,UNSC)[2] (OAS)[4]
253 Zambian Borders, 1965-	12(343)6	(UNSG)(UNSC)[2]
260 Eritrean Civil War, 1967-	12(33433)	(UNSC, Sudan)(UNSC)(OAU, UNSC)
264 June '67 War, 1967	2(344)	(UNSC)(UNSC, UNGA)
269 Arab-Israeli Confrontation, 1967-73	(22333444)	(UNGA,UNSC)(USA, UNSC, UNGA)(UNSC, UNGA, US)
273 Exiles in Haiti, 1968	2(34)	(UNSC)[2]
274 Czech Invasion, 1968	(123345)	(WTO)[2] (UNSC,WTO)(WTO)[2]
277 Eq. Guinean Post-Indep. Tensions, 1969-72	12(34455553)4	(UNSG)(UNSG, OAU)(WHO, UNSG, OAU)(OAU)
281 Iranian Borders, 1969-75	1(2345445)6	(UNSC)[4] (Turkey, UNSC)(UNSC)
287 Cambodian Civil War, 1970-75	12(34)	(UNSC)[2]
289 Guinean Security, 1970-78	12(3445445)	(UNSC)(UNSC, OAU)(OAU)(UNSC, OAU)(LTG)
291 Bangladesh, 1970-74	1212(345)6	(UNSC)[3]
295 Cod War, 1971-73	(2333)34)5	(ICJ)(ICJ,NATO,UNSG,UNCttee)(ICJ)
304 Yom Kippur War, 1973-74	2(3344)	(UNSC, USA)[2]
308 Cypriot Coup & Invasion, 1974-	2(3344)	(UK,UNSC)(US, UNGA)
313 Chadian Civil War, 1963-	12(333344)3(4334)3	(OAU,S,N,UNSC)* (S,N)(OAU)(S,N)(Kano Conf)
322 Chilean Repressions, 1973-	2(33333)	(ICommJ,I-AmCHR,UNGA,OAS,UNHRC)
330 Nicaraguan Insurrection, 1974-79	2(333)5	(USA,OAS,UNSC)
332 Ungandan Tyranny, 1974-79	(223344)33)5	(OAU,ICommJ)(UNGA,OAU)(OAU,UNGA)(UNGA,OAU)
333 Timorese Independence, 1975-	12(343)	(UNGA)[3]
335 Lebanese Civil War, 1975-	2(3333)	(Syria,USA,UNSC,AL)
336 Kampuchean Invasion, 1975-	(3)4	(UNSC)
341 Beninese Domestic Security, 1975-77	(2344)	(Ghana)(UNSC)(OAU,UNSC)
346 Western Sahara, 1976-	(33)	(UNSC,OAU)
350 S. African Persecutions, 1976-	(3)	(UNSC)
357 Sino-Vietnamese Border, 1977-	2(3)	(UNSC)
363 Afghan Civil War, 1978-	2(3)	(UNSC)

Liberia/Togo/Gambia; *S = Sudan, N = Niger.

Haas, Alker/Greenberg, and Butterworth to include in our data gathering efforts a phase-specific list of both direct and indirect parties to international peace-threatening disputes. Briefly, conventional practices (and Kende/Zacher "war" coding) look primarily at legal recognized parties to a dispute, plus those taking sizable military actions in them. These we call direct or primary parties, allowing as well that they may include nonstate actors, if such actors have considerable influence and political autonomy. Secondary parties are those states or actors significantly assisting primary parties—beyond the mere giving of diplomatic support.

Also, in an effort to go beyond a state-centric empirical positivism, we have extended our list of management agents beyond the lists of organizations constitutionally charged with collective security functions (according to either Haas/Butterworth/Nye or Zacher's interpretations) to get at the dynamic reality of both individual state and nonstate actors, collective defense organizations, and non-Security Council UN agencies assuming such functions. Details of such distinctions are present in the Farris et al. (1980) codebook that we are continually updating as new variables or cases are added.

CONFLICT PHASES, ACTION SEQUENCES, AND INTERPRETIVE PERSPECTIVES

Typically, the universe of studies we have been reviewing and reformulating has rather statically examined the collective actions of interstate collective security organizations, only indirectly acknowledging that national, transnational, transgovernmental, and alliance-linked supranation actions have often been the primary modes of security-seeking behavior. More realistically, but sometimes with an anticollectivist bias, a much larger effort has been made, primarily in the United States, to collect data on serious conflict events (like Kende has done) without special attention to the action of third party or collective management agents (see also Singer and Small, 1974; Eckhardt and Azar, 1978, 1979; Mahoney and Clayberg, 1979; Blechman and Kaplan, 1978). Since the phases in which, and the extent to which, parties to a dispute get involved in conflict-managing practices vary considerably, with significant impacts on outcomes, we strongly believe *both* kinds of data are relevant to the study of *more* or *less* collective security-seeking practices.

Our phase-structuring derives basically from Bloomfield and Leiss's earlier (1969) study: *dispute* (phase 1) notes the beginning of a quarrel or disagreement claimed by at least one party to be an issue of substantive international political significance; *conflict or crisis* (phase 2) indicates that at least one party has demonstrated willingness to use military force to resolve the dispute but has not yet already done so; *hostilities* (phase 3) involves the systematic and objective-specific use of military force, causing casualties and/or property loss. *Posthostilities conflict* (phase 4) is different from a *posthostilities dispute* (phase 5) in that the former still evidences parties contemplating the use of force. A *settlement* (phase 6) is one where the parties concerned formally agree about certain of their key differences. Although a dispute must reach phase 2, the conflict phase, for us to consider it a crisis, knowledge of when it first was considered an international issue is very helpful in assessing the extent to which "preventive diplomacy" or relevance-denying agenda decisions have occurred. Hence our phase 2 dates, although often imprecise, are theoretically useful information.

Although only a correlational summary for UN-managed hostile disputes, Table 8.3 is richly suggestive of results. For example, management involvement patterns often seen to be too late and/or too limited: not how often management activities are restricted to hostility and posthostility phases. Another significant finding is that disputes often do not end in tidy (phase 6) settlements; some drag on in intermittent hostility or languish in unsettled posthostility phases, while others are subsumed by larger, substantially redefined conflicts. (The string of Arab-Israeli conflict episodes are of this latter sort, and so was the more threatening part of the Bay of Pigs case, which was overcome by the Cuban missile crisis—a case not shown becase it was not judged to have reached a third phase.) Also note the trend toward multimanaged conflicts and the evidence of distinctive modes of conflict management by members of the Organization of African Unity, the OAU. Statistical analysis of settlement phases or desirable phase transitions, e.g., not going beyond phase 2 or avoidance of recurring phase 3s, are inadequate when the relative causal impacts of particular party and management actions are not taken into account. Comprehensive analyses must also note the effects of related issues and compare managed with unmanaged dispute phases, as will be done in Figures 8.2 and 8.3.

In addition to more specific codings of mediation, investigation, sanctioning, and other management actions, we have also recoded all of the Butterworth *narrative* conflict accounts for phase-specific information on the actions of the primary and secondary parties themselves, sequenced by phases. Following along lines suggested by Azar and Sloan (1975), we have also separately coded both the initiation and cessation of conflictual and cooperative actions. Variables that characterize such actors unilaterally, e.g., subversion of a government, issuance of a diplomatic protest, expressing a willingness to talk, or providing economic or technical assistance to an opposing party are distinguished from variables like the existence of infrequent border skirmishes or military confrontations, the reduction of the level of hostilities, and the coordination of policies, all of which refer simultaneously to the interactions of parties on both sides of a dispute.

Going beyond the historical sequencing of conflict episodes, we have tried to reduce the arbitrariness of "statistically independent" events by linking together separately described "phases" from particular conflicts and recoding more expansively Butterworth's information on preceding or subsequent disputes deemed "relevant" for the understanding of party and agent actions.

As to the perspectives of conflict parties and management agents, their goals, demands, expectations, strategies, and legitimate rationales, we have not gone much beyond previous studies, except for intensive related studies of Chinese and Soviet policy operational codes by Tanaka (1980) and Mefford (1982), both of whom used data from Mahoney's CACI studies. It is worth noting that Zacher's study of changing aggression-related norms in the OAU, the OAS, and the Arab League fits the logic of inquiry of the Alker/Greenberg/Christensen approach to changing and alternative operational UN charters. Without undertaking an intensive reason analysis comparable to Alker's (1975) interpretive treatment of the UN's Congo intervention, we have, however, coded a modest amount of nation-specific actions within conflict-managing agents as a way of seeking which states try to shape discussions and outcomes on which disputes, and in which arenas. The Haas et al. (1972) variables on the kind and extent of consensus mobilization efforts within their organizations are a different and helpful way of disaggregating the ways organizations act on different disputes.

HISTORICAL CONTEXTS, DISPUTE OUTCOMES, AND SYSTEMIC EFFECTS

For large-scale historical studies, detailed information on the perspectives of all major actors is either unavailable or prohibitively expensive to obtain. Disputes about the intentionality, the larger purposes, unintended functions, or planned consequences of particular action sequences go to the heart of many protracted conflicts. In such situations, like Kende, we have had to retreat to whatever relatively objective behavioral information is available. By collecting outcome judgments specific to the different sides of a dispute, we may inductively be able to sort out some of the more controversial arguments about collective security-seeking practices, going beyond the sizable amount of judgmental assessments by Zacher, Haas, and Butterworth in particular. But codings from various European, Asian, Latin, and African judges are needed if a more universal scientific version of "multiple reality assessments" (Alker, 1975) is to be achieved. Like claims that certain acts are "aggressive" or that certain disputes are "threats to international peace and security," judgments that certain management actions serve "patching-up," "prophylactic," or "proselytizing" functions (James, 1969) or realize "hostility-stopping" or "dispute-limiting" outcomes are essentially contested. Outside of the obviously divergent interpretations of Cold War crises, one need only look at current UN or U.S. or Egyptian-Middle East moves. Rather than dictate "objective" codings of such disputes, it is better to see if comparative empirical assessments of outcomes and effects sustain one or another such assessment of a particular case. Less controversial, more interesting, system-relevant, Haas-inspired codes of Third World "balancing" practices or "preventive diplomacy" designed to limit the spread and involvement of major parties might also be attempted in a similar fashion.

For such purposes, we have disaggregated and amplified the outcome and success variables of the earlier Butterworth studies, basing them on objective behavioral evidence where possible. Most concretely, phase sequence information tells of hostility avoidance, setbacks (a return to hostilities, phase 3), loose ends (no phase 5 or 6), and genuine, if sometimes partial, settlements (phase 6). Although the United Nations and its associates are not automatically to be given credit for either the successes or failures in Table 8.3, it is evident in such cases that hostility setbacks have occurred 17 times, while 67 hostility phases have moved on the nonreversed, posthostility phases. When compared with the much smaller figure of 25 settlement phases, most of them not managed by the United Nations, we see clear evidence for the diplomatic claim that international organizations usually *manage* conflicts rather than *resolve* them, at least in part because they serve extinguishing rather than fire prevention functions. All of these findings avoid consideration of the disputes (like the Arab-Israeli conflict, the Cold War, and certain colonial situations fraught with ethnic conflict) where the settlement of some issues or continued unrest gets transformed by the emergence of substantively new disputes related in important ways to their predecessors.

Of particular relevance to recent diplomatic claims that the UN exacerbates and prolongs too many disputes—a view that presupposes that much more interventionist patterns of international crisis resolution are both possible and desirable—we have also coded, but not yet analyzed, agent-specific judgments as to the likely intensity, continuance, spread, or settlement of the disputes without management intervention. A contrasting interpretation may be expected on the basis of Butterworth's (1978b: 120) principal finding that international conflict-managing organizations have shown a moderating influence "by providing an institutional framework that supplements, but does not transform, traditional interstate relations."[6]

In an effort to enrich policy-relevant understanding, Tanaka (1980) defines Chinese precedental contexts in the same way that Alker, Christensen, and Greenberg found "similar" conflicts in their practically oriented simulations of UN peace-making efforts. In Figure 8.1 are a series of antecedent disputes exactly like or similar enough on key characteristics to be considered policy-relevant precedents to the Sino-Vietnamese border incident of December 1970. On the left of the figure, a "narrative context" is constructed by looking for recent conflict episodes with at least one of the parties on each side the same as those on the current case being studied. An analogous presentation could be made for disputes in our modified and updated Butterworth data set. One can thus better see, and perhaps better analyze, specific events against the background of co-occurring, as well as relevant past, events.

Reflective Learning, Agenda Processes, and Epigenetic Systems Change

As a preliminary illustrative discussion of ways in which precedentally sensitive "reflective political learning about war avoidance" has had an effect on subsequent agenda processes and system change, we shall now discuss brief narrative accounts of UN involvement and noninvolvement in two different "breaches of peace": the Chinese invasion of Tibet, 1950-51, and the North Korean invasion of South Korea, 1950-53, a war which also saw Chinese intervention, but at a later point. From a comparative perspective on the UN's effectiveness, these two cases nicely contrast the extremes of the UN's relatively effective coercive

involvement and its relative weakness as a resolver of recalcitrant conflicts. As noted by many observers in the advanced capitalist countries, a
similar contrast fits the UN's unprecedentedly ambitious UNEF operation in the Suez crisis of 1956 and its inability to stop or even ameliorate
the Soviet invasion of Hungary at about the same time. After discussing
these (and some other related examples), we shall make some concluding,
more systematic remarks about research possibilities and reflective
learning concerning agenda process and systems change in collective
security-seeking practices.

TIBET AND KOREA AS PARALLEL CHALLENGES TO COLLECTIVE SECURITY-SEEKING PRACTICES

Recall that Figure 8.1 contains cases other than those connected by
historical trees of either narrative-based or precedentally linked con-
tinuities. The reason for doing so was the expectation that a careful
examination of "parallel cases" (those that are co-occurring and
strategically interdependent from the point of view of certain actors)
would sometimes reveal more about the generative principles or
operational codes of such actors.

The Tibet invasion and the Korean war are doubly interesting in this
regard. Not only do both cases involve nearly simultaneous invasions by
Chinese troops (into Tibet on October 26, 1950 and by Chinese volun-
teers into North Korea at about the same time), they are both
precedentally linked by the role of India as a management agent, inside
or outside of the United Nations. Leaving to Tanaka the discussion of
his own figure and the importance of Chinese double involvement
decision, we focus here on the latter "parallelism."

Attempting to forestall the reestablishment of Chinese control over
Tibet, Tibetan authorities sought the aid of India (a local balancing
operation) to offset expected advances by the People's Republic of
China (the PRC) following the Communists' victory in the Chinese Civil
War (a major "antiregime" conflict or "internal cold war" that the
United Nations never had on its agenda). Prior to the Chinese invasion,
Tibetan-PRC talks were held in New Delhi under the auspices of Prime
Minister Nehru. After the Chinese invasion caused an outcry in the
West, India successfully blocked the inclusion of the Tibet question on
the UN agenda. Referring to the nonmembership of the PRC in the UN
(an issue fraught with significance for UN collective security practices
for more than 20 years), India appealed to the already heavy UN
involvement in the Korean War. Its stated rationale involved the

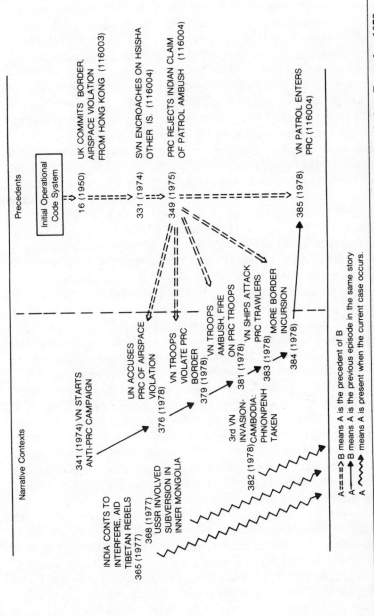

Figure 8.1   Precedential Chains in Narrative Contexts Behind Sino-Vietnamese Border Incident in late December 1978

Source: Tanaka, 1980.

argument (which to many Westerners looked more like a fait accompli position than an advocacy of a truce and subsequent negotiations) that the situation could be resolved peacefully without resort to UN debate.

India's position and China's moderation did facilitate the termination or resolution of this initial round of the Tibet-PRC conflict and the signing of the "Seventeen Article Agreement of 23 May 1951" (see Butterworth and Scranton, 1976: 145-150; and James, 1969: 197ff for relevant details). Consequently, India's role as a "facilitator" of the PRC's interests in UN-related matters was given a certain precedental validity on the part of both the PRC and the United Nations.

The story of UN involvement in Korea is better known. A UN commission had been in the country for some time trying to work for the peaceful reunification and postwar rehabilitation of Korea. It reported a massive, well-planned North Korean invasion of South Korea, a move associated with Acheson's prior disavowal of U.S. vital interests in Korea, the possibility of certain Southern provocations, and considerable unrest in South Korea related to a domestic electoral process of dubious democratic validity. UN coercive involvement on the side of the South Koreans was helped decisively by U.S. leadership on the provision of forces, and by the from-this-case-perspective "accidental" absence of the Soviet Union from the Security Council. After the Soviet return and successive vetoes attempting to delegitimate and stop UN coercive involvement, the United States led a constitutionally significant effort (which in another form had earlier been unsuccessful) to bring such issues to the General Assembly. The Uniting for Peace resolution, a precedent now invoked at least tacitly by all parties, passed on the grounds that it was a procedural question not susceptible to Great Power veto, allowed the Assembly to take up and make recommendations concerning security questions on which the Council had reached a veto-based deadlock. In order to gain wide support outside of the Soviet Bloc (which it did), the resolution also contained language suggesting the desirability of increased Third World development aid in a subsequent period of diminished Cold War tensions.

After UN forces had reached the Yalu, China had intervened and a military stalemate had occurred near the former North-South Korea demarcation line, dispute mediation efforts by the Indians and their nonaligned states were given more attention by the Chinese and U.S. allies. (Eisenhower's election and his secret threat to use atomic weapons against the PRC are given an important role in realist commentaries on the subject as well.) In any case, India had early expressed reluctance about the permissive engagement or proselytizing activities (to use Haas's and James's terms) of UN forces in an Asian context on an issue where the Great Powers and their allies seriously disagreed. India was used to transmit "proposals" from the Chinese concerning an armistice and prisoner repatriation practices, proposals which eventually became the basis for the termination of hostilities. Given China's exclusion from UN membership, surely Chinese willingness to use Indian "good offices" in UN-related matters was furthered by their relatively satisfactory role as a management agent in the Tibetan dispute.

Stepping back from these brief narratives, one may draw some heuristically suggestive inferences. First, note the importance of agenda processes, as they are affected by the relative power of different actors vis-à-vis particular arenas. Thus, the PRC's nonmembership in the United Nations in 1950 encouraged a rare, explicit, negative agenda decision concerning the Tibetan case. Similarly, the capturing of "collective security" symbols by a U.S.-led "collective self-defense effort" against communist "aggressions," an anomalous result when compared with either the Tibetan or Hungarian cases, can be laid to the accidental absence of the Soviet Union from the Security Council. Relatively decisive action, the Uniting for Peace resolution, and Indian mediation efforts are associated with subtle but important endogenous change in UN security-seeking practices.

In particular, the legitimating basis and fundamental character of UN collective security actions became less the Wilsonian Collective Security ideal (one unrealistic in a Cold War era anyway, and flawed from the point of view of the nonaligned countries) and more the "balancing" of Cold War antagonists by nonaligned parties playing newly legitimate, universalistics roles directed toward the "peaceful settlement of disputes" rather than collective defense or security operations. Thus the beginnings of the nonalignment movement in the 1950s (usually associated with the Bandung Conference of 1955 and the shift in world politics to a "loose bipolar system," with the United Nations playing a significant mediating role) are seen in our study as well. And the increasing role of *both* local or regional conflict managers *and* the UN system is prefigured, as is the post-Bandung UN emphasis on "preventive diplomacy" directed against Third World Great Power involvement (turning Great Power Concert principles upside down until some later date).

A further suggestive inference is that agenda politics, the dynamics of which disputes get addressed by which management agent (if any), holds the key to a better understanding of the evolution, decay, and transformation of collective security-seeking practices. Thus the very uneven involvement and success patterns of regional and universal collective security-seeking organizations can be seen realistically as part of a global political process in which neither "power politics" nor collective peaceful settlement practices are absent from the scene.

COLLECTIVE SECURITY-SEEKING AGENDA PROCESSES

One of the serious mistakes of an unreflective logical empiricism studying collective security-seeking practices is a preoccupation only with the UN system and a taking for granted that only the issues discussed there are wanting of study. Alger (1970) has shown such tendencies to exist in the earlier American literature. Reducing the study of power politics to the study of the participation of various actors in the making of decisions avoids recognition of what are now called "nondecisions" in American political science. Such a practice confuses

(1) the *overt power arena,* where issues are actively and publicly contested;
(2) the *veiled power arena,* where rarely visible negative agenda decisions ("nondecisions") take place; and
(3) the realm of *averted structural* power, which determines or limits actions even without overt agenda discussions or conscious recognition that choices are being made (see Lukes, 1974, for the best review of these distinctions, drawn originally from Dahl's—among others—work on community power).

We think it highly desirable to analyze collective security-seeking practices in these terms. Thus, the recognition that a controversial issue is a peace and security dispute appropriately discussed in a multilateral way corresponds to the move from the averted structural power arena to the veiled power arena. Agenda processes in the veiled power arena are typically associated with expectations of the "mobilization of bias" inherent in a particular institutional arena. This bias has a lot to do with the reluctance or enthusiasm of parties to a dispute to bring it into such an arena for management efforts (assuming unilateral self-help motives have begun to shift at least toward collective defense concerns). The jurisdictional scope, the normative consensus, the distribution of membership and divisional powers among friends and enemies in different management arenas all come into play at this stage. Why else have the major alliances taken on internal collective security functions? Agenda decisions that are positive lead to overt discussion and possibly action; negative decisions lead to nonmanaged conflicts, or management "nondecisions."

The communal nature of positive, collective security-seeking actions (the avoidance of a veto, achieving 2/3 majorities, and so forth) means that nondecisions on the merits of an issue are often the result of management efforts through collective security organizations. These nondecisions (in a different sense from above) are painfully obvious to various interested observers, who nonetheless frequently do not understand the reasons for nondecisions of either sort. Dispute parties are likely to size up such prospects more accurately, relying on multiple security-promoting instruments, self-help, and certain collective efforts in a calculated manner open to scientific investigation.

Does this general sketch conform to the views of Zacher, Kende, Butterworth, Haas, and other students of our subject? Yes, at least partly, we believe. Haas, Butterworth, and Zacher have all pioneered multiarena comparative studies of collective security practices, although the agenda process has not been given sufficient attention in their studies. Zacher makes a further valuable contribution to our understanding of the frequent failures by internation collective security organizations to stop overt aggressions (e.g., the Chinese going into Tibet or U.S. assistance in the overthrow of a Marxist government in Guatemala) by demonstrating the statistical likelihood of discussion and/or condemnatory actions in most disputes involving intra- or interblock actions. He recognizes that attacks by bloc members on nonaligned states (like Egypt in 1956 or Tibet in 1950) are most likely to evoke positive deterrent action if the additional requirement of membership of most of the relevant parties in a collective security organization can be met. Moreover, Zacher is quite suggestive in estimating the likelihood of bias (pro-West or not) in the different organizations he studies. We hope to extend his work, explicitly modeling the trajectory of issues into or out of management practices on similar grounds, thus making amends for previous studies, e.g., Alker and Greenberg (1971), which only mentioned agenda processes without empirically studying them.

As a first step in such activities, Figures 8.2 and 8.3, derived from our revised Butterworth and Scranton data set, give gross trends in agenda attention to the universe of over 300 disputes we are working with (many more than in Table 8.3). One can see that multiplication of management agents has indeed occurred. And a significant number of pure "nondecisions" vis-à-vis the stated charters or relevant organizations are also

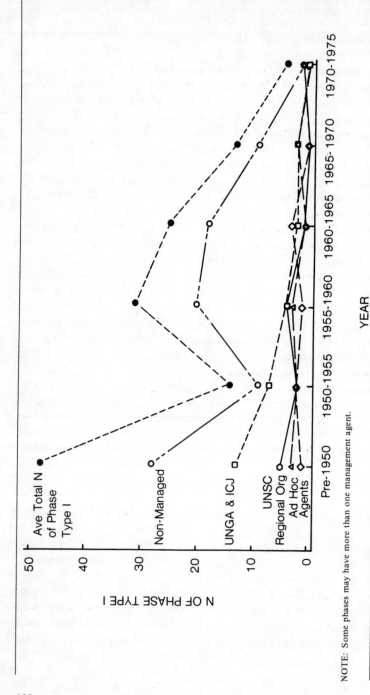

NOTE: Some phases may have more than one management agent.

Figure 8.2 Trends in the Number of Disputes (Conflict Phase 1) Handled by Different Types of Management Agents, 1945-1975 (Revised Butterworth/Scranton Data Recoded in Phases)

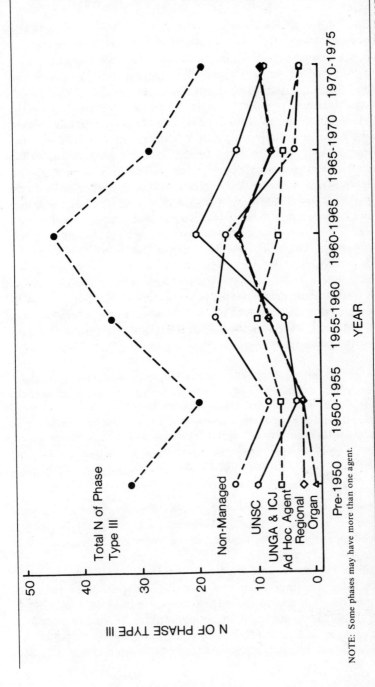

NOTE: Some phases may have more than one agent.

Figure 8.3 Trends in the Number of Hostilities (Conflict Phase 3) Handled by Different Types of Management Agents, 1945-1975 (Revised Butterworth/Scranton Data Recoded in Phases)

obvious.[7] But what is surprising is the post-1965 decline in early UN (Security Council *and* General Assembly) involvement in serious disputes, although many more disputes than before were being managed, perhaps by newer organizations. Surprisingly, the 1960s saw the Security Council busier with hostility dispute phases than did the 1950s!

Kende's claim of post-1965 détente is consistent with both figures. In our view, he is right to focus on both "internal" and "foreign" wars (despite Charter provisions against UN intervention into "domestic" jurisdiction issues); he is right to look for breaches of the peace associated with regular, collectively organized military violence. But he is wrong to leave out military interventions that are nonmassively resisted (e.g., Soviet intervention into Czechoslovakia), and he is limited in scope (as we all must be at times) in not focusing on the role of threats that coercively produce compliance (phase 2 actions) without an overt resort to force. The hegemonial role of both the United States and the USSR in their respective parts of the world has kept numerous disputes in the nondecisions category, e.g., the issue of U.S. colonialism in Puerto Rico. Structurally averted power exercise according to the rule of anticipated reactions is real, even if difficult to observe behaviorally.

As a Marxist, Kende takes seriously the role of structural determination or the influence of systemic dispute contexts. Thus he argues:

> We do not believe that either of these (recent) important political phenomena—assertion or peaceful coexistence or the decrease of wars (post 1967)—was the consequence of some kind of suddenly arising personal good will, or of essential changes in any system. We are more inclined to the view that significant changes in the international balance of power ("the main line of development of international politics") have led to these results, have compellingly brought about these new phenomena [Kende, 1978: 238, note 6].

It puzzles us that he attributes changes in war frequency and intensity to changes in a structural variable, the distribution ("balance") of power, but without seeing this distribution as an "essential change," as many realists would have it.

Additionally, we feel, there is a need in the realm of averted issues to acknowledge and investigate the changing recognition of systemic determinants of at least some specific dispute management outcomes, such as arms races, unrecognized demographic-technological pressures for expansion, and asymmetric economic or political relationships. In the middle 1940s, bloody colonial riots and even explicit guerrilla activity were sometimes not seen as threats to international peace and security by any major power. This has changed, with resistance to genocide and the struggle for other basic human rights having also slowly emerged. Classically, fights over overseas resource monopolies were causes of wars; now, guaranteed market access complicates such issues. Arms race politics and the success or failure of arms limitation efforts have caused previous nonissues (Soviet troops in Cuba) to become crises and help rationalize other interventions (e.g., the Soviet Union in Afghanistan). The study of collective security-seeking practices cannot close its determinative loops until structural and political factors shaping security objectives are endogenously explained.

GENETIC AND EPIGENETIC SYSTEMS CHANGE

Discussions about systems change are often rather unproductive. We started this chapter, for example, with a summary of post-1945 developments in collective security-seeking practices that to us indicates many such transformations, yet Haas and Zacher in some respects see few such changes within the United Nations, at least few that are not reflective of the external environment, world politics. Kende's earlier remarks also seem hard to interpret.

Without structurally reifying systems concepts, and without assuming the reproduction of such systems to be mechanically automatic, how can we study the systemic aspects of collective security-seeking practices? Our first response is to ground systems thinking in unilateral and collective practices. Both the Congo example of Alker (1975) and the Tibetan and Korean cases discussed above indicate how organizational action can be rationalized as a collective political practice. Thus, we may essentially or summarily find regularities in practices that deserve a "systems" label. Significant transformations in the number or distribution of major autonomous *actors,* in their action-linked *perspectives,* in their support mobilization or security-seeking *strategic action sequences,* in the differently biased *arenas* characteristically appealed to for management practices, in issue-specific success or failure *outcome* patterns, and in the *consequences* of the above for future systemic patterning, have *all* been used to describe systems changes.

Additionally we may distinguish essentialist and aggregate systems views. The former looks for deep structuring, generative, organizing principles (contained within the perspectives of different practices). The latter looks for statistical trends or aggregations, as in Figures 8.2 and 8.3, on trends in management/nonmanagement practices. Liberal or conservative positivists in the twentieth century tend to take nominalist, aggregate positions on systems issues, while Marxists like Kende tend to make essentialist (i.e., capitalism-linked) interpretations. This polarization, however, is not complete. It is our view that the most productive approach is to look for indirectly observable, changing essences or sociopolitical practices. If there are deep, generative structures within security-seeking practices, we want to find them. Advanced techniques within the Artificial Intelligence tradition—frames, scripts, or schemes —suggest ways of empirically modeling the charter norms, balancing or alignment rules, characteristic dispute management procedures, or class conflicts that may be the constant or changing essence underlying such practices (Alker et al., 1980).

One further distinction within an empirical essentialist way of thinking should be made, namely that between genetic and epigenetic processes of system reproduction and transformation. A geneticist views living systems as realization of DNA-embedded, preformed genetic potential, possibly triggered off in different maturational stages. Analogously, an epigenetic perspective emphasizes unprogrammed, creative accretions in an organism's functioning. Being careful within the limits of the analogy when applied to organized international systems, one can still meaningfully distinguish preformed and novel functional patterns. For example, we suspect that the internalization of an insecurity-driven, power-balancing logic in the life experiences of most current political leaders makes the recurrence of such a systemic phenomenon highly likely, mistakenly giving the impression that this program of behavior had been "wired into" these statesmen and women at birth. Epigenetic accretions in function, like collective defense organizations that serve collective security functions, also occur. The apparently temporary turning upside down of classical concert of power practices to give preventive diplomacy practices also strikes us as epigenetically describable. Combining these two kinds of processes of systems change with adaptive, bias-sensitive, security-seeking agenda processes helps explain our sense that many important systemic transformations have occurred in the 1945-1980 period, while at the same time allowing us and others like Zacher and Haas or Kende to account for the nearly "eternal return" of power-balancing, bihegemonial systemic practices.

It is not our intention here to further review alternative systemic patterns possibly recognizable within collective security-seeking practices. But we do pause to provide a two-dimensional alternative to

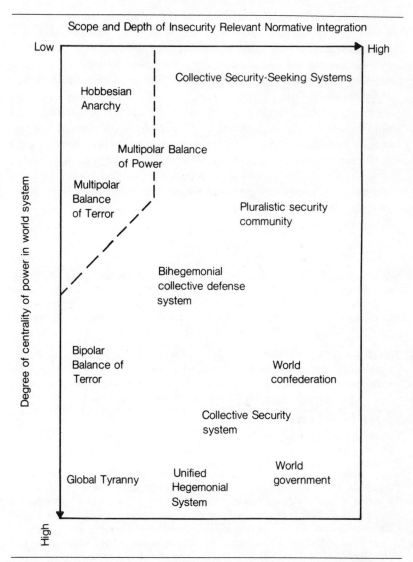

Figure 8.4 An Approximate Classification of Collective Security-Seeking Systems

the anarchy-collective security-world government continuum with which we opened this chapter. From the writings of communitarian peace researchers like Ernst Haas and Karl Deutsch (Deutsch et al., 1957), we recognize that a unipolar power system may be legitimate or not, a tyranny or a world commonwealth. Further, we see the possibility of pluralistic security communities, systems of nominally sovereign states that manage conflicts among them without recourse to threats of war. Figure 8.4 shows how many of the alternatives discussed in this chapter can be characterized (approximately, to be sure) in terms of a power centralization and security-relevant consensus axes. We wish the larger realm of transitions among such alternatives would be more constantly in the view of specialists on unilateral and collective security-seeking practices.

NOTES

1. Our brief summary on these points (including the Wilson quote taken from Ruggie's first page) derives basically from Haas (1955), Claude (1964), and Ruggie (1974).

2. The first long quote is recalled by one of us from a talk by Stanley Hoffmann; the second comes from Claude (1964: 224); the remaining quoted phrases refer of course to Article 51, Chapter VII and Chapter VIII of the United Nations Charter.

3. A principle conclusion of the Haas et al. (1972: 60) study is that "there has been no organizational learning in the past [1960-1970] decade—although probably some 'unlearning.'" Haas (1962) earlier described UN experience of the 1950s as "Dynamic Environment and Static System," implying that if there was a real change taking place, it was not within the UN system. Given our own perceptions of rapid transformations in collective security-seeking practices, we are trying to capture the real phenomena, wherever they occur.

In an important study, Zacher (1979: 215) repeats the Haas et al. view of collective security organizations as little more than standing diplomatic conferences with no power, personality, or learning capacity beyond those of individual governments. His whole book gives a rather static but detailed view of the efforts of inter-, intra-, and cross-bloc alignments on prospects for collective conflict-handling success. But he concludes, in a way that resonates with our concerns, that a future, multivariate theory of collective security efforts "will likely assign a central place to coalition configurations and the affiliation of conflicting parties with particular political-security groupings" (1979: 207).

4. In our attempt to get serious further discussions going about empirical scientific work on collective security-seeking practices, we shall have to impute views to East European scholars that some or all of them, including Kende, may not hold. We do so with apologies before-hand, in the hope of having our statements corrected through serious, empirically informed scientific discussions. The only other systematic, empirically oriented study of major postwar conflict episodes and conflict management practices of which we are aware is by Professor Gantman and his associates in Moscow. A full English or French language account of these studies is not available to our knowledge.

5. We have not carefully reviewed the relevant histories, but see as relevant to present concerns Goldmann's (1970) depressing account of the great variety of rationalization postwar states have used to justify (post hoc?) war initiation decisions. Similarly, Ferencz's (1975) study of eventual definitional success needs to be correlated with the political realities of its construction period. The interested, operationally inclined researcher might also wish to read Rivera (1973).

6. Perhaps U.S. Ambassador Kirkpatrick is correct in seeing more profound systemic effects evidenced by new trends or patterns of joint (but still usually late) action or referral. A glance at Table 8.3 suggests such a significant trend away from U.S. hegemony: management agents dominated or constituted by the United States are significantly less monopolistic after about 1963. Her remarks to this effect were reported on the *CBS Television Evening News* in late February 1982.

7. We like to think that the weakness of the United Nations is a virtue from the point of view of nondecisions research. Whereas conservative behavioral critics of the nondecisions argument have been known to say, "Show me a nondecision," which by their nature is difficult to do, the world of collective security-seeking practices is *full* of nondecisions in either of the two textual senses used above. Perhaps, then, agenda process research has found here its *Drosophila,* a naturally occurring species whose "veiled" genetic codes are much easier to discover with microscopic investigation than the veiled or averted power processes also thought to influence domestic politics.

CHAPTER 9

THE UN SYSTEM
Structural Transformation and Crisis

KINHIDE MUSHAKOJI

The Problematique

The role of international institutions in conflict management is quite
limited in the present international setting. It is true that the United
Nations has been involved since its creation in different crises and has
played a certain role in peace-making and peace-keeping. It also plays
an important role in various matters related to disarmament. However,
when these achievements are compared with the expected performances
of an ideal world government, they are far too limited to satisfy the
expectations placed on international institutions in the field of peace
and security.[1]

In opposition to the *idealists* who expect to see in the future the
creation of international institutions fully empowered to manage
conflicts, the *realists* have always maintained that the international
system is in fact international and that any international institution,
including the United Nations system, cannot but reflect the realities of
power politics that attribute to the major powers the principal
responsibility to manage crises, leaving the international bodies with
only a marginal role to play.[2]

This controversy between the two schools of thought has gone on for
several decades and will undoubtedly continue for several more.

AUTHOR'S NOTE: The views expressed in this chapter are those of the author and not
necessarily those of the United Nations University.

Meanwhile, history progresses and the international system itself is changing.

In fact, the emerging trends in the contemporary international situation appear to confirm neither of the above positions. Nowadays, it is difficult to imagine an imminent materialization of the idealists' dream of opening a path toward a world "beyond nations" (Haas, 1964). It is, however, less and less realistic to rely on the major powers and expect them to be able to manage successfully the new types of crises that are likely to proliferate as the international system enters a phase of structural transformation.

It is more and more apparent that the superpowers are beginning to lose their capacity to provide a framework for stability and security. The proliferation of different types of violence, the heightened competition for scarce resources, the desperate struggle for human survival, and many other symptoms of a systematic crisis create conflictual situations far beyond the management capabilities of the major powers that were developed in historical settings so different from today.

The idealists may find in the present international crisis the growing pain of a system moving into a transnational and global phase. The realists may believe in the capacity of the "balance of power" system to recover its equilibrium after a phase of destabilization. It is, however, also possible that the whole international system will collapse if no alternative institutional formula can be found to replace the present crisis management settings in their disarray.

The present chapter does not intend to provide an in-depth analysis to determine which of these three readings of the "signs of the time" is correct. Its objective is, rather, to present a conceptual scheme for studying what institutional measures should be taken in case the third hypothesis comes to be. If the major powers fail to exercise their crisis management functions, what role should the United Nations play?[3]

Our basic assumption in this chapter is that in the event the crisis management responsibilities have to be totally shouldered by the UN system, that institution must be prepared and know ahead of time exactly what is to be expected of it. We know from the example of history that system collapse and structural transformation call for a transfer of essential political functions from the dominant institutions in decay to subsidiary institutions that are suddenly called on to play a leading role. Such was the case when the Christian church had to replace in different ways the falling Roman Empire.[4] To build a conceptual scheme to determine the future role of the UN system in managing crises is not easy. Even more difficult is the task of relating the emerging role of international institutions as a consequence of structural transformation to the failure of existing institutions to fulfill certain functional requirements.

Since the structural transformation of the international system is a macrohistorical process, the historical context that gave birth to the existing structures must be analyzed. Since structural transformation also implies that the existing institutions have failed to perform certain functions, it is not enough to analyze the past; the conceptual scheme should have the possiblity to grasp the shapes of the future. Since the inquiry treats the role of the UN system in a totally different setting compared to its present environment, empirical research on the past is insufficient.

Structural Aspects of the Problematique

The first step of the present inquiry, which tries to relate crisis management to international institutions in the context of the contemporary process of structural transformation, is to determine the structural context of the relationships in question.

The basic consideration we start with is as follows: Any international system functions on the basis of a definite division of labor among its component units—social, economic, political, and military. This process determines the differentiation of roles, defines the patterns of allocation of scarce values, attributes to the different units divergent ranges of capabilities, and designates different tasks to each unit.[5] We will call *structure* the set of component units, together with the division of labor that enables them to operate as a system. Our inquiry will focus on international political structures; we will use the plural to stress the fact that even in the field of politics different types of the division of labor can be distinguished according to the specific aspect of the political system under scrutiny.[6].

Any international system evolves through a historical process whereby different units seek to improve their position in the existing division of labor, eventually attempting to change the very nature of that division. Therefore, structures are more or less stable depending on the level of crisis caused by a given unit's attempt to transform the existing division of labor. Structural transformation appears whenever such attempts are successful. Crises are thus closely related to structural transformation unless they are caused only by competitions within the framework of the existing structures. They are either violent or nonviolent depending on certain conditions determined by the division of labor that assigns to different sectors of the system different types of violence. We can therefore talk about structures of violence and conflicts.[7]

International institutions can be defined in two ways. On the one hand, they are a set of means used by the units to guarantee the stability and efficacy of the activities they undertake within the framework of a given division of labor. On the other hand, the institutions can also be defined as component units taking part in the division of labor alongside other units. In the case under study, the UN system is both a means to guarantee a smooth and stable interaction among nation states and an independent unit of the international political division of labor.[8]

Having given a definition of the key concepts we are going to use, we can now enter into a macrohistorical discussion of the structural aspects of the problematique under consideration in this chapter.

The present international political division of labor has evolved out of three historical contexts within which the different aspects of the contemporary structures are defined. We must study the three aspects of the ongoing structural transformation that were caused by the obsolescence of the modes of the division of labor inherited from the three historical moments of formation of the contemporary international system.

The first pattern with a determinant effect on the present international structures is the division of labor that followed the formation of a *world economy* in sixteenth-century Europe. This is the Western States Structure (hereafter abridged as WSS) that was crystallized at the time of the Treaty of Westfalia. The second is the division of labor that emerged out of the process of the globalization of Western capitalism from the beginning of the industrial revolution until today. This is the center-periphery structure (hereafter CPS) that determines the division of labor between the industrialized and the developing nations and regions. The third pattern is the bipolar structure (hereafter BPS) that opposes the international economic division of labor into capitalist and socialist patterns, instead of linking them both into a single political division of labor. This pattern originated in the interwars period, but only crystallized after World War II with the introduction of nuclear bipolarity as a crucial factor determining the modes of the political division of labor involving the socialist and capitalist states.

These three modes of the division of labor are closely interrelated since they evolved out of the same historical process that gave birth to the present international system. The CPS adds a periphery composed by colonies—and later ex-colonies—to the Western states in the WSS, making them the core of an international system of global dimension. The BPS is nothing but a transformed WSS—or a CPS whose center has been changed as a consequence of the emergence of two superpowers.

The WSS's basic characteristic is the attribution of power and the legitimate use of violence to the sovereign states. The concept of sovereignty with its diverse attributes is crucial in defining the units of contemporary international political division of labor, i.e., those states formally equal to each other who respect each other's prerogative of noninterference in their respective domestic affairs.[9]

The development of an international, capitalist division of labor, being the formation of *world economy* with a multiplicity of poles of industrial development that free competition guarantees for the growth of the total system, is based on this international political division of labor wherein the states correspond to national markets relating each pole of development (the industrial sector) to its hinterland (the agricultural sector). In this way the states become the political institutions guaranteeing the autonomous and self-sustained growth of their respective poles of development (Burns, 1980).

Another aspect of the sovereign state no less important is its internal political division of labor as characterized by the emergence of a bureaucracy of which the diplomats become a part. This creates a management style characterized by a means-end rationality that prepares for the rise of technocratic management of the BPS (Perroux, 1954: 281-306).

Coming back to the fundamental principle of equality among sovereign states, we must point out that in spite of this principle, which normally should create an egalitarian division of labor among states, the WSS is hierarchical and distinguishes major powers from the middle and small states. From the Concert of Europe to the veto right of the permanent members of the UN Security Council, the major powers are attributed special prerogatives in the management of crises in the international system.

The limited role conceded to international institutions in the present international system finds its origin in the historical circumstances of the birth of such institutions. It was only when large-scale, violent international conflicts proved the inability of the balance of power among major states to guarantee the successful management of such conflicts that international institutions, e.g., the League of Nations or the United Nations, were formed by these states to play an auxiliary role in filling in the gaps of the WSS created by the emergence of total wars unknown to the signatories of the Treaty of Westfalia.

As the second mode of the division of labor that influences present international political structures, the CPS brings into the international economic and political division of labor an asymmetry that is much more basic than the distinction between the major powers and the middle and small countries of the WSS. Whereas the WSS attributes no direct control of a given major power over a specific small nation, since the major states are collectively responsible for the management of the total system and a checking mechanism does not permit any permanent ties to link any two states, the CPS links given states (or colonies) in the system's center and periphery by means of colonial or neocolonial ties (see Samir, 1976: 13-73).

We will discuss later the functional aspects of the international division of labor of the CPS. Suffice it here to stress one point. Unlike the WSS, which was a comparatively homogeneous and stable international structure, the CPS is a heterogeneous and unstable structure. This is because unlike the former, the latter is built on a division of labor with international capitalism imposing its rule on a set of precapitalist modes of the division of labor. We have explained elsewhere that the present international political structures can be described as a superimposition of *industria*—an international industrial order—on *agraria*—the agrarian-based international order (Mushako-ji, 1977: 47-49).

The international process of industralization-modernization-Westernization forces upon the peripheric sector of the CPS an alien mode of the division of labor that is also exploitation. This is why the CPS is heterogeneous and unstable, and hence generates different types of conflicts. The CPS is accompanied by two opposed processes, a process of intrusion and another of resistance. Associated with the former are the terms mentioned already: industrialization-modernization-Westernization. With the latter are linked the political symbols of nationalism, liberation, and cultural identity.[10]

The United Nations serves as a forum where the two processes can be accommodated, at least on the level of states, but there are no institutional means to cope with the processes on other levels, either transnational or subnational. This is why the CPS is by nature unstable. The division of labor between the center and the periphery can be maintained only by a crisis management mechanism guaranteeing the center's "mission" to "pacify" the periphery.[11]

The instability of the CPS increases, however, as its structures become more complex. As it is discussed by many authors, the social stratification of the international capitalist division of labor has evolved into a complex structure with subdivisions in the center and the periphery of both industrialized and developing societies, so that we now have the center of the center, the periphery of the center, the center of the periphery, and the periphery of the periphery. This stratification is not only economic but also political and social (Galtung, 1972).

The forces opposed to the maintenance and transformation of structural asymmetry and the violence opposing the center and the periphery of both the industrial center and the developing periphery build into the process of intrusion and resistance a complex combination of alliances and oppositions where diverse interests destabilize the balance of the national interests of the WSS. The effect of the contradictions between a "modernizing" elite at the center of the periphery allied with the industrialized center and the nationalist forces resisting external domination in the periphery of the periphery is to generate crisis and violence, all part of the process of cultural convergence in the periphery (see Mazrui, 1976: 191-210).

Whereas the CPS evolved as a consequence of the expansion of the WSS that accompanied the economic and technological growth of the international capitalist division of labor, the BPS developed in the central sector of the CPS following the economic bipolarization of the capitalist and socialist division of labor as it was translated into a political division of labor with the two superpowers at the top of two power blocs. The emergence of the two superpowers was the result of the process of industrialization that enabled them to centralize control in technological, political, and economic terms (see Morse, 1976).

The BPS is replacing the balance of power among a plurality of major states by a nuclear balance between the two superpowers and their respective blocs. To this extent the structures are based on symmetry in the political division of labor between the two blocs and between the two superpowers. The structures are asymmetrical, however, both within the blocs and between the two blocs, on the one side, and within the peripheral sector on the other. This double asymmetry is reinforced by the structures of military capability, with the nuclear superpowers on top and the peripheral countries with only rudimentary military capability at the bottom. We will return later to the functional consequences of this structure of violence being associated with the BPS. Suffice it to mention here that the asymmetry built into the BPS makes it unstable and conflict-laden. Some authors use the term *atimia* to represent the sense of frustration on the part of the states whose status has been downgraded as a result of the emergence of the superpowers. Atimia is doubly felt by the states in the the peripheral sector, since they are dependent on the central sector and thus have the lowest status after the superpowers and the other states of the industrial regions (see Lagos, 1963).

The structural transformation of the international system that we are experiencing today is nothing but the cumulative effect of various contradictions, structural and functional, that were built into the system as the WSS, originally a relatively homogeneous and formally symmetrical system, evolved into a heterogeneous, asymmetrical system following the emergence of the CPS and the BPS. This is why the emergence of the two structures has added to the possible sources of crisis in the contemporary international system not only the danger of symmetrical nuclear conflict but also the proliferation of asymmetrical crises among industrial states within the two blocs, between them and the peripheral states, and especially among the latter ones, whose atimia motivate them to compete with each other. In sum, it is not surprising that after the accumulation of so many factors of asymmetry, instability, and crisis, the present international political structures are entering a phase of structural transformation.

Functional Aspects of the Problematique

In the previous section we studied the implications of three historical modes of the international division of labor that contributed to the shaping of the contemporary structures of the international system. We will proceed one step further in this section and discuss the ways in which these three modes determined the process of the specification of functions prevalent in the present international system.

The *specification of functions* is a concept that demands some explanation. *Function* is a term generally used as an analytical concept representing what should be done in order to maintain a given system's existence. Among other schools of thought, the structural-functional paradigm assumes that *structures* have to meet certain functional requirements (see Parsons, 1951; Levy, 1951). This method of relating structures to functions, assuming structural stability and a universally defined set of functions, cannot be of any help in analyzing a process of structural transformation since the structures are not stable.[12] Such a method assumes: (a) that the structures are stable and (b) that there are universally defined functions. These assumptions give birth to the commonly accepted view of structural transformation as a pathological situation where the structures can no longer fulfill certain functional requirements, and hence a dysfunctional process is triggered.[13]

But such an interpretation does not take into consideration an important factor which concerns us here, namely, the role of institutions. Why do certain institutions fail to cope with structural change, increase the level of violence, and delay the process of restructuration while other institutions make possible a process of peaceful transformation, thereby accelerating the creation of new structures? This question can only be answered if we assume that institutions are not merely exercising universally defined functions but that they play a role in identifying—or being blind to—new functional requirements emerging out of unforeseen situations created by the rapidly changing structures.[14]

To be blind or to have insight into emerging functional requirements is the touchstone that determines the historical role of various institutions in times of social change. Therefore, crisis management capability in times of structural transformation must be defined as the capacity of any institutions—superpower, nation-state, political party, revolutionary movement, or international organization—to have insight into the new functional requirements of structural transformation.

The most serious problem with institutions prevailing in a stable system is that they develop a selective mechanism that focuses their attention on certain key functions essential to the stability and maintenance of the existing structures—in other words, to the reproduction of a certain type of division of labor. Institutions identify and specify a selected number of *functions* and conceive of the *management* of the system as a steering and controlling action guaranteeing their fulfillment.[15] This is why we must reverse the assumption that different structures should fulfill certain functions equally indispensable for their maintenance and study how different structures, i.e., different modes of the division of labor, determine the way certain functions are specifically identified, distinguished, and singled out whereas others remain unidentified, confused with other functions, or have to wait for the transformation of the structure to be specified in their turn. The reason we insist on this approach will become clear as we apply it to the following inquiry into the functional aspects of the problematique of crises and institutions in an international system undergoing structural transformation.

The first case in which the specification of functions takes place in a historical context still binding the present international political structures is the WSS. As we know, the WSS represents the political division of labor accompanying the *world economy* born in sixteenth-century Europe.

The specification of functions is guided by two major requirements of the international economic and political division of labor. As we saw already, one of them was to organize the international political division of labor around nation-states that were expected to play the role of protectors of national market economies—the keystones of capitalism. The other was to build a network of economic activities within and without national boundaries, and within and without Europe, in order to foster the accumulation of wealth by private enterprise (see Wallerstein, 1980: 68-122). In order to fulfill the first set of requirements, not only did the sovereign states become units of the WSS, but as we have already seen, they monopolized the military function and the police function while the economic and technological functions were monopolized either by groups of private enterprises, by the state, or by both together, depending on the stage of development of the international economic division of labor.

This twofold monopoly required a number of functional distinctions. First, it was necessary to create a sharp distinction between international and domestic functions, to guarantee the monopoly of military power by the states, and to permit them to protect their domestic markets. After the Mercantilist stage, where the economic and political functions were closely associated, their dissociation became the rule. This created a distinction on the international level between *high politics*, dealing with the power competition within the international political division of labor, and *low politics*, occupied by the need for the states to protect the economic activities of their nationals and hence related to the international economic division of labor and the free competition taking place within its framework.[16]

The selective specification of functions of the WSS had a direct impact on the violence and military functions. Domestic violence was outlawed, whereas international violence was legitimized, provided that it was exercised by the states as an example of *violent diplomacy* by means of their national armies, whose exercise of legitimate violence was carried out in order to observe certain rules codified by the WSS (Aron, 1976).

The military function of the WSS is subordinated to the political function. This means both that war is an extension of diplomacy and that the civilian political elite controls military matters. It implies that arms races and armed conflict are permitted so long as they do not disturb the balance of power and the division of military and political labor wherein the major powers play a concerted leading role. The military art alongside the art of diplomacy developed in the WSS as a method of optimally balancing violence and negotiation within this framework (Schelling, 1971).

The functions to be played by international institutions are also determined in view of the WSS's specification of functions. The development of the international economic division of labor was accompanied by the various consequences of a growing international interdependence; several functions in the fields of trade, transportation, communication, and mobility of people became more and more cumbersome for the states to handle through their low politics diplomacy. The birth of international institutions in the WSS is thus associated with the need to transfer to them the low priority and cumbersome functions in order for the WSS to concentrate on the conduct of high politics (see Haas, 1964).

The functionalist and neofunctionalist schools of thought put a high value on the spill-over effect of the nonpolitical functions exercised by the international institutions that they hoped would permit them to extend their activities to functions related to power politics. It must be realized, however, that in this field the major powers of the WSS have jealously kept for themselves the function of crisis management, permitting the international institutions to perform only subsidiary functions in the fields of disarmament, peace keeping, and the like. The UN system has inherited from the WSS specification and attribution of function only the subsidiary ones. The severe limitations put on the UN peace-keeping actions is a proof of this reality.

As we have already seen, since the emergence of the WSS, crisis management functions have been attributed to the concert of major powers. They had to use diplomatic means, often multilaterally, to oversee the crises among them or in their spheres of influence so that: (a) violent diplomacy did not go beyond certain boundary conditions; (b) armed conflicts observed certain rules of the game; (c) the distribution or redistribution of power assets—notably land—did not break the balance among the major powers; and (d) that no disturbances, domestic or international, developed against the interests of the WSS that might disturb the international division of labor.

As we saw in the last section of this chapter, it was only when they realized their incapacity to handle large scale-conflicts that the contemporary structures relied on international institutions. An important corollary of our basic contention that identification follows the needs of the structures is that it is extremely difficult to convince the major actors who have an interest in the maintenance of a certain mode of the division of labor that international realities do not fit the frame of the functions identified according to the requirements of the actors' respective structures. In this particular case, this means that the major powers cannot identify any functions related to crisis management unless they are in accordance with the basic structural requirements of the WSS. The functions should not contradict the sanctity of state's sovereignty, nor cross the border between the international and the domestic, nor recognize the legitimacy of any military or paramilitary activities not conducted by internationally recognized states. Any functions that tend to call into question the crisis management role of the major powers are left unidentified. For example, functions related to nonviolent crisis management, to the management of structural transformation, or to the promotion of institutional innovations appear to be beyond the range of comprehension of the major actors of the existing structures.[17]

The above functions identified by the international elite—the statesmen, foreign office bureaucrats, diplomats, and political leaders— of the WSS constituted a cognitive system that permitted this elite to manage the WSS sufficiently well, to preserve its stability, and to guarantee the growth of the international economic and political division of labor of the world economy.[18] The elements of this cognitive system, from the concept of sovereign state to the rules of crisis management, constitute to this day the core of the framework within which the international elite identify the functions that the institutions they manage must perform. However, their cognitive system becomes more complex and less consistent following the emergence of the CPS based on an asymmetry of functions in the center and the periphery.

In brief, the functions identified in the WSS remain valid in the center, while the identification of functions in the periphery follows a quite different set of structural requirements. The periphery obeys a basic principle—the fusion of the economic and the political functions. Whereas in the center the free market economy and power politics have to be distinguished, in the dependent part of the international capitalist division of labor the major powers have to build up the zones of influence that are indispensable for their economic growth. These zones have to be formed and preserved by political means supported by military violence. The distinction between domestic and international functions is also blurred, so that army and police functions are often confused.[19] Consequently, the dependence of the periphery on the center is not only economic but also political, cultural, and military. The whole structure of dependence is maintained by the asymmetry in technological development preserved by the center's monopoly of the R&D functions.

The CPS emerged, as we saw before, as a consequence of the WSS's expansion into the non-Western world. The major functional requirements of this type of structure are to guarantee the expanding reproduction of the international capitalist division of labor by expanding its periphery to the extent that it covers the whole globe.[20] This expanding reproduction of the economic division of labor requires both the stability of the center, i.e., the WSS in the industrialized regions, and the expansion of the control and domination by the center over the periphery.[21] Through this control, the regions hitherto outside of the WSS had to be transformed into the *hinterland* of the poles of industrial development in the center of the CPS. This is why the CPS is built on an asymmetric dualism of functions in the center and in the periphery.

Politically, the CPS's functional requirements are guaranteed by a mechanism of stabilization in the center through expansion in the periphery, and such an expansion is backed by a stable crisis management mechanism in the center.

The balance of power of the WSS—and of the BPS—becomes even more stable due to the existence of frontier lands where the major powers of the center can compete without destabilizing the center. However, when the division of the periphery by the major powers generates excessive tensions among them, to the extent that it endangers the balance of power, the crisis management mechanism must work to reassign each power's sphere of influence. When this mechanism fails to work, major conflicts—like World War I—break the balance of the CPS (Mushakoji, 1977: 70-85).

Constant expansion and increased intrusion in the regions where a precapitalist agricultural division of labor predominates is not only an economic functional prerequisite, in view of the industrial growth of the center, it is also a political prerequisite in terms of keeping the level of competition among the major powers under a certain threshold beyond which it becomes difficult to keep the system stable. This expansion, called modernization, industrialization, or Westernization, puts into contact, as we have seen earlier, two types of societies where the process of industrialization works generally to increase the difference between the industrial and agricultural sectors of the periphery society. The structures of violence and conflict reflect this asymmetry. Most conspicuous is the dependency of the military functions. Although the military functions are formally in the hands of the states in the periphery, once they have gained independence they are still dependent on certain states in the center in terms of the transfer of arms, the training of military cadre, the presence of military bases, and/or of eventual military intervention (see Luckham, 1979).

In fact, the role of the military in the dependency structures is not always subservient to its center ally. Its role is frequently to lead the reactive process in the face of the process of intrusion from the center. The military in the periphery plays the role of a modernizing elite, and their efforts are concentrated on the formation of a national army as independent as the international division of labor permits. The military in the dependent countries assume nonmilitary roles in the accumulation and flow of economic surplus and in the national political management. With the development in the center of the CPS of a technocratic elite with political, military, and an industrial concentration of power, the periphery tends to emulate this trend by developing a military-technocratic elite that builds an autocratic rule sometimes opposed to the process of intrusion from the center but quite often in total or partial alliance with it.[22]

In general terms, irrespective of the economic and political position of the military, the militarization of the economic and political functions of the societies in the periphery increases the level of dependency in military, technological, and sociocultural terms by the introduction and emulation of the institutions, technical know-how, and cultural characteristics of the military. The functional dependency of the periphery on the center through the mediation of military functions is a key factor in the contemporary structures of violence and conflict (Kumar-D'Souza, 1980). The predominance of the CPS fusion of all these these functions in the current international system makes it impossible to cope with the true roots of the violence and crises in the developing societies of the periphery. An effective crisis management system cannot be built under such conditions. It should rather succeed in coping with the above-mentioned linkages between the military, the political, the economic, and also the sociocultural aspects of crises within the context of the international structures of dependence. Unfortunately, the assumption inherited from the WSS, that the military function is independent from all other functions, with the exception of the political, i.e., the decisions taken by states, makes it impossible to create an effective strategy to change this situation.

The structures of violence in the CPS pose another problem for the prevailing distinction of functions. As we saw before, domestic violence is illegitimate and an object of police control in the WSS. The expression "United Nations police operations" covers a definition of peace-keeping functions derived from this method of identifying functions that cope with domestic crises. As we know, the periphery is defined in the CPS as a field where military and police functions are fused together, and the term *police operation* is not just a metaphor, since it corresponds to an identified function of *pacification*.[23] But crises in developing countries cannot be managed with the same approach as those in the WSS, because their roots lie in a complex combination of structural violence with ethnic, tribal, and other factors specific to the *agraria* crises, as well as factors related to the conflicting trends of intrusion and resistance.

If one persists in applying the WSS functions to the CPS, no attempt can be made to cope with structural violence, and the exercise by military rule (with or without support from the center) of reactive or preventive violence thus acquires legitimacy. Not only does peace-keeping become identical to pacification, as we saw before, it is also made into a means of recovering the status quo. The forces fighting for independence or for structural transformation are ignored unless they acquire legitimacy through the official support of a sovereign state.

In a different way, the BPS also have problems of function identification. As we saw in the second section, the BPS grew out of the WSS. Although based in part on the opposition between two patterns of the economic division of labor, the political division of labor is also based on nuclear weaponry (Fontaine, 1965/1967; Dukes, 1970).

Hence, the maintenance of the BPS is closely related to the nuclear arms race and to the avoidance of a nuclear war. This is why two sets of functions play a key role in the BPS. One category of functions links the military, the managerial, and the technological functions. The technocratic approach to international politics and conflicts that characterizes the two superpowers is a consequence of this fusion of functions. According to this approach, crises are games played among rational decision-makers, so that crisis management is just an operation to find a rational solution to the game. In place of the diplomatic function, which was most important in the WSS, the manager/planner is supposed to be able to handle violence and conflicts.

The imperative that nuclear war should be avoided is assumed to deter international actors from engaging in conventional warfare as long as there is a danger of escalation. The hierarchy of weapons corresponds to the hierarchy of conflicts that must and can be avoided, since the more powerful the weapons, the more likely an escalation of the conflict. Thus, the Euratlantic region, where the more industrialized and the possessors of stronger weapons are found, has been spared military conflicts while the periphery countries have experienced a number of serious ones.[24]

The periphery of the international system is in several ways the weak spot of the BPS. First, it is a region where wars could not be eliminated by the BPS, as we saw earlier. Second, it is a region where rational calculation does not work and where the superpowers have been making important miscalculations. Third, it is where the atimia mentioned earlier may lead to nuclear proliferation, the greatest challenge to the crisis management of the BPS (Mushakoji, 1980).

These points indicate the major functional causes of the apparent weakening of the crisis management capability of the superpowers. It is impossible to interpret the CPS on the basis of the functions identified within the context of the BPS. Whether this implies a complete loss of control or only a temporary setback remains to be seen. It appears, however, that the fundamental contradiction that may incapacitate the major powers of today is the fact that crisis management in a time of structural transformation of the international system requires the capacity of the managing agency to grasp the various aspects of the emerging division of labor and identify the functional requirements of the structures that have yet to be formed. Such exigencies contradict the basic interests the major powers have in the maintenance of the existing structures. This is where an international institution not sharing this interest, and therefore without its constraints, could play a major role in crisis management.

Institutional Aspects of the Problematique

The crisis management system of today is controlled by a mixture of the basic rules of the game of the three structures mentioned above. It inherits the basic assumption from the WSS that crises are primarily part of a universe of action of sovereign states that engage in violent diplomacy. The level of violence should be controlled by preventive diplomatic negotiation and other means of crisis management. Underlying this assumption is the perception that all the parties involved have a shared interest in system maintenance. Hence the recognition that war is a continuation of politics through other means and that therefore political accommodation can be found through diplomatic means acceptable to the states involved since, as we saw earlier, they prefer to negotiate rather than fight (see Kaplan, 1965: 23).

This shared interest in the maintenance of a balance of power implies a great many preconditions that are studied in the literature on conflict, conflict prevention, and conflict management, e.g., the perception and definition of a crisis by decision-makers, the channels through which crisis information is collected, the rules of the game in crisis bargaining, the selection, interpretation, and application of historical precedents, and so on. Unless a common understanding about the WSS and its maintenance exists, the crisis management mechanism cannot function, since it is based on a process of institutionalization and regulation that presupposes shared values and common perceptions of reality.

The emergence of the BPS has helped to strengthen, at least among the major states, the shared understanding about the need to keep the international system in balance. To avoid a nuclear war becomes a shared objective in crisis prevention and management between the two superpowers and their allies, combined with a new style of military-diplomatic competition first called the Cold War and then détente.[25] Thus the BPS adds to the art of crisis diplomacy inherited from the WSS the technocratic style of decision-making through planning. Crisis management becomes a conceptual exercise of rational calculation where deterrence and compliance are used in such a way that both parties involved in a crisis arrive at a decision to deescalate rather than escalate.[26]

The crisis and crisis management literature, both of nuclear strategists and of peace-makers, is full of research—theoretical and empirical—about the rules involved in crisis decision-making.[27] It is through this technocratic rationalization that crisis management becomes a specific object of science built upon a limited set of assumptions about the rationality of the parties involved in a crisis situation. This rationality, often defined in terms of the theoretical game concept of minimizing possible losses, is culture-bound and also dependent on a nuclear obsession that forces the parties involved to choose alternatives minimizing possible nuclear annihilation (Mushakoji, 1968). Crisis prevention and management in the periphery, where direct escalation into nuclear conflict is unlikely, still maintain the same rationality assumptions combined with the rules of the game of the CPS. It is generally thought that crises must be prevented or managed by the nuclear superpowers, because they are the only ones who can bring rationality into an otherwise "irrational" crisis situation.

Internal conflicts, their sources, their actors, and so forth constitute an important theme both of military science and peace research.[28] Considered by North Atlantic social scientists as a pathological phenomenon of the development process, crises in the periphery must be managed not by negotiations to stabilize the balance of power but by police actions to impose order. The only exception to this trend are the crises perceived by crisis managers as the expansion of one of the superpowers, in which case the BPS's rules of the game are adopted to rationalize the crisis situation.[29]

This approach assumes that the actors involved in crises of the periphery are not strong enough to refuse the imposition of peace by the major powers and that the existing order, once reestablished through an intervention from the center into the periphery, can maintain itself. So long as the international system maintains its stability, the above preconditions are met and the crisis management system functions satisfactorily. Once the process of structural transformation is triggered, however, the management becomes ineffective to the extent that its rationality is called into question.

We may term technodiplomatic the conflict management style that prevails now. This style is a combination of: (a) the preventive diplomatic approach based on the cognitive frame of the WSS, (b) the peace-keeping activities linked with the CPS, and (c) the arms control and disarmament measures that were developed within the context of the BPS. The problem today is that this style is losing its efficacy in the present setting of transformation.

It is no longer possible to cope with nation-states in conflict using only diplomatic efforts to restore the balance of power. Preventive diplomacy cannot handle the subtle problems of the distribution and redistribution of scarce resources. Mediation requires an arrangement of political accommodation that may create new tensions if it does not fit into a broader plan for the redistribution of scarce resources and for peaceful structural transformation (Young, 1967).

Preventive diplomacy must also be sensitive to the demands and expectations of the people in the periphery and to movements for structural transformation. It should take full account of structural violence and of the different aspects of the structures of violence, especially of militarization. Otherwise, it will arrive at a compromise acceptable to the states involved but deprived of legitimacy and of the social and political support it needs in a period of structural transformation.

In exactly the same way, peace-keeping cannot be effective in asymmetrical conflicts unless the conventional aims of these operations are reformulated. In the present setting, peace-keeping operations aim at preventing or curtailing the fighting and thus at creating an environment in which it is possible to conduct negotiations that may lead to the solution of the conflict. This is clearly insufficient when the operation takes place in the periphery of the CPS (see Dewast, 1977; International Peace Academy, 1978; Rikhye et al., 1974). This is so in the first place because such conflicts are very often asymmetrical, and to curtail the fighting at a certain time and freeze the situation until a negotiation takes place means to solidify a power relationship that may benefit only the stronger party and maintain the status quo. It is also because, in more general terms, where conflicts are caused by structural violence, the environment for the negotiation of a peace-keeping operation must involve the removal of such violence and not just the curtailment of armed violence.

As was already stressed earlier, unless peace-keeping is only a measure to maintain the existing structures, it is indispensable that an operation be conceived of within the context of a broader plan for peaceful structural transformation. It is also important for this operation to be sensitive and responsive to the people living in the conflict area. The last point seems to be observed in many of the actual peace-keeping operations of the United Nations, but it is not part of the formal assignment given to those in blue helmets.

Turning to a third example related to the BPS, namely, the problems of disarmament, we also find here the need to go beyond the present approach. Take for example the prevention of nuclear proliferation. In the setting prevailing today, the nuclear weapons states stress the obligation of the nonnuclear weapons states not to take part in any activities that may lead to nuclear proliferation. From the point of view of the latter, this perpetuates the nuclear hierarchy, and the asymmetry creates inequality not only in military terms but also in technological terms. As we pointed out before, to prevent nuclear proliferation it is indispensable to convince the non-nuclear states that a more egalitarian, denuclearized regime is sought by nonproliferation and not merely the preservation of the present BPS (see SIPRI Yearbook, 1980: 317-343). This implies again the existence of a plan for peaceful structural transformation and a responsiveness not only to the claims of the non-nuclear states but also to world public opinion.

These three examples indicate that crisis management in a time of structural transformation must be insightful enough to develop a project about how the ongoing process of structural transformation can be guided in a nonviolent and peaceful direction and that it must have the capacity to deal actively or passively with different categories of people around the world.

Such a statement is not a futurist or populist normative declaration but an observation based on the example of the major states of today that appear to be losing their crisis management capability because they are too strongly attached to the structures of the past to develop any insight into the present process of structural transformation or to open new channels to communicate with the nonstate actors who play different roles in this process. It must also be recognized that a project is not a utopian dream but rather a realistic plan of action based on a macro and micro analysis of the various aspects of the present crises.

We can identify the following general trends that characterize crises in the contemporary international system:

(a) Structural change:
   The crises tend not to be, as in the classical WSS, the results of partial disequilibrium in a system where actors sharing common values can always reestablish the equilibrium by negotiation, but rather tend to represent a complex set of opposite interests among international and national social forces—including states and coalitions of states—that do not share common values, and among whom some do not recognize the legitimacy of the present division of labor and that intend to change the existing international and/or domestic structures (see Pettman, 1979: 139-179).

(b) Beyond rationality:

The contemporary crises are generated by a multiplicity of factors motivating a variety of social forces to enter into conflicts where problems of equity, justice, autonomy, identity, and other values make the decision rules more complex, as in the case of the theoretical game rationality typical of BPS crises.[30]

(c) Linked fragmentation:

The crises of today tend to result from the loss of hegemonic control capabilities by the superpowers and a resulting fragmentation of the world, wherein specific local values and realities transform existing structures. This trend is combined with an opposite trend of increased interdependence on the global level that links together specific local crises. The local character of these crises makes it difficult to deal with them by a common approach imposing the rule of the strongest as it was the case in in the earlier phase of the CPS.[31]

It follows from this that crisis management based on the logic of the three structures does not function satisfactorily in the present crisis settings. It also follows that some new approaches to coping with crises should be invented. Such approaches should be able to obtain the support not only of the major states but also of emerging social forces. It should give legitimacy to new values and institutions by fostering the restructuring of the international system rather than its maintenance.

Some new means of crisis management should be devised to cope with different crisis situations, taking into account the complexity of the sociocultural, economic, and political settings. They should also be more responsive to the demands and aspirations of the social forces involved and have built into them a learning mechanism responsive to specific local conditions. The new approaches to be devised should avoid a top-down approach imposing the rule of the nuclear balance on conflict situations in the periphery and build instead a bottom-up process of crisis management linking the fragmented crises to their global matrix so as to help the emergence of a coherent plan for restructuring the international system.[32] It is in this context that the role of an international institution capable of leading the international system into the use of such a new approach is crucial.

Can the United Nations succeed in doing all this where the big powers have failed? This is the crucial question. In order to give an answer, it is necessary to conduct a careful study of both the requirements and the available resources, i.e., what will be expected from the United Nations in terms of institutional support for a peaceful, structural transformation of the international system (and by whom) and what the United Nations can do in response to these expectations.

More fundamentally, what should the crisis management approach be that the United Nations should adopt in a process of structural change? The task is, negatively, to minimize violence and military conflict in this process of transformation and to facilitate a process of restructuring the existing militarized international system into a more peaceful world order. Since, as we have pointed out already, the top-down nuclear hierarchical approach does not work, a bottom-up process, taking specific local conditions into full account, will have to be devised.

The technodiplomatic rational calculation approach should be replaced by a process of negotiation much broader than the WSS diplomacy involving only sovereign states; it should involve all the social forces involved in crisis situations. The negotiation process should relate local specific problems to the global problematique instead of linking the détente of the nuclear order to local conflict management from the top down. This requires a much greater sensitivity and learning capability regarding fragmented realities and sociocultural diversities.

More than the military capability to impose a solution and implement it—a capability not unimportant—the international institution must have a broad information-gathering capability to relate to each other the ever-changing realities on the local, national, regional, and global levels. The capacity to cope with fragmented facts, to perceive transient local realities, and to learn how to relate them to more general trends on the regional and global levels—in brief, to build a decentralized information processing system—is crucial. But most important it is the ability to propose a *plan* for the peaceful restructuring of the international system, taking into consideration the major causes of conflict and the interests involved both for and against such a move. Such an ability would be indispensable to any guarantee that the crisis prevention and management activities of the institution would truly be an operation on the part of the management of the international system with a view toward a new international order and not just a ploy for the maintenance of the status quo.

All of these points make it indispenable for an institution to lead the international crisis management system beyond the conventional approaches of diplomacy, peace-keeping, and disarmament. To realize all of the points, a basic precondition must be that the United Nations succeed in detaching itself from its present subsidiary role to the existing international political structures and develop the capacity to make a critical assessment of the present international division of labor and its associated functions so that it can gain some insight into the emerging structures' functional requirements. Only by its detachment from the existing structures and by exercising a metafunction, i.e., providing the ground for the identification of new functions, can the United Nations be successful.

In a very tentative way, the following points are suggested for research and eventually as guidelines for planning, in line with the above discussion:

(a) It is likely that the UN system will have to replace the major powers in playing a determining role in crisis management and the management of structural change.

(b) The UN system must create new values in preparation for this future role.[33]

(c) The UN system must prepare itself to assume this role through intensive research on crises in the international system undergoing structural transformation and on the functions it can perform to promote bottom-up crisis management.

(d) The UN system should mobilize all of its existing instrumental capabilities to cope with the task ahead.

(e) It should study the optimal organization to make full use of these capabilities and to acquire or develop new ones. This would imply, among other efforts of reorganization:

    (i) bridging the gap between what was termed high and low politics by relating its political forum functions to the service functions of the specialized agencies;[34]

    (ii) acquiring better insight into the process of global structural transformation; it must reorganize its information-gathering and processing capability that is scattered in different sectors of its system;[35]

    (iii) participating actively in the process of structural transformation in dialogue with the agents of this transformation; it should make full use of the field activities developed by its various agencies, especially in the periphery of the international system.[36]

(f) The United Nations should develop a plan for the peaceful structural transformation of the international system. The two principal themes of *project* should be the denuclearization and the demilitarization of the contemporary international structures.[37]

(g) On the operational level, the United Nations should develop a new approach to crisis management in accordance with the functional requirements of an international system undergoing structural transformation. This implies among other measures:

(i) finding means to develop a diplomatic style where negotiation and mediation are conducted in the context of a project for peaceful structural transformation on a global scale;

(ii) developing modalities to merge peace-keeping, peace-making, and peace-building functions by organizing relief and service activities, along with a mechanism for consultation with the people, especially in the periphery of the periphery;

(iii) developing a research and development capability in different regions for social innovation during the structural transformation.

The above remarks are meant to provide the baseline for a more systematic, empirically based, and critical study of the role of the United Nations in managing crises in an international system during its transformation.

NOTES

1. On a world central guidance system or a world central authority, see for example Falk (1975: 240ff.) and Galtung (1980: 341-352).

2. It is justly pointed out, for example, that "the United Nations exists in a system of intricate international relations. Its activity is indissolubly linked with the general international situation and its real impact on this situation depends on the relationship of forces in the world and in the Organization, which at each stage determine the degree of implementing its chief purpose to save mankind from the scourge of war" (Morosow, 1976: 156).

3. This question, raised by Mr. Soedjatmoko in a discussion at the United Nations University, motivated the author to write the present chapter.

4. The macrohistorical approach is especially useful in the analysis of systems in transformation. See for example Galtung et al. (1979).

5. We follow here Immanuel Wallerstein in defining an international *division of labor*. A world system is one within which a large-scale division of labor takes place. This division is not only functional but also geographical (1980: 314). We stress the fact that the economic division of labor cannot be detached from the social, technological, political, and military division of labor. As to the methods of social and technical divisions of labor, see also Gurvitch (1955: 256f., 267, 277).

6. The attempt is made here to consider the different structures not in their historical context but rather as matrices generating different cognitive structures that identify certain functional requirements to be met by definite actors according to the specific rules of the game. Although greatly inspired by the typology of international systems of Kaplan (1965: 22-43), we define the present international system as a composite of three historically evolved structures, two of which are defined by him as the "balance of power" and the loose bipolar systems.

7. In discussing crisis management, a common error is to view *violence* as an antisocial deviant group's behavior that is to be *managed* to preserve law and order, ignoring the fact that different types of violence, military or other, actual or structural, are associated with different institutions and roles in the international division of labor (see Nordin, 1980: 482ff.).

8. On the concept of institution, see for example Lourau (1970).

9. About the rules of the game followed by sovereign states, called by Kaplan "national actors," see Kaplan (1965: 23ff.).

10. In that connection, Mazrui (1976: 271-328) talks about *counter-penetration* of the center by the periphery.

11. As to the "mission" of "pacification" of the major powers in the center, see Mushakoji (1960).

12. Komuro ("Kozo-Kino Bunseki no Riron to Hoho") develops a more basic criticism of structural functionalism and proposes to stress the study of intra- and intersystem conflicts. He proposes the analysis of what he calls the dysfunctional and the structural change space of social systems in transformation.

13. According to Komuro, the above interpretation of the structural-functional paradigm is based on a misinterpretation of the concepts of functions and structures, but it is possible to build a theoretical framework avoiding the above difficulties. We follow roughly his suggestions in our usage of the concepts of structure and function.

14. The problem with the ability of actors to perceive definite functional requirements in different social settings brings us into the realm of the sociology of knowledge. The cognitive framework of social actors maps only a limited sector of the field of social reality, and the mapping is determined by the social framework within which one acts.

15. For a general discussion of conflict management, see Pirages (1980: 425-460), who sees conflict management as dealing with the maintenance of asymmetric social structures from the point of view of the superordinate actor. We find this vertical approach inappropriate in a historical moment of structural transformation, but the article presents a good state-of-the-art account of the literature.

16. About the distinction between *high* and *low politics* and the definition of international crisis, see Morse (1972: 123-150).

17. We must admit that the agents of crisis management have the capacity to learn from their experiences. This aspect of the crisis management problematique is studied by, for example, Alker and Greenberg (1971) and Tanaka (1980). Our contention is that even if learning takes place, there are cognitive boundaries that the agents cannot cross. Cognitive consistency sets those boundaries.

18. About the cognitive system of the WSS, called by Morse "classical statecraft," see Morse (1976: 22-46).

19. As to the zones of influence of major powers and their attempts to reserve them through military means, see for example Elsenhals (1979: 110-135).

20. On this expansion, Latham (1978) shows that without the part played by the underdeveloped world between 1865 and 1914, it is doubtful whether the so-called "free trade" era in the center could have ever continued.

21. Choucri and North (1972: 80-122) stress the fact that countries with advanced technology need more resources. The demands and specialized capabilities of such societies produce *lateral pressure*, i.e., a tendency to undertake activities farther and farther from the center into the periphery to control more resources. This is the cause for police actions and wars against low-capability societies.

22. About the role of the military in the development process in the periphery, see for example Bienen.

23. The term "police action" is distinguished by some authors from "order enforcement" based on an imposed set of rules and norms, and peace-keeping is found to belong to the latter category. We tend to define police action to include order enforcement and "pacification" (see Mitchell, 1976: 150-173).

24. The Euratlantic region constitutes the center of the détente system. (On this point see Mushakoji, 1980: 32-48.)

25. On the combination of crisis prevention-management and military-diplomatic competition, see for example Kissinger (1954: 349-366).

26. A typical example of this approach is found in Kahn (1965).

27. The same theoretical paradigm interpreted in opposite ways is used both by nuclear strategists and peace researchers. As an example of the former see Schelling (1960); of the latter, Rapoport (1960).

28. On empirical research about internal conflict, Ted Gurr includes state-of-the-art reviews of such diverse themes as "The Psychology of Political Protest" (Muller, 1980), "Theory and Research of Revolutionary Personnel" (Resai, 1980), "Theoretical Approaches to Explaining Collective Political Violence" (Eckstein, 1980), and "Macro-Comparative Research on Political Protest" (Zimmerman, 1980).

29. The Cuban missile crisis is a typical case of the superpowers' rationalization of a CPS conflict.

30. This is why in the search for nonviolence, crises and violence must be analyzed, taking into consideration the *countervailing trends* aimed at these values (see Kothari, 1974: 94-114).

31. On the crisis linkages and the need for an international learning process to cope with them, see Mushakoji (1978).

32. We use the term "management" with a new connotation of self-management when we refer to a bottom-up management process.

33. "One of the most important and least recognized functions of the United Nations is to keep alive ideas and principles which cannot immediately be realized, but which remain an objective to be strived for and eventually won" (United Nations, 1980: 2).

34. The economic, social, technical, and cultural activities of the UN system give it the possibility, if properly related to its political activities, of considerable *remunerative power* that could become a base for its crisis management actions. As to the remunerative power of a World Central Authority, see Galtung (1980: 351).

35. The UN system's information gathering and information processing activities should be carefully studied, not only to rationalize its operation but to make of the UN system a crisis management system better informed than the superpowers. The early-warning capability not only on armed conflicts but also on ecological, energetic, and other crises is an asset of the United Nations.

36. UN contacts with the nongovernment sectors of all countries should be systematized. This includes not only NGOs but also change agents mobilized by different specialized agencies in the field.

37. To seek an alternative international order (and structure) means to look for an alternative to the BPS and the CPS. Denuclearization is an alternative to the former and demilitarization to the latter.

CHAPTER 10

NONALIGNED COUNTRIES IN CONFLICT

RADOVAN VUKADINOVIĆ

In theoretical attempts to define nonalignment, it is often stressed that this is a policy, doctrine, program, force, or significant factor in contemporary international relations. Regardless of what definition should be accepted, or whether one should accept several of them, it is beyond any doubt that the group of countries that have opted for pursuing a policy of nonalignment has developed into an important moral and political force of the contemporary world. In an effort to change political, economic, and social relations, and in the struggle for peace, the democratization of international relations, and general progress, the nonaligned countries have made a vast contribution, while at the same time they are part and parcel of those revolutionary forces objectively in the front line of the struggle to change what is old and create something new—the struggle for a fairer and more humane world.

I

Various countries are in action within the group that has, in the course of the past twenty years, quadrupled its ranks. These countries differ in many historical, economic, cultural, political, and religious factors, they are situated in different parts of the world and have gone through different sociopolitical and economic phases. The accumulated layers of history, geographical and political location, economic development level, outside influences, and the action of internal political forces—all of these are factors distinctive to virtually every nonaligned country, thus revealing them as a highly heterogenous and pluralistic group, both in the political and ideological sense. In view of the characteristics dividing individual nonaligned countries, a casual observer of international relations might conclude that this is a disunited movement within which it is hard to set up joint principles and/or aims of action.

However, nonaligned activities so far, their engagement on the international scene, and the concrete results recorded in certain vital provinces of international relations today confirm that under contemporary international conditions, nonalignment has become the world policy that most completely expresses the interests of many states and nations. In the divided world, replete with bloc politics, rivalry among the great powers with their real or covert dilemmas, rising tensions, and the widening economic gap between the developed and developing countries, nonaligned countries are the initiators and vehicles of the struggle for new, universal solutions, going far beyond the boundaries of their own territories and joining the general quest for a democratic and progressive world public.

Aware of the realities of the contemporary world and the dangers threatening them, but also aware of the strength and influence they themselves wield, the nonaligned countries, despite mutual differences and specific distinctions in national development, are acting in concert on the basis of the joint platform that they are constantly adding to and elaborating. In the course of twenty years of action, the nonaligned countries, with their principles and aims, have managed to specify the main determinants of nonalignment, thus making it possible also to determine the bonds linking these countries. In this light, the unity of the nonaligned countries symbolizes:

—the activities of states not desirous of subordinating their political orientation to any predefined ideological aims;

—countries that are not members of military-political alliances:

—according to the estimate of their national interests, the retention of complete freedom in decisions and trends in international relations;

—striving, on an organized scale, for détente, peace, progress, and economic advancement,

—strict adherence in their relations with other countries to the principles of the United Nations Charter;

—active striving for new forms of political, economic, social, and cultural relations, thus helping to create a democratic and equitable world of the future.

These fundamental traits, which constitute the unity of the nonaligned countries, are at the same time part and parcel of their political action program and permanent rallying core.

II

By the authentic principles of nonalignment, which are the ever-present foundation of joint action, the nonaligned countries have also given expression to their fundamental views on international relations, and equally on the content and form of their mutual relations. The countries that were among the first to take up peaceful, active coexistence as the only alternative in contemporary world development have declared themselves in support of all the progressive tenets of the UN Charter and in other documents of international law that plead for the elimination of all conflict and its peaceful resolution.

Starting out from the conviction that the preservation of peace in international relations today is the *conditio sine qua non* for general progress, and that this is a prerequisite for translating into practice all of the principles and aims of the movement, the nonaligned countries have, through their political struggle to change tense, polarized international relations and eliminate the dangers of war, developed into a major force in safeguarding world peace. The criteria of nonalignment, the principles and aims of the movement seek the establishment of such international relations as will be devoid of force, the threat of force, interference in the internal affairs of other countries, and of the threat of war and war itself. This option of the nonaligned is the logical result of their new overall outlook on the contemporary international community and their place within the latter. For this reason the nonaligned countries have emerged as the main vehicles in the struggle for peace and new international relations.

The nonaligned countries' demand for the peaceful resolution of all conflict stems from the principle of nonaggression and equitable negotiation of all disputed issues that may emerge in relations between various states. The mastering of conflicts is viewed by the nonaligned countries as a legal, moral, and political obligation, and it has been stressed in many documents of the movement, as well as in numerous multilateral and bilateral documents of a political nature.

In view of the large number and frequency of conflicts, this has become the central and most crucial issue in the political practice and theory of international relations. The postwar world, rid of the nightmare of the great world war, is still teeming with international conflicts bringing in their wake death, destruction, and want.

Without entering into an analysis of the various conflicts, this not being the subject of the chapter and a hotly disputed theoretical issue (Young, 1967; Luard, 1968; Zhurkin, 1975), let us define a conflict as an unexpected event on a major scale, one that disrupts the international system. How the conflict erupted, the number of participants, its effect on bilateral, subsystemic, or systemic relations can vary just as the ways in which it may end. An analysis of each conflict automatically shows that this is a case of conflicting interests and that in striving to realize one's own interests there is recourse to the most widely varied means, including war.

The dynamics of the eruption of conflict show that during the period when bipolar tension relaxed and when the nonaligned movement was developing, disputes between nonaligned countries increased, with some of them being settled by force of arms. Thus, conflicts between nonaligned countries have become one of the characteristics of contemporary development in international relations, at the same time refuting all their own fundamental principles and aims.

Faced with a growing number of conflicts, the theory of international relations is striving to find an adequate mechanism to classify causes and types of conflicts and to establish their common traits. In this context there is sometimes an explanation classifying elements connected with the nature and behavior of people; it also points to the underdevelopment of social and political institutions and finally apostrophizes the imperfection of the international system which, being decentralized, anarchic, and disorganized, is not equipped to prevent the outbreak of conflicts or their further expansion. To this one might add that many international disputes that ultimately ended in war were the results of unsettled differences and minor incidents which, following the development of the internal of international situations, gradually developed into open conflicts.

In the analysis of conflicts between nonaligned countries, apart from these general theoretical guidelines, one should nonetheless dwell on certain specific distinctions connected primarily with the fact that this is a highly heterogeneous group of countries and that there are certainly enormous differences between them. The legacy of the past, the changing world, did not favor the development of the nonaligned countries that by their conflicts offered an opportunity for building up their own list of causes of conflict, including the most extreme form thereof, war.

At a time of open disputes and conflict between members of the firmly integrated bloc units, where there are notable forms of unified ideological, political, military, and economic bonds, the existence of conflict in the nonaligned world is no unexpected or surprising phenomenon. Polycentric development and the lack of scope for the accelerated changing of the world have necessarily influenced the creation of conflicting situations in countries which, as the vehicles of change, are most closely linked with the development rate of universal democratic processes. Therefore any stagnation, denial, or attempt to reverse the positive transformation of international relations, together with internal troubles and problems, will immediately find its place in the conflicts between nonaligned countries and prevent their being settled promptly.

III

The typology of causes for the outbreak of conflict between nonaligned countries can be divided into three categories:

(1) The almost classical cause of conflict is *unsettled frontier and territorial questions* in relations between nonaligned countries. The large number of nonaligned countries, their colonial past, the unsettled relations between various states bordering on each other, the arbitrary setting of frontiers during colonial rule, and the efforts of various peoples to attain self-determination have all created conditions making it possible for conflict situations to erupt. To this one should also add the internal political forces, frequently imbued by differing political ambitions, that likewise, by unilateral moves, helped to create or expand the scope of the conflict. At the same time, it must be borne in mind that the territorial component, a visible national interest, is always subject to manipulation from various quarters. Involved in territorial disputes are larger and smaller nonaligned countries, with identical or different ideological options, strong or weak military potentials, and so forth. In view of the large number of such conflicts and of the possibility of the big powers' direct or indirect involvement in them, it is to be expected that this group of causes will continue to be very much present in relations among the nonaligned countries and that they will give rise to other conflicts.

One could add to territorial conflicts, as a new form, the contrasts emerging between various states in view of the economic value of certain areas and the scope for their exploitation. The discovery of new oil fields, of gas or other raw material deposits, can easily give rise to demands of a revindication character between neighboring countries. In cases when other countries[1]—usually the former colonial metropolises or multinational companies—share in the exploitation of these natural resources with the nonaligned countries, one can easily expect the exacerbation of conflict situations.

(2) *Ideological and political differences* are the reflection of a broad palette of differences existing within the group of nonaligned countries. While accepting the general platform of international action and having opted for the fundamental principles of the movement in their policy, they are nonetheless unable to master all at once the various antagonisms existing between them. And so the territorial, a visible and significant element, together with economic interests, having emerged under new and altered technological conditions, are creating a broad scope for the intensification of initial ideological or political differences that under different circumstances might possibly not in themselves have been dominating factors leading to a conflict.

The political differences between nonaligned countries have highly varied aspects, but on the whole they are firmly founded on national interests that cannot be adjusted on the spur of the moment to the interests of other, most often neighboring, nonaligned countries. Among the concrete forms of manifestation of such political differences between certain regimes that have opted for a nonaligned policy and that are full members of the movement, those most often emerging are political aspirations to play a prominent role in a definite region of the world. In realizing such political ambitions, they run into obstacles in other (nonaligned) countries; tensions then arise that may ultimately result in a conflict. One can immediately add to these political determinants some characteristics of a political nature, emerging in the form of a clash between progressive and conservative regimes, in declarations for one of the superpowers, and in the automatic acceptance of the latter's proclaimed ideology. There are also clashes over some of the approaches to the resolution of certain concrete international questions that have their own territorial or economic aspects but that soon acquire a political character because of bad interstate relations.

Though it is clearly stressed in the basic principles of nonaligned policy and in many official documents of the movement that these are the free and voluntary activities of a large group of countries—meaning their acceptance of sociopolitical, economic, and ideological pluralism—nonetheless differences of an ideological character tend to make themselves known in various disputes. Sometimes ideological motives are a screen for tangible material interests or alliances with the policy of a superpower, so that in the world of the nonaligned, the ideological factor is acquiring ever greater significance. A certain intolerance toward other nonaligned countries under the guise of ideology is usually dubbed "extending aid," "the wish to establish stability," "a normal situation," and the like, all intended to conceal the fundamental aspiration to dominate.

Some of the nonaligned countries that have in principle accepted the political and ideological pluralism of the movement are applying their own ideology as the guiding motive in their action, linking it up with outside forces and at the same time enabling them to pursue their policy following an ideology accepted by them and based on concrete tasks usually determined by outside forces. Practice so far in the nonaligned world development indicates that such ideological activity can result not only in the outlining of an ideologically specific action platform and attempts to include a larger number of nonaligned countries in it, but that it can also serve to justify a policy paving the way for the use of arms among nonaligned countries.

(3) Though varying widely by their time of action, character of relations, and scope for action, *the presence of the superpowers in the vast expanses of the nonaligned world* is developing into a more and more essential characteristic of contemporary developments in international relations. Starting from their global strategic interests, in which economic, military-political, and ideological factors are inherent, the superpowers and their respective blocs are seeking a scope for broader activities. Considering that there are many accumulated problems of an internal character in the nonaligned countries, considering that their mutual relations are increasingly encumbered by disputed situations, and that ultimately the constantly changing international situation conduces such undertakings, the superpowers are striving to pursue a policy that will ensure their lasting presence in certain regions and explore the possibilities for its further expansion.

The strategic, economic, and political interests of the superpowers are the main elements in their action, which is intended to create a situation sowing discord among the nonaligned so that subsequently the superpowers, directly or indirectly, will be able to make themselves felt in various parts of the nonaligned world. Though these activities of the superpowers take various forms and while their tangible possibilities of extending aid and exercising influence likewise vary, it is a fact that their ultimate aims have been so determined as to put the nonaligned countries in the orbit of the superpowers' schemes, interests, and long-range activities.

Aware of the existing state of affairs in international relations and of the nonaligned countries' activities, the superpowers have not come up with any demands for the nonaligned countries to join in their bloc structures. Strictly confining the activities of their military political mechanism to the given boundaries, they probably consider that acquiring new members would also require additional efforts on the part of the superpowers, including firmer engagements in various unstable regions. For all that, the superpowers and blocs are interested in filling the so-called vacuums and they consider each existing situation of conflict from the angle of their own narrow interests. In this way they foment, take advantage of, and fan conflicts between the nonaligned countries, while retaining nonaligned policy as the main political action in order to subject these countries to the powerful influence of bloc structures. The superpowers, without directly fomenting conflicts by their policy, in view of the specific bloc interests are objectively the force influencing the outbreak and escalation of conflict. On the other hand, once a conflict has broken out between nonaligned countries, due to their specific characteristics and their necessary reliance on outside political and military support, it paves the way for the further penetration of the superpowers into the world of the nonaligned. By such strategy the superpowers support and take advantage of conflicts, striving to keep them going and, through them, to infiltrate into various regions of special importance. Within this context there are also attempts to create groups of nonaligned countries that would act as concentric circles, their task being to pursue a policy in the interest of the superpowers.

Even at first glance, a classification of the causes of conflict between nonaligned countries shows that this is a complex tissue of action of various factors and vehicles in international relations, and that within this large group of countries various currents merge and mingle. The colonial legacy of the past, numerous unsolved questions, the development of new technological knowledge and new economic divisions, and new political aspirations attempting to obtain special regional and even broader sway, domination, and hegemony—all of these are the source of the medley of activities connected with the non-aligned countries' internal actions as the main vehicles of conflict. On the other hand, in a situation in which conflicts are increasingly becoming a permanent distinction of the nonaligned states, scope is created for the access of the superpowers and their allies who will find fertile ground for long-term action in this situation of conflict. For all these reasons, the combination of internal problems and the effects of outside forces constitutes a great danger to the survival of the nonaligned movement and to its scope for united action on the international stage.

IV

The nonaligned countries that started building up their policy with enthusiasm and zeal, that approached concrete tasks in the same way, for a long time considered conflicts in their mutual relations as a transitory and negligible phenomenon. The struggle against colonialism, imperialism, hegemonism, and the stress brought on by the need to create new international relations and concrete action toward setting up a new international economic order, efforts towards disarmament, and so forth for some time concealed some aspects in the domain of their mutual relations. This explains why little attention was given to the need for resolving conflict situations at the first nonaligned gatherings. It was furthermore believed that the nonaligned countries, having pledged themselves to identical principles and goals and emerging together in international relations, would be able to settle their crises independently, should they occur, that giving closer attention to these conflicts would make it even more difficult to settle them, and that this would sow discord among the ranks of the nonaligned.

Parallel with the spreading activities of the nonaligned countries and their increasing numbers, the number of conflicts also grew. Internal reasons and the heavy burden of the past, which cannot be overcome easily, began making themselves increasingly felt in the activities of the nonaligned countries that were entering a higher phase of statehood. On the other hand, the policy of détente, established on a narrow range of bilateral or bloc agreements and negotiations, restricted the bloc rivalry to outlined and fixed boundaries that were finally confirmed in Helsinki. However, in other regions the majority of nonaligned countries had become the scene of extensive rivalry and of the use of sundry instruments in bloc activities headed by the superpowers (Vukadinović, 1979).

One of the founders of nonaligned policy—Josip Broz Tito, an experienced statesman—was one of the first to feel it necessary to point to this outstanding problem that was taking firmer and firmer shape. Tito never submitted to dogma and was always ready to face up to international realities, regardless of their nature. At the fifth nonaligned summit in Colombo, Tito appealed to the heads of state to show "greater tolerance and mutual understanding" in their mutual relations.

Aware of the differences existing between the nonaligned countries, of their specific views on international relations, and of their different positions, the Yugoslav president was concerned over the future of non-alignment, should such trends continue within the movement. He was also well aware that this was a complex question that could not be resolved all at once and to which it was impossible to find a solution acceptable to all, even given the greatest goodwill.

For all these reasons, striving to point up above all what all nonaligned countries have in common, Tito stressed the need to settle disputed situations by peaceful means. To this end, he noted in Havana, the idea of creating "certain mechanisms" for settling disputes between nonaligned countries should begin from the realities in those countries' development, from their distinctive characteristics and the need of the entire movement. Viewing conflict as something that exists and that will continue to exist within a group of such different and numerous countries, Tito pleaded in the first place for the resolution of conflict by negotiations between the directly interested countries, i.e., the partners to the conflict. Should such a procedure not prove to be effective, the conflict should be referred to various international regional organizations, and if even then no results were forthcoming, the question should be put before the United Nations.

This methodology in resolving conflicts was intended gradually to arouse a sense of duty in each nonaligned country pledging it, in the case of a conflict, to settle the disputed issue independently with one or more other nonaligned countries. The unity of interests and aims was to have been a sufficiently powerful basis for initiating a peaceable solution without outside participation. Regional organizations or the United Nations would only come into play when all possibilities of independent action by the parties to the dispute had been exhausted.

As distinct from some other statesmen of the nonaligned movement, who wanted conflicts to be discussed at the conferences of heads of state or government, Tito was against this kind of action. He believed that this would give unnecessary publicity to the conflict, thus making it more difficult to settle, while at the same time undermining the unity of the nonaligned countries on principled issues. Studying the numerous conflicts between nonaligned countries in all their new forms, Tito was already quite sure that apart from producing internal friction, conflicts between the nonaligned countries would also create ample scope for the actuation of outside forces that would take advantage of the conflict situations and thus find it much easier to infiltrate into the expanses of the nonaligned.

The Yugoslav initiative for passing a special resolution on the peaceful settlement of disputes dates back to the ministerial conference of the nonaligned in Belgrade in 1978 and to the 1979 Havana summit. In the meantime, the proposal of Sri Lanka had been revived, proposing the formation of a committee for the peaceful settlement of frontier disputes between nonaligned countries, with stress being placed also on the political unity of the nonaligned countries and the need for their own activities aimed at settling border disputes. There was also a proposal to set up a commission for the peaceful settlement of frontier disputes by conciliation. This commission would be of a permanent character and composed of foreign ministers from five geographical regions, elected at a conference of heads of state or government (Nick, 1981: 21).

The most constructive request for the peaceful solution of conflicts between nonaligned countries was contained in the Yugoslav work paper, submitted at the ministerial conference in New Delhi. Its starting point was the need to create conditions for flexible action that would not infringe upon the authentic principles of nonalignment equality and voluntariness. More and more crises in relations between nonaligned countries clearly indicate that conditions have matured for seeking and adopting a solution that will above all take into account the interests of the nonaligned countries and of the movement as a whole. In its introductory part, the Yugoslav proposal refers to the principles of active and peaceful coexistence, the UN Charter, the Declaration on Principles of International Law on Friendly Relations Among States and Cooperation Among States, the Resolution on the Rights of States in Case of the Outbreak of Hostilities, and the stands adopted at earlier conferences of the nonaligned countries and finally states:

—the obligation of nonaligned countries, finding themselves in conflict, to invest the utmost efforts independently to seek a peaceful solution;

—a peaceful solution can be found by means of bilateral contacts, with the help of regional international organizations, UN mechanisms for the peaceful solution of disputes and with the aid of the nonaligned countries;

—at the request of the parties in dispute the nonaligned movement can set up a committee of informal "ad hoc" groups for good services, while there is also the possibility for the nonaligned countries to act: as a plenary group, minor group, Coordinating Bureau or individually, and that they may offer their good services or mediation in the dispute.

The latest Yugloslav proposal likewise gives due account to the realities of contemporary international relations. Today it would be impossible to demand, within the nonaligned movement, the establishment of any fixed mechanism for the peaceful resolution of conflicts or to seek any kind of declaration or vote on individual situations of conflict. Prospects for the peaceful resolution of conflicts between nonaligned countries can now only be sought within the range of overall experiences gained so far in the movement's political activities. Faced with new trends in international development, bearing the great burden of their colonial past, and further encumbered by inequality in international relations, the nonaligned countries must accept the fact that differences between them take various forms of manifestation, including actual conflicts. Such a state of affairs cannot be mastered in a single move, nor is it possible to find any universal instrument that would prevent all conflicts. What the nonaligned countries can do today is the following:

(1) Accept and consistently apply the principles of nonalignment and peaceful active coexistence to all aspects of international relations, in particular to relations among the nonaligned countries themselves. It would be of special importance here to formally accept the principle of refraining from the use of force in crisis situations. Though most of the nonaligned countries have pledged themselves to honor tnis principle, its renewed acceptance by all nonaligned countries would be of vast moral and political importance and would help to translate these principles into practice.

(2) When a conflict breaks out, the nonaligned countries should give priority to peaceful talks between the parties involved, if necessary using the services of other nonaligned countries.

(3) Without forming any special agencies for the peaceable resolution of conflicts, the nonaligned countries should take the utmost advantage of the services of the Coordinating Bureau. Only if this fails, and after the greatest effort, should they resort to solutions within regional organizations of the United Nations.

(4) In finding any solution, the nonaligned countries should always bear in mind the need to adhere to the principles and goals of the movement and firmly strive by their actions to help resolve the the conflict.

Conflicts between nonaligned countries have become a reality of present-day international relations,[2] and the sooner instruments have been set up for their peaceful solution, the more this will accelerate the general strengthening of the nonaligned countries and their influence in overall international relations. For, as President Tito stressed, non-alignment is not only a moral and political force of today's world, it is also part of the future of modern civilization, and at present the only alternative to tense, international relations.

NOTES

1. Some observers of international relations have recently stressed in particular the differences evident in the nonaligned group concerning their natural wealth, i.e., their economic position. According to them, this might be another form of polarization of interests if effective means are not found for reducing the economic gap.

2. Completely opposing views come from the circle of bloc countries that stress the existence of conflict between the countries of the so-called Third World while formulating narrow, exclusively Western strategies of approach to the conflicts. According to them, the West should provide the means for combating outside interference in regional affairs and should encourage the quest for regional solutions (see IISS, 1981: 85f).

CHAPTER 11

SYSTEMIC CRISIS
Lessons of Regional Détente

KARI MÖTTÖLÄ

Crisis as a Systemic Phenomenon

The concept of a crisis suffers from careless and inflationary use, in both journalism and academic research, despite rigorous attempts at theoretization and conceptualization often connected with empirical works. Crisis research has accumulated a respectful amount of empirical evidence and theoretical explanation, both at the actor-level and systems-level of analysis. We have definitions of the concept of a crisis; theories and evidence from the internal processes—decision-making and perceptions—of states under the stress of crises; theories and empirical knowledge of the interaction between states—action-reaction cycles or sequences of actions—in a crisis situation; and we have useful research on escalation, that is, processes caused by the actions and reactions of the actors involved.[1]

The main point of this chapter is not general or theoretical but specific and practical: to build a bridge between the achievements of crisis research and the present-day problems of international politics. For this purpose, the relationship between the present international system and those crises that are experienced within it is the main problem of analysis. This means that crisis is seen in a broad perspective and linked with its political, system-wide environment.

Whatever the different detailed formulations, a crisis is defined in two basic ways. An international crisis is a situation linked with *sensations* of concern and anxiety, with a manifest feeling of uncertainty and threat to vital values by decision-makers (actor-level), or it is seen as a phase in a *process* of events among states leading to ever more conflictual and dangerous situations, and ultimately to the use of force (systems-level). The explanations of behavior are, in the former case, based mainly on psychological and, in the latter case, on structural factors.

The structure of the international system determines the *framework* variables of crises, such as alignments, sources of interdependence, military capabilities, and their distribution, rules, and norms of behavior. Taking the systemic, structural method of explanation, this chapter makes an effort to characterize the present international system from points of view relevant to the question made. The types of crisis experienced in real life are also outlined. At the end, an attempt is made to answer the question of what kind of policies should be pursued to prevent, manage, and resolve crises in the international system now and in the future.

One of the more disturbing problems with crisis research from the point of view of structural and systemic analysis is that it deals with effects of social phenomena. An analysis is made of the processes and sequences of events that unfold because some domestic or international factors have led to increased tension or the sharpening of latent conflicts. But to be able to follow the course of an international crisis— or to manage it—one should be cognizant of the root causes of crises and conflicts. They may be found to be structural and "objective" or perceptional and "subjective"; they may take effect slowly or arise suddenly. There is a certain background where crises breed and arise, and in the last analysis this background is global and systemwide. For this reason, approaches used in peace and conflict research should accompany those linked with the more narrow perspectives of traditional crisis research.

When using the systemic approach, the concept of a *systemic crisis* is also needed: a process of the developments having global ramifications in the sense that the great powers—the United States and the Soviet Union—and the great power alliances are involved, directly or indirectly, or—if the scope of events is not global—the great power relations are affected by the crisis. The key questions are how the international system "behaves" under the stress of crisis; what future trends one can discern or what reforms one can prescribe for the system to make it less crisis-prone or to alleviate the repercussions of crises.

The Regional System, Détente, and Crises

The point of departure for the analysis of crises in the present international system is détente. It is used here primarily as an analytical concept to help in the demonstration of the nature of the relationship between international systems and crises. Détente is a form that the international system can take in certain historical stages. It can prescribe a certain structure for the international system, but above all it is a characteristic of the *substance of politics* between states. The interesting question is what effects such détente-type ways of politics may have on the birth, course, and management of crises.

Analytically, a continuum may be perceived where characteristics of détente diminish or grow in the international system over time. But another classification can also be made: Regional systems and the global system may represent different degrees of détente. Finally, the international system can be analyzed from the East-West and North-South dimensions.

In Europe, where the analytical concept and historical experience meet, détente is limited to the East-West system. In this regional system of détente, the framework conditions for interstate politics were given by the *common goals*: first, the *stabilization* of the politicomilitary relationship between East and West in the area covering the participants of the Conference on Security and Cooperation in Europe (CSCE), and second, *cooperation* in various functional fields. Détente is a reflection of common goals and the maintenance of a process based on them. In détente there are effects of two different, at first glance even conflictual, parallel strategies of politics: a constraining strategy that aims at regulating—and making predictable—the policies of all the states participating in the system, and a functional strategy that believes in a reinforcing process of interaction that brings states closer. Underlying détente there seems to be an ambiguous mixture of conflict and harmony, as one analyst ends his treatise on détente:[2]

> In détente perceptions the conflict pattern clearly penetrates all the relevant models. . . . Functional assumptions, however, open possibilities for consensus-based action as they specify the conflicts in terms of interests which may be harmoniously accommodated in specific cases and on the condition of consensus among participating actors.

> Instead of a dominating value conflict, East-West relations may be equally understood to be systematically ambiguous to the extent that functionalist accommodations are possible [Apunen, 1981b].

The stabilization goal in détente reflects the technology model for peace. The main condition is the stability of the deterrence relationship between the United States and the Soviet Union. An accompanying condition is bloc cohesion within the military alliances, and further, a military balance in a wider sense. But the goal of stability encompasses also another, more political dimension: the protection provided by détente for the integrity of the political systems that are in interaction— i.e., recognition of the political status quo in Europe.

The cooperation model for peace, on the other hand, is based on the growing interdependence[3] of states that leads to what is called positive peace. Neither the military balance nor the so-called political interests, but rather peace-creating effect of a network of functional interactions is the guarantor of peace. What is involved is a step-by-step process from one specific case to another, from one practical task to another, but always having a certain permanent pattern of politics in solving these problems.

What is particularly relevant in détente for the purposes of crisis research is the idea of *consensus* on the rules of behavior between states and on the methods of solving problems and settling disputes between states. Consensus determines procedurally the character of the relations between states in détente.

The basic rule of behavior in détente—confirmed in the Eastern treaties and the CSCE Final Act—is the non-use of force (Apunen, 1977). In contrast with the Cold War conflict model of politics, where power was used to gain dominance over others, in détente a harmony model of politics has a role, too; power is used to gain control over one's own potential capabilities and thus to maintain an autonomous status. Whereas in the Cold War power was seen as a *repressive* instrument and the use or threat of the use of force prevailed, in détente power is also seen as an *emancipatory* instrument, and political conciliation and cooperation have important roles to play in solving the issues that come up in international relations (Apunen, 1977: 23, n. 2).

Historically, during the Cold War crisis management was successful enough to prevent a major war between East and West, but the threat of an open conflict was always present. During détente, consensus over the joint rules of behavior and a different outlook for the coexistence of states in general provide a completely different ground for crisis management—if crises come up.

Détente does not exclude the role of force in international relations. It remains in the background because maintaining a military balance is considered vital and attended to continuously. The basic value conflict between the Eastern and Western systems remains, and conflicts of interest come up in practical politics. But through the rules of behavior that recognize the legitimacy of the two systems in Europe, the repressive use of power is denied. This gives stability to the East-West relations. At the same time, the rules of action in essence point to the peaceful settlement of disputes and to political cooperation between states. This makes negotiation the main instrument of politics, not coercion or the demonstration of force.

Both the politics of the Cold War and of détente are bilateral in the sense that the two military alliances and their leading powers are the dominating actors. But in détente there are also elements of loosening bipolarity. Within the blocs there are several significant actors—in particular in different issue areas—and the nonaligned and neutral states have much room for maneuver and a greater influence in the negotiation and solving of issues. Another way of seeing a bipolar system in détente is that of dividing states into two political and economic systems; this is a relevant approach in certain issue areas, too.

It goes without saying that the above description of détente is analytical. It represents an ideal model. In practical politics the common goals, the joint rules of behavior, the mutual recognition of the legitimacy of social systems, and the mutual interests in functional cooperation are not unproblematic. This has been amply demonstrated in the CSCE follow-up process, for example. The meetings in Belgrade and Madrid have provided the differing interpretations of what détente is and should be that prevail among the participating states.

Conflicts that have arisen have affected both of the two central framework conditions of détente: stabilization and interdependence. The military balance is strained due to new rounds of the arms race, and the stability, if not the legitimacy, of social systems has been called into question again. Economic cooperation has not widened as a continuing process but has experienced difficulties and setbacks. These developments have taken place in the European region as a whole new perspective opens on the global scene.

What is important to note is that the East-West system has been taken in a kind of vacuum as a regional system, separate from the rest of the international system. That is why the system can be called a system of *regional and perfect détente* in analytical terms. Two prime examples of the definition of a crisis follow:

(1) An international crisis is a sequence of interactions between governments of two or more sovereign states in severe conflict, short of actual war, but involving the perception of a dangerously *high probability of war* [Snyder and Diesing, 1977: 6, emphasis added].

(2) (perceptions held in a crisis situation by decision-makers)
  (a) a threat to basic values, with a simultaneous or subsequent
  (b) *high probability of involvement in military hostilities,* and the aware-
      ness of (c) finite time for response to the external value threat
      [Brecher, 1979a:447, emphasis added].

Several situations from the Cold War can be recalled that fulfill these conditions in the European regional system (in particular, the Berlin crisis). But since the onset of détente circa 1970, no such situation has originated in Europe, that is, in the regional system of détente. Even the periods of the reaggravation of tension in Europe cannot be characterized as crises in the above sense, as situations where military hostilities between the participating states would have been imminent or highly probable. Rather, tension has been caused by more slowly developing phenomena that have made the basic conditions of détente more vulnerable as systemic characteristics. And then of course, tension has been caused by extra-European events and crises.

There may be several simultaneous explanations for the absence of crises in the regional perfect system of détente, and they can be found among the framework conditions outlined above: the stabilization of the military and political status quo as a common goal, with the risk of nuclear war as the deterrent; the deepening benefits of functional cooperation as the basis for mutual interests; and consensus as the method of solving international issues. Bilateralism also has its effect, which was a constraining factor during the Cold War, too. The existence of the military blocs has made it impossible to create limited, interbloc conflicts. Peace between East and West has become indivisible in Europe.

The Global System, the Great Powers, and Local Crises

As the perspective is enlarged to encompass the global system in its entirety, the picture changes. The analysis continues to pinpoint the great power relations, but they are seen in both regional and local contexts as well as the global context. Détente is used as an analytical concept that provides a basis for comparative analyses between the regional East-West system outlined above and the global system with its regional and local elements. It continues to be the normative goal of politics, which makes it a natural yardstick in a comparative analysis.

In addition to the fact that the great power relations are seen in their global dimensions, the inclusion of the North-South relationship brings new elements to the analysis of crises and their causes. Recent historical evidence shows that systemic crises where force was used or demonstrated have originated outside of Europe but have had repercussions on the regional system of détente in Europe. The list of examples is long, from Angola to Afghanistan, and so on.

The conflicts underlying these kind of crises seem to be extremely complex as to the factors involved and the processes and mechanisms of escalation and settlement. The key to understanding those conflicts is the crossing point of the East-West and North-South dimensions of interstate relations. This is also vital for efforts to manage these kinds of systemic crises. For the continuation of the politics of détente, even in the regional East-West system, it is increasingly important to come to understand the real crises that exist in the present international system. For the purposes of comparison, the global system is described with the help of the same explanatory variables that were brought up in the case of the regional system: bipolarity, stabilization, and interdependence.

The global international system is increasingly *multipolar*. The simplest indication of this is the existence of a multitude of relevant decision-making centers and power centers. But more interesting and important is to witness the loss of bipolarity in the distribution of power as it affects the outcome of issues. The reason for multipolarity in this sense is not so much a diffusion of military power, although there is a clear tendency toward a military effort by the developing, nonaligned countries that is relatively stronger than in the leading military powers.[4]

The main reason is the new kind of risk for the great powers should they become involved in Third World crises, and this makes them more reluctant to do so. Because of the multitude of local factors involved and the increased range of possibilities for the unravelling of the crisis in question, conflicts are not as clear-cut as they were during the Cold War when local details played a minor role.[5] And they are not as easy to judge as tense situations in the regional East-West system in Europe where the dividing line is clear. Hence, there is *greater ambiguity and unpredictability* of crisis developments outside of the European system where the multipolarity of the global system is shown in a concrete form.

The situation is further demonstrated in the classification of great power participation in crises:[6]

(a) a direct confrontation between the great powers, the United States and the Soviet Union;

(b) crisis in Europe where one great power and an ally of the other are initial direct participants, with the other great power taking the lead in crisis bargaining;

(c) crisis in Europe between allies of the two great powers;

(d) crisis outside the European region, with one great power and an ally or a semi-ally of the other as the direct participants;

(e) crisis outside Europe, with allies or semi-allies of the great powers as the direct participants;

(f) crisis outside Europe, with purely nonaligned countries as the initial direct participants.

Alternatives (d), (e), and (f) are the new type of crises that are of interest to the analysis here. They are also the only kinds of crises that have existed recently. The great power involvement may take different forms, such as a direct participation in the bargaining—a probable outcome in case (d)—or supporting the allied or friendly state through the transfer of resources, arms, and the like in case (e) or, after new alignments, in case (f), too.

But the nature of the links of the great powers with the Third World actors can be ambiguous or vague. In any case, it does not correspond to the traditional allied relationships of the European system. The links are typically bilateral arrangements where the political, economic, or military obligations remain subject to a politically motivated interpretation; they may be limited in scope; and their implementation may be problematic due to institutional, organizational, or political deficiencies. In short, there is a strong element of uncertainty in the linkages and alignments.

It is true, on one hand, that a decreased benefit is seen for the great powers in tight alignments. On the other hand, new kinds of alignments are emerging: Militarily or economically strategic points are being transformed into "forward bases" of the great powers. This can become a new wave of bloc politics. Another aspect of multipolarity is that countries can find alternatives for alignments, with the European community, China, and Japan being the most important partners. A number of Third World countries in Africa, the Middle East, and Central Asia have also gained more room for maneuver in their alignments with the great or middle-level powers.

The mutual recognition of the status quo was a central factor contributing to the stability of the regional East-West system. Globally, there is no such consensus between the great powers. Their perceptions of the dynamics of extra-European developments differ from one another radically. There is no such consensus on the maintenance of the political and social status quo as in Europe. But it would be difficult also for the fact that the Third World is changing politically due to intra-Third World and domestic reasons.

A major cause for instability is *the weakness of the legitimacy* of many Third World governments and domestic regimes in general. The question becomes international because in most cases the claims of the regime for legitimacy are based on both domestic *and* external support, and the latter is acquired through neocolonialistic or other unequal ties with the developed countries. Especially in cases where economic performance is the critical variable in the claim for legitimacy, its fulfillment becomes heavily dependent on international factors, and above all, on the success of the North-South redistribution of wealth.[7] As the whole idea of developmentalism has run into a crisis of credibility, states tend to lose this practical legitimacy based on rational and productive policies for all. This loss of legitimacy creates a crisis of the state and its role in general and may lead states to emphasize conflicts and national and parochial values in search of a new basis for their existence.[8] The state itself becomes the problem, not the solution.

But the challenge to the legitimacy of a regime can arise from other typical Third World factors such as social, ethnic, or religious disintegration. All these factors can lead to antiregime conflicts with or without outside involvement and—as a result of the open conflict—to changes in the status quo in the Third World also from the point of view of the great powers. This kind of dynamics makes it impossible to agree upon the political stability as a precondition for détente as was the case in the European system.

The other dimension of stability, the military balance between the great powers and the alliances, also becomes problematic in the global context. For the time being, the nuclear strategic balance is not affected by developments in the Third World—at least so far as the proliferation of nuclear weapons is prevented. So far Europe remains the only region for which the great powers also prescribe a separate regional nuclear balance, but this tendency could grow to encompass other regions, too. At present the great powers are concentrating on creating capabilities for the global projection of conventional land, naval, and air military power. This can lead to efforts to establish regional conventional balances between the great powers—the Persian Gulf is the prime candidate—which would create yet new channels for making local crises systemic.[9]

Although the mutual benefits to be accrued from economic *cooperation* are recognized also in the North-South relationship, efforts are stalling in practice. They are naturally complicated by the goals of the redistribution of resources and the decentralization of decision-making that the Third World has set and that a large part of the developed world has recognized as vital parts of any solution. Even if the common goals are at least partly defined and determined, there is no effective agreement on the rules of behavior or the institutions needed for the implementation of those goals.

What has become an acute problem and endangered even more the chances of functionalism is the new kind of power politics directed toward sources of energy and raw materials in the Third World. The great powers have included the dependence on outside energy sources and raw materials in the calculus of national security. It can be tolerated only if the supply is secured by alignments or domination, that is, by force in the last analysis. Trust in positive interdependence seems to be weak. This is yet another factor in explaining the course of crises where the North-South and East-West dimensions meet. Crises in economically strategic regions tend to become systemic in their effects.[10]

The global system that has been scanned above is clearly one of *imperfect détente*. Those framework variables that characterize the regional system of détente in Europe—bipolarity, stability, and interdependence—take a different form in the global system. They are not necessarily opposite in their contents, but at best they are ambiguous.

Systemic Crisis Behavior and Reforming the System

The behavior of states in conflicts or crises can be derived from the framework variables of the international system, the deep-seated features of the context where those conflicts or crises unfold. It is vital to understand the *expectations* that actors draw from this environment and the *presuppositions* they make for the functioning of the system as a whole and its participants.

In a study on escalation, Smoke (1977) defines *saliences* as central elements in the drawing up of a picture of the situation for all participants.[11] In this way, limits are drawn and thresholds marked in the conflict. As far as saliences are objective—noticeable by all the participants—but at the same time discontinuous, escalation in conflict or war can be defined as a step that crosses such a saliency. It changes the ground rules of the game, since a threshold is crossed and tension increased to an upper level. Such a step leads to a reaction by the other participants. But such a crossing of saliences also affects the policy-makers' expectations, their image of the context where they operate, and the situation as a whole. This reasoning shows that it is important to have not only adequate *sequence cognition*—realization among the actors of how crisis develops—but also *systems cognition*—realization of what the context is and what the salient elements are. After this, an attempt can be made to analyze how the international system "behaves" in crisis.

In the regional system of perfect détente, the non-use of force is the point of departure for choosing methods of interaction between states, even in settling disputes. Political conciliation is based on the consensus reached on the context and its saliences. As far as the global system of imperfect détente is concerned, the use and the threat of the use of force are alternatives, often chosen and in many cases leading to *limited war.* Peace is divisible. In this system, an international crisis may be a situation where the threshold has been crossed into war between some actors, whereas for others this limited war is one factor affecting their international relations but not the kind of crossing of a salience that would draw them into the same armed conflict. This could be the case with the great powers; attempts to limit and settle those wars between Third World participants might become the central aspect of the crisis. The mechanisms of the spread of war thus become crucial for controlling local crises in the short run.

A related question is the definition of the rules of great power behavior outside the regional European system. As has been so often noted, the failure in extending the same kind of rules that were agreed upon for Europe to the Third World has contributed to the stalling of détente in the European region. The lack of consensus on the framework condition for global détente has also meant that the saliences that the great powers perceive in Third World developments vary. An event that for one is a natural and objective social phenomenon is a threat to national security for the other. A legitimate alignment for one is a unilateral interference for the other and a threat to the political or military balance.[12]

The effects of an eventual proliferation of nuclear weapons are another significant factor that determines systemic crisis behavior. There are different and even opposite interpretations of what those effects could be. Proliferation could weaken the credibility of great power alliances and commitments in general and increase the reluctance of the great powers to enter into new alignments. It could increase the probability of the actual use of nuclear weapons, initially in a regional conflict, but also later between the great powers that would be drawn into the conflict. In this way, proliferation could lower the threshold to first use or preventive use of nuclear weapons by the great powers. But it could also lead to a more strict avoidance by the great powers of involvement in local conflicts (Jones, 1980; Montbrial, n.d.; Dror, n.d.). But there are analysts who think that proliferation would in fact strengthen stability, globally and regionally, by providing means for solving security problems (Waltz, 1981, Weltman, 1981).

These and other examples of the growing scale of possible uses of force in international conflicts and of the growing number of actors also mean that the spectrum of possible outcomes in an international crisis has grown wider. This has made it more difficult for the great powers, too, to judge where the saliences are that would turn the crisis into a great power confrontation. Both sequence cognition and systems cognition have become more problematic—for the actors and the outside analyst—in the present global system.

What, then, should be done to make the global international system safer and to secure a peaceful solution of international crises? The international activity directed toward tackling this problem can take the form of *managing, preventing,* or *solving* crises. The difference between these activities lies not only in the time perspective—doing something during, before, or after the actual crisis—but also in the changes or *reforms* that they would require in the international system.

In the regional system of perfect détente described in the beginning of the chapter, analytical and also historically verified categories were given for such a reform of the international system. Table 11.1 gives a summary of such systemic changes. In the management of a crisis, measures that regulate, guide, or control the short-term behavior of states are crucial for the outcome of the acute situation. Established common rules of behavior, applied to a particular political context, as in the CSCE Final Act, will also have such a restraining effect in aggravated situations. The non-use of force should be the guiding principle that is defined in a concrete and binding way. A long-term practice of political consultations and dialogues, buttressed by bilateral and multilateral institutions, will provide channels and also apply pressure for keeping communications open.

In the prevention of crises, measures should be implemented that will have an effect on the military capabilities and motivations of states.

TABLE 11.1   Reforms of the International System and their Effects on Crisis

Crisis-Related Activity	*Systems Reform*
managing crisis	rules of behavior of states institutionalized negotiation
preventing crisis	security alignments confidence-building measures arms control functional cooperation
solving crisis	collective security disarmament functional interdependence redistribution

Similarly, vested interests in functional cooperation will keep the options of a peaceful solution high on the agenda before the decision-makers. The kind of military measures envisaged here do not go deeply into the military structures but rather have characteristics of collective security-seeking; they can be the opening for a later change in the security system, but they need not be. This is illustrated by the fact that the traditional military alliance can also be listed here as a practice that can prevent crises—both as a deterrent and as a negotiating mechanism.

But to solve the crisis, measures should be taken to eliminate permanently the causes for the conflicts that may escalate into crisis. These measures lead into deep, even structural changes in the system that will also have long-term effects on crisis behavior. They change the way force can be used in international relations by changing both the motivations and the capabilities for the use of force in the settlement of disputes. These reforms in the international system will also heighten the effects that functional cooperation has on the behavior of states—from the mere consideration of mutual but limited interests to a compelling interdependence.

There are different actor levels for these system reforms or other crisis-related activities: multilateral/global, great power, regional, local, and bilateral. To take the most effective measure in each case, a division of labor between the actor levels must be envisaged. An example of the shifting emphasis is given in Table 11.2.

The global international system is becoming more complicated and more ambiguous from the point of view of crisis management. It is

TABLE 11.2   Actor Levels for Systems Reforms

Systems Reform	Global	Great Power	Regional	Local
rules of behavior		X	X	
institutionalized negotiation		X	X	X
security alignments			X	X
arms control, cbm's		X	X	
functional cooperation	X	X	X	
collective security	X		X	
disarmament	X			
interdependence	X			
redistribution	X			

becoming less prone to greater power control, which again makes the outcomes of crises less predictable. At the same time, there are possibilities for reforming the international system in a way that makes it more susceptible to peaceful solutions and peaceful development in general. Experiences gained from the practice and analysis of détente can help and give cues for this work.

NOTES

1. Those used here are Brecher (1979b), Smoke (1977), and Frei (1982).
2. The following treatment of détente relies heavily on Apunen (1981a).
3. For a definition of complex interdependence, see Keohane and Nye (1977: 23ff.).
4. For a recent study, see Kolodziej and Harkavy (1980).
5. This is noted, among others, by Smoke (1977: 299-302).
6. This kind of categorization is made also by Snyder and Diesing (1977: 504).
7. For an interesting analysis of this aspect, see Vidich (1979).
8. A point made by David E. Apter in the Zurich Round Table Discussion.
9. Apunen (1981b) gives an analysis of the factors and trends of great power military presence.
10. See Russett (1981) on the global issues involved. The resurgence of geopolitics is a telling indication of the trends in today's great power politics.
11. Smoke (1977: 30-35) deals with the escalation of limited wars, but his concepts are useful and applicable also for the analysis of crisis—especially since the threshold between crisis and war is not clear in the global system. It depends also on the level of analysis.
12. This problem, as is well known, is the major issue in the American debate on the results of détente that led to the reconsiderations of the Carter and Reagan administrations. See, for example, Congressional Research Service (1981).

CHAPTER 12

PRACTICAL SUGGESTIONS FOR CRISIS MANAGEMENT
An Inventory

KING-YUH CHANG

I

The growth of international interaction is a long-term trend. In ancient times, civilizations existed without even being aware of each other. When history entered the modern age, the tempo of interaction among states quickened. A global economy began to take shape in the eighteenth century. Far-reaching wars began to occur in the nineteenth century, culminating in the two world wars of the twentieth century. The multiplicity of actors, the rising political and economic resources at their disposal, and the increasing instruments available to different kinds of actors all contributed to an increase in international interactions (Scott, 1977: 429-432).

Although it seems that cooperative/participatory interactions among nations are more common than conflict behavior, and that *conflict actions* constitute only a small percentage of world events,[1] the management of international conflict has become an ever more important task. Two basic reasons can be cited here. First, without an interdependence of effort, there is no conflict in the real world. As the level of interdependence increases, so does the need for coordination. Any increase in interdependence will tend to increase the risk of coordination failure and hence the probability of conflict. In other words, as international interaction grows, the number of conflicts that would need proper management will also grow. Second, with the increasing destructive power at the disposal of international actors, the potential consequences of failure to manage international conflicts, especially military-security conflicts, will become more serious. Hence, the management of international conflict is a central task for the foreign office.

Conflict behavior is likely to result when one party occupies a position incompatible with the wishes or interests of another party. When two parties adopt different and incompatible views over the solution of problems such as territory, tariff, the price of petroleum, or the treatment of nationals and minorities, conflict occurs (Holsti, 1977: 460). When the conflict becomes severe and the decision-makers of a state perceive that a change in the state's external environment contains the following three traits or components, an international crisis situation is said to exist. The three components are (1) a threat to basic values, with (2) a simultaneous or subsequent high probability of involvement in military hostilities, and (3) the awareness of finite time for response to the external value threat. These three elements, though logically separate, are interrelated in a crisis situation. Brecher has observed that

the more active and stronger the threat and the more central the value(s) threatened, the higher will be the perceived probability that military hostility will ensue. That, in turn, would lead to a more intense perception of crisis. Similarly, the more active, the stronger, and the more central (basic) the threatened value(s), the more limited will be the perceived time for response. Moreover, the greater the time pressure, the higher will be the perceived probability of war and the more intense the perception of threat. The reverse relationship also obtains: the higher the perceived probability of war, the more central, active, and strong will be the perceived value threat, and the more limited will be the time perceived to be available for response to that threat [1979: 454].

Conflict is an inevitable feature of social life. International conflict, as conflicts in general, can be handled more or less constructively or more or less destructively. At one extreme would be the punitive methods of force and destruction that imply the annihilation of an opponent, and at the other extreme would be the methods of integrative solution, making the dispute irrelevant. In between would be the methods of conflict denial, bargaining and compromise, and limited warfare. The objectives of conflict management should be to avoid the crisis, limit the conflict, or settle the difference. The purpose of this chapter is to explore what types of foreign policy behavior should be undertaken and what types should be avoided in a crisis situation in order to manage the crisis peacefully or to successfully solve interstate conflicts in a peaceful way.

II

As already indicated, in a crisis situation the decision-makers perceive a threat to basic values, a high probability of military hostilities, and a finite time for response to the external value threat. In order to manage the crisis peacefully and to influence the choice of the other party, a state should adopt foreign policy actions not being perceived as threatening the basic values of the opponent, not involving a high probability of military hostilities, and not pressuring the opponent to make precipitous decisions. The following types of foreign policy behavior are desirable.

(1) Keeping communications channels open: When two parties are engaged in a conflict, the first requirement of peaceful resolution is to keep the communications channels open, either directly or indirectly through third parties in order to avoid any misunderstandings. As the level of threat and hostility rises, there is a tendency to reduce formal diplomatic communications. The "mildest" step in a crisis, such as the recall of ambassadors, makes official communications more difficult. One may presume that at a time when suspicion, distrust, and a sense of urgency are at their highest, authoritative and explicit communications are all the more important. While the opponents negotiate, they will, in general, avoid provocative actions (Holsti, 1977: 468). The fact that the Iranian government refused to send its own negotiating team to meet the Americans face to face only delayed the resolution of that crisis.

On the other hand, the very fact that two parties are in conflict may make communications difficult to initiate. As a result of experimentation, Deutsch and Krauss suggested that

> where barriers to communication exist, a situation in which the parties are compelled to communicate will be more effective than one in which the choice to talk or not is put on a voluntary basis [1962: 75].

Organizations such as the United Nations, the Organization of African Unity, and the Organization of American States play particularly useful roles in providing forums for communication. The parties in conflict simply cannot avoid contact and communication in these forums. One is often reminded that an encounter in the corridors of the United Nations was partly responsible for the settlement of the first Berlin crisis.

(2) Keeping communications specific: The more hostile the general relationship between two states, the worse the interpretation that the antagonists are likely to make of each other's words and deeds. Generalities may conform to the principle of flexibility. However, when two nations are involved in a crisis, specific communications are more likely to induce responses. Hence, a state should make its demands, its offers and its threats very clearly. One party should make the set of consequences of doing what it wants (including the benefits and disadvantages) more attractive to the other party than the set of consequences of not complying. One scholar has proposed a guide regarding the specificity of the communications:

(A) Demand: The decision desired.
   Who?   Who is to make the decision?
   What?   Exactly what decision is desired?
   When?   By what time does the decision have to be made?
   Why?   What makes this a right, proper, and lawful decision?

(B) Offer: The consequences of making the decision.
   Who?   Who benefits if the decision is made?
   What?   If the decision is made, what benefits can be expected?
           What are the costs?
   When?   When, if ever, will the benefits of making the decision
           occur?
   Why?   What makes these consequences fair and legitimate?

(C) Threat: The consequences of not making the decision.
   Who?   Who gets hurt if the decision is not made?
   What?   If the decision is not made, what are the risks? What are
           the potential benefits?
   When?   How soon will the consequences of not making the deci-
           sion be felt?
   Why?   What makes these consequences fair and legitimate?
           (Fisher, 1969: 48).

Clearly, vagueness and generality in a conflict situation will be suspect. Specificity increases credibility. A specific offer with details demonstrates greater commitment, and it is therefore more probable that the other party will respond.[2]

(3) Treating a dispute as a conflict of interest, not of principle: In a labor-management conflict, wages and benefits can be the subject of bargaining, but not the principle of free trade unionism. The recent events in Poland show that the Solidarity Union wants to defend free trade unionism and the Polish Communist Party wishes to maintain its leading role in the nation. Neither side can bargain an ideological principle without compromising its moral position. If either side attempts to challenge the other on its principle, an open clash will be unavoidable.

In international conflicts, it is rather difficult, if not impossible, for a state to abandon its basic foreign policy principles, such as supporting the "Free World" or adhering to "proletarian internationalism." There is an all-or-nothing quality to moral principles on which countries are usually unwilling to yield. Daniel Katz has observed that "the logic of bargaining and compromise is well suited for reaching agreement about economic and power differences, but it is scarcely appropriate for the settlement of ideological differences of a symbolic character" (Herman, 1972: 383; Holsti, 1966: 227).

When a dispute is considered a conflict of interest and each party is willing to settle for less than his ideal position rather than continue the conflict, a compromise can be reached. Thus, if the Berlin crisis of 1948 had been considered a matter of principle and not a matter of access, it would have been much more difficult to handle. When it was considered a matter of access, solutions became possible.

(4) Soliciting third party involvement: When an interstate crisis occurs, the parties have often cut their communications or are too committed to a fixed position to change. A third party can then serve as a messenger, fact-finder, mediator, conciliator, arbitrator, and/or supervisor of settlements. As long as these third party efforts continue, the possibility of war is greatly reduced. In a recent study of 247 interstate conflicts, Robert Butterworth found that more than three-fourths (192) involved a manager. Managers were defined to be actors who "achieved access to the parties and issues and whose manifest intention was to prevent the conflict from escalating." While the managers are not very successful in managing Cold War and/or superpower conflicts, their influence in other types of conflicts has been substantial (Butterworth, 1978b: 195-214). In another study dealing with 32 crises, conflicts, and disputes involving 54 ultimate political objectives to be achieved, the United Nations was found to have been

successful in 57 percent of the cases where it took action beyond mere debates and passage of resolutions (Holsti, 1972: 493-498).

Bargaining is a positive-sum game with a mixture of conflict and cooperation: The payoffs may be different to each party, but both are better off with a solution than without one. A third party can clear up misunderstandings, propose new solutions, widen the agenda, and mobilize public opinion to cause a sufficient reconciliation of positions to permit a bargain (Boulding, 1962: 316-321).

If the role of the third party institution is made legitimate by shared values or upheld by shared interests, and if an institution is prepared to use its power to prevent conflicts from being settled by violence, the likelihood of the parties in conflict eschewing violence could be very high.

The management of the recent hostage crisis between the United States and Iran was handicapped by the lack of sufficient direct communications between the two parties. At one time or another, the United States enlisted the help of others, among them Pakistan, Syria, Algeria, Libya, Switzerland, France, West Germany, Britain, and the Palestine Liberation Organization. Several intermediaries put together a complex plan in February and March 1980 that sought to arrange for the transfer of the hostages to a neutral third party, followed by their release, in exchange for a formal UN inquiry into Iran's grievance against alleged American crimes and a humble admission of guilt by the United States. This was probably the most promising initiative, although the Ayatollah Khomeini scuttled the plan. While the intermediaries did not solve the hostage crisis, their efforts may have succeeded in deflating it.

(5) Disregard provocative actions: It takes two to make a fight. If one country ignores the insults and belligerent attitude of an aggressor, it may avert a struggle. A weak state may thus refuse to acknowledge the real meaning of hostile acts against itself by a strong neighbor in order to avoid a disastrous conflict. A strong and stable country may choose to ignore external insults. In the case of the hostages, the U.S. government maintained its tranquillity despite repeated insults to the American flag and to the U.S. Chief of State by the militant Iranian students.

Obviously, "denial of conflict" may not always succeed in managing an interstate crisis. China's self-controlled responses to Japan's provocative and aggressive behavior in the late 1920s and 1930s did not stop Japan's large-scale attack on China in 1937. Sometimes the demonstration of weakness or lack of resistance may have the reverse effect of emboldening the aggressor. On the other hand, the controlled response of the United States in the hostage crisis avoided an escalation of the conflict.

(6) Fractionating the conflict and diffusing the crisis: A crisis is often a sudden eruption of unexpected events caused by a previous conflict. As the overall controversy is not easily solved, small conflicts will remain and accumulate. Between friendly states, issues are often dealt with separately on their own merits. Solutions thus become easier. Between hostile states, however, small controversies tend to become integral parts of a bigger controversy and are consequently hard to settle.

Very often the disputing parties cannot solve a crisis or conflict completely at any particular moment. But they can limit the size of the conflict. If the parties treat conflicts as particular small issues rather than as single big ones, they are less likely to resort to violence, since the existing community of interests will weigh more in the scale against particular small issues than against single big ones (Waskow, 1964: 124).

In a crisis situation, the most urgent task is to diffuse high tension. Positive interactions contribute to the creation of an atmosphere in which negotiations can be more effectively conducted and political settlements achieved. If a dispute is dissected, perhaps some positive actions can be undertaken to meet the demands of the other party. In this way, some degree of mutual trust can be built up so that serious negotiations on the core issues can follow. In the Iranian hostages crisis, as long as the Shah of Iran remained in the United States, any negotiated settlement was impossible since the new rulers of Iran were determined to punish the Shah, and the young Islamic militants believed that by seizing the American hostages they might force the United States to return the Shah. On the other hand, the United States could not hand over the Shah to the new Iranian authorities, so the Shah was persuaded to go to "neutral" Panama. The seriousness of direct confrontation was thus greatly reduced.

(7) Employing force wisely with flexibility and self-control: Force should be used only as a means to protect vital interests and only when other alternatives are either unavailable or exhausted. Even when force is used, it should be combined with other means to reach a settlement. In other words, the military instrument should be used as an integral part of diplomacy.

In the Cuban missile crisis of 1962, the United States imposed a naval quarantine on the reasoning that:

> the course we finally adopted had the advantage of permitting other steps. If this one was unsuccessful, we could have gradually stepped it up until we had gone into a much more massive action which might have become necessary if the first step had been unsuccessful.[3]

This naval quarantine was a flexible and self-restrained response to a serious Soviet challenge to American security. This particular move enabled the Soviet Union to respond with deliberation. The U.S. response to the Soviet action was characterized by another participant-observer as "a graduated effort which avoided trying to achieve too much and which stopped short of confronting an adversary with stark and imperative choices" (Hilsman, 1967: 228).

In our view, flexibility, self-control, and self-restraint in the application of force were the principal cause for the peaceful resolution of the Cuban missile crisis. On the other hand, inflexibility during the 1914 crisis after the Sarajevo assassination made the use of unlimited force and war inevitable.

III

When a conflict becomes a crisis, it is marked by high tension and urgency. It is also fraught with serious consequences if it is not handled properly. In order to reduce the likelihood of violence and war, the following types of foreign policy behavior should be avoided.

(1) Issuing ultimatums: Students of international crises have found that as an international crisis approaches its peak, decision-makers increasingly perceive that they are under great time pressure. They see their freedom of action being increasingly restricted while their opponent's freedom of action is increasingly widened (Holsti, 1965: 365-378). In general, the longer the decision-making time, the more alternatives likely to be considered. Working in a crisis situation, decision-makers tend to reduce information search, suppress unpleasant input, and increase in-group conformity (Suedfeld and Tetlock, 1977: 170 ff.). Ultimatums shorten the time available for making vital decisions. They also increase the opportunity for the other party to take preemptive actions.

(2) Threatening the core of the opponent's value system: If the core of a state's value system is threatened, it will have no choice but to respond

forcefully. Had the Soviet Union insisted on keeping its missiles in Cuba, or if the United States had chosen to overthrow the Castro regime during the missile crisis in 1962, an open clash between the United States and the Soviet Union would probably have been unavoidable. In the end, the United States agreed not to invade Cuba and the Soviet Union agreed to remove its missiles; the crisis was peacefully resolved. In the Iranian hostage crisis, the Iranian authorities threatened to try the hostages but never carried out their threat. The United States openly warned the Iranian authorities that it would take retaliatory measures should Iran put the hostages on trial. Recognizing the seriousness of the U.S. warning, Iran refrained from challenging the core values of the United States.

(3) Mixing moral principles with conflict of interests: When moral principles are introduced into a conflict, an all-right or an all-wrong solution will be sought. A compromise becomes impossible and a stalemate ensues. When the Iranian authorities accused the American government of immorality and Khomeini called President Carter "the great Satan" in the White House, it was difficult for Iran to come to terms with an "immoral" America. The hostage crisis was thus prolonged.

(4) Pressuring the other party beyond certain limits and/or using force: A frequent reaction to a conflict situation is to do something unpleasant to the other government, sometimes to "punish" it for its allegedly evil behavior. These actions could include verbal denunciations, economic sanctions, cessation of trade and economic aid, censure in the United Nations, and even military measures. The purpose is to make the other side discontinue their actions and consequently to change their course of action.

The theory of inflicting pain upon another government rests on the premise that the latter will change its mind to avoid further pain. However, the record of past sanctions is unimpressive. When a government takes an action, it may have already calculated the costs. To inflict pain may simply be to impose anticipated costs. Even if the costs are high, people can adjust rather quickly. Furthermore, the more they have suffered, the more they will regard themselves as committed to their present course of action. Foreign policy decision-makers, like individuals in groups, are unlikely to propose that the best course might be to yield to pain and change the course of action. On the contrary, external pressure may often solidify the group (Fisher, 1969: 27-35). Drastic actions may be undertaken when a state believes it is in great danger. When Americans were taken as hostages, the Iranian authorities must have anticipated certain American actions. However, if the U.S. economic sanctions had become completely effective, the Iranians might have been forced to turn to the Russians or to take other drastic measures. Thus the crisis might have been enlarged.

If pressure escalates to physical violence, a situation may get out of control. New alliances and alignments may be formed. Third parties may intervene. The crisis may become unsolvable short of declaring war. The Middle East conflict in 1967 is a good example. Egypt took certain actions to deter Israel from attacking Syria. Yet, given the existing tension in the area, when Egypt dispatched forces to Sharm al Shaykh, closed the Straits of Tiran, and asked the UN Peace Force to leave its territory, the Israelis felt, rightly or wrongly, that a war was imminent and that preventive or preemptive actions had to be taken forthwith. At that point, war became almost a certainty.

IV

In any international crisis, if one party is determined to use physical force as a means of resolving an anticipated or actual critical situation, and if this decision is based on a careful weighing of chances and consequences, the prospect of a peaceful resolution of the conflict would approach zero. Only a superior force could deter or defeat such an aggressive action.

What we are proposing are behavior patterns that would minimize the possibility of war in a crisis situation. Obviously, we do not believe that the transition from crisis to war is inevitable or beyond human management. The June 1914 Sarajevo crisis escalated to war; the October 1962 Cuban missile crisis did not. When compared with the 1914 crisis, the 1962 crisis seems to be characterized by a longer time for negotiation, a variety of alternatives, and better communications (Holsti et al., 1969: 62-79). In order to manage any crisis peacefully, then, a state should improve communications, retain alternatives, and extend the negotiation time. Any action that would obstruct or reduce communications, foreclose options, or precipitate decisions should be avoided.

In handling an international crisis, decision-makers should not attempt to use it to solidify their own domestic support. Domestic public opinion, when sufficiently aroused, may restrict the rational options of policy-makers. Only between rational parties is a transition from crisis to normalcy possible.

NOTES

1. In a survey of world events in 1966, using the New York *Times* as the sole source, McClelland and Hoggart (1969) divided international interactions into the following three groups:

	Percent
Cooperation	33
Participation	35.5
Conflict	31.5

When conflict, cooperation, and participation are considered in terms of the verbal and physical actions distinction, the distribution is as follows:

	Percent
Verbal cooperation	24.2
Cooperative actions	8.8
Verbal participation	17.4
Participatory actions	18.0
Defensive/Reactive verbal conflict	7.7
Offensive verbal conflict	16.4
Conflict actions	7.5

2. During the Vietnam War, President Johnson offered North Vietnam the so-called San Antonio Formula on September 29, 1967. He stated:

The United States is willing to stop all aerial and naval bombardment of North Vietnam when this leads promptly to productive discussion. We, of course, assume that while discussions proceed, North Vietnam would not take advantage of the bombing cessation or limitation.

Roger Fisher believes that this was not a concise formula about which North Vietnam could make a yes or no decision, mainly because the terms "promptly" and "productive" are ambiguous. In his view, a clearer signal tying up the cessation of bombing, reduction of fighting, and the onset of negotiations would have been preferable. He would have had a neutral party send an invitation to the two Vietnamese governments, the National Liberation Front, and the United States requesting them to implement a general reduce-fire (to include a cessation of all major offensive military action, including a cessation of the bombing and other armed attacks against North Vietnam) at a fixed time and designate a representative to attend the meeting immediately following to consider a general cease-fire and to implement the Geneva Accords of 1954. While there is no guarantee that North Vietnam would have responded positively to such a formula, he asserted it would have been much easier to solicit a yes or no answer from the North Vietnamese (Fisher, 1969: 24ff.).

3. President Kennedy, quoted in Holsti et al. (1969: 74ff.).

CHAPTER 13

VIEWS FROM DIPLOMATIC PRACTICE

ROBERTO de O. CAMPOS
NIELS HANSEN

I

The difficulty for a diplomat to approach a discussion with political scientists, who talk a lot about the simulation of conflictual positions, options, and responses, is that diplomats are trained not for simulation but for dissimulation. I would not go quite as far as Kissinger, who said that successful diplomacy (and crisis management, for that matter) are a mixture of secrecy, surprise, and ambiguity. I think there is some truth in that but would prefer to use the complicated formula suggested by Professor Laponce: CCCCMMUHH.

Perhaps too much attention is given to crisis management and too little attention to crisis prevention. I think that here lies the crucial subject of our times: How to help in preventing crisis? I would make three observations on that score:

(1) The first is that a great deal of the "crisis-proneness" of our societies derives from the fact that altogether too many people interpret conflicts as zero-sum games, when to a very large extent conflicts may be or can be made to become positive-sum games. The idea that conflicts are basically zero-sum games is present both in the East-West confrontation and in the North-South debate.

In the East-West debate there is perhaps a psychological reason for this difficulty of understanding. One not irrelevant consideration is that the Russian national sport is chess. Chess playing is a particularly cruel game: You can win, lose, or have a *draw,* but there are not those intermediate gradations of satisfaction that you can have for instance in a soccer game, in which you can lose a number of games but gain by goal average, or gain a half-time, or redeem the team through a beautiful goal. Chess is a cruel game, and when you are defeated, even the terminology is rather brutish: checkmate. This creates—or favors at least—an unconscious perception of a number of international debates and conflicts as being zero-sum games.

In the North-South dialogue, which might better be called the T and T debate, because it is really a dialogue between temperate and tropical zones—most of the underdeveloped areas of the world being in the North and not the South—there is yet another syndrome. Because quite a few of the now underdeveloped countries suffered exploitation and dependency, they nurture an "adversary" complex. They seem to be imbued with a "reparations" mentality. Thus they often insist on reaching for unilateral advantages, even when this is not really a practical goal, instead of being satisfied with smaller concessions that are practical and feasible. Their presentation of claims in the guise of reparations for past imperialist exploitation is sometimes unrealistic because donor countries do not like to acknowledge, or be reminded of, their guilt. Nations never learn from history or even from experience. They only learn by fatigue. There is no gainsaying that the more we think of international conflicts as capable of becoming positive-sum games, the better off we are in preventing conflicts and eventually in banishing them.

(2) Perhaps a second rule would be for the states having a conflictual relationship to try to state clearly their real objectives rather than simply reasserting their core values and insisting on symbolic ritual presentations. When a state has to formulate its objectives explicitly, it must endeavor to rationalize them and thus to mold its core values into a a more pragmatic and negotiable framework. The mere counterpointing of core values—themselves rigid concepts—makes the process of mutual understanding extremely difficult. A clear statement of objectives would therefore be helpful in all types of conflicts.

We have first, however, to accept as facts of life two qualifications. First, no nation is ever going to be perfectly honest and frank about its objectives. There is, inherent in affairs of state, a certain amount of constructive dissimulation. Some national objectives are likely to remain unavowed. Second, the law of entropy in relation to objectives appears to be at work not only in the physical but also in the political world. National priorities, like anything else, are subject to entropy, and this has to be recognized. Sometimes the entropy of objectives—that is, the degradation of purposiveness and vigor—is a very fast process. In the Vietnam case, for instance, the United States initially insisted on retaining a South Vietnam completely independent from the North, trying to repeat history, to repeat the Korean experience in a different context. Later, as the war fatigue corroded the national fabric, American policy reconciled itself to a much more modest objective—a decent coalition government. In the final days, the entropy had worked to such an extent that Kissinger was quite content to have just a "decent interval" before the inevitable take-over by the more ideologically vigorous Northern communists.

We have a bit of the same phenomenon in revolutionary Iran: The initial objective, after the taking of the hostages, was to have the Shah extradited in order to face public humiliation and physical punishment, in addition to recapturing his wealth and properties. Death eventually took care of the aim of physical elimination, so the objectives were downgraded simply to the insistence on recapturing the Shah's wealth. Since there are forms of property that are difficult to trace, the objective was subsequently further downgraded to obtaining some commitment for the devolution of properties, if and when identified, plus the immediate unblocking of unofficial assets. So much for the law of the degradation of objectives. It remains true, however, that the statement of national objectives is a very important element in crisis prevention, for the very effort of spelling them out requires an exercise in rationalization.

—*Roberto de O. Campos*

II

Before dealing with this subject, let me try to answer very briefly the general question regarding the impact of political science on "practitioners" and their decision-making. To be candid, I do not think this impact is really relevant. This may be due to the fact that practitioners are quite often not familiar enough with the specific research done by political scientists. At the same time, though, some doubt is in order as to whether the simulations applied by political scientists can in fact cover all the essential circumstances—and constraints—facing those who actually have to make far-reaching political decisions.

One of the axioms put forward in the preceding chapters is that we should keep lines of communication open during crisis situations. In principle, I agree. This might become somewhat problematic, however, once a clear distinction is drawn between an aggressor and the victim of aggression—a pertinent example being the events of 1938 and 1939. There are cases, indeed, where to continue communication really plays into the hands of the party at fault, enhancing even its respectability. As was demonstrated in 1980, the maintenance of East-West contacts proved quite difficult because it was considered important to avoid giving the impression that the occupation of Afghanistan was merely an "accident de route" and a case of "business as usual." As a consequence, one of the measures taken was to discontinue certain contacts.

It is useful, we think, to differentiate between genuine crisis management on the one hand, and on the other, routine contacts (such as those instituted within the framework of the U.S.-Soviet agreements of 1973/74, setting up a network of bilateral commissions in various fields). The former type of contact should be maintained, and I should like to note here as an example the Moscow talks of Chancellor Schmidt and of Foreign Minister Genscher in the summer of 1980.

A basic difficulty in crisis management arises if the parties concerned do not proceed from a common sense of values and from a set of agreed-upon rules. This is particularly true, of course, in the East-West context. Evidently, just talking is not enough. Giscard's Warsaw meeting with Brezhnev in July 1980, having achieved no tangible results, may even have contributed to a hardening of positions.

In democratic societies, special difficulties stem from the obvious fact that our governments have to react not only to the perception of their decisions abroad, but also at home. Within the Atlantic Alliance, signals to the other side must be the subject of prior consultation. At times, doing so has proved rather complicated and resulted in slowing the decision-making process. This underlines the need, in certain circumstances, of appropriate contingency planning.

Communication and crisis management in a larger sense should have their prophylactic aspects as well. In order to avoid crises and to give the right signals, one must seek to influence the other side's thinking early enough. It seems important to induce moderation *before* certain actions are taken that are then liable to escalate from situations of rivalry into ones of conflict.

But let me broach this aspect within a broader context and cast into the debate the notion of confidence of which there is so much talk these days—mostly with a view to Confidence-Building Measures, the "CBMs." Here again, in considering the East-West relationship we must take into account differences of political culture. One must try, however, to build up confidence in spite of these differences. Otherwise, communication in time of crises will prove futile more often than not.

Let me add that crisis management should not only be a means to avoid war, a big East-West conflagration having become rather unlikely in the nuclear age anyhow. Crises can arise from any situation in which one party gains unilateral advantage, allowing it to "bully" others politically. In this context it seems extremely important to keep a balance, to maintain equilibrium—as a sort of precrisis management. This is called for not least in the military sphere, although we should not restrict the notion of security to weaponry and the like. It is here, in particular, that the problem of communication enters in a larger sense, in the sense of creating true confidence. Is it naive to demand that *all* parties be more candid with relevant information, e.g., in discussing military budgets?

As another example, I would mention the extension of the CBMs to the whole of Europe, as requested in the French proposal submitted to the CSCE. Should not all sides accept more far-reaching verification measures in arms control? This certainly would result in more confidence, and more confidence means fewer crises, more effective communication in crisis situations, and thus better management of emerging or continuing crises.

—*Niels Hansen*

ABSTRACTS/RÉSUMÉS

1
La prise de decision en situation de crise: L'approche informationnelle
Karl W. Deutsch

Une crise est définie comme une situation où une décision inéluctable sera prise dans un temps bref, par commission ou omission entre des résultats probables qui different beaucoup dans leur caractere et impliquent des valeurs importantes pour au moins l'un des participants. Ces différents résultats, valeurs, et émotions impliqués déterminent l'ampleur de la crise et la courte durée du temps disponible et son intensité. Du point de vue de la théorie de l'information classique privilégiant les canaux d'information, les décideurs dans une crise doivent décider sur la base d'une information limitée, qui les atteint par des canaux limités dans un temps limité, contaminée par du bruit et sélectionnée par des désirs, des peurs, de la rage et/ou une véritable misreprésentation par des institutions ou groupes intéressés. Plus la crise est intense et forte, et plus la recherche d'informations et les capacités de traitement du systéme décisionnel sont limités, plus il est possible que les décisions soient fausses. Si les capacités disponibles pour la recherche et le traitement de l'information sont grandes, alors une crise pourrait améliorer la recherche pour l'information et la qualité des décisions. Le manque de capacités adéquates tend à produire une surcharge d'information et des réactions faibles du fait des délais, omissions, erreurs plus fréquentes, stéréotypes, l'imposition de priorités, et un controle de rétro-action insuffisant. Ceci peut parfois avoir des conséquences désastreuses. Une théorie de l'information orientée sur le contenu de cette derniére comparerait le *sens* du message envoyé et recu, en termes des mémoires respectives de l'émetteur et du récepteur, mémoires qui peuvent différer. Cette approche génere dix questions pour les récepteurs d'un message, au sujet de son codage ou intelligibilité, sa source, son contexte, contenu, le fait qu'il soit agréable ou non, sa vérité, moralité, ses implications ses exigences pour l'action. Les memes questions s'appliquent aussi à l'émetteur du message, ce qui fait que les possibilités de malentendus, au sens combinatorial, sont grandes.

En conclusion, il est suggéré que les décisions de crises devraient être envisagées comme des occasions urgentes pour la recherche de l'information, que du temps devrait être gagné et les émotions non engagées autant que possible, enflammer l'opinion publique et rechercher des coupables devrait être évité, et il faudrait accorder plus d'attention aux processus cumulatifs de création de crises. Dans les crises internationales de l'âge des armes nucléaires, il devient moins important pour l'une ou l'autre des parties de l'emporter et plus important de trouver des solutions tolérables permettant á toutes les parties de survivre.

Crisis Decision-Making: The Information Approach

From the viewpoint of a classic, channel-oriented information theory, decision-makers in a crisis must act on the basis of limited information, reaching them through limited channels within a limited time, contaminated by noise, and selected by desires, fears, rage and/or outright misrepresentation by interested agencies or groups. The more intense and acute the crisis, and the more limited the information search and processing capacities of the decision-making system, the more decisions are likely to be wrong.

If the available capacities for information search and processing are ample, a crisis may improve the search for information and the quality of decisions. The lack of adequate capacities tends to produce information overload and responses beset with delays, omissions, more frequent errors, stereotyping, imposition of priorities, and insufficient feedback control, sometimes with disastrous consequences.

A content-oriented information theory would compare the *meaning* of the message sent and received in terms of the respective memories of sender and receiver, which may be different. This approach generates ten questions by the receivers of a message about its coding or intelligibility, source, context, content, pleasurability, truth, morality, implications for self-respect, compatibility with plans, and requirements for action. The same questions also apply to the sender of the message, so that the combinatorial possibilities of misunderstandings are large.

In conclusion, it is suggested that the making of crisis decisions should be treated as urgent occasions for information search, that time should be gained and emotions disengaged as much as possible, inflaming mass opinion and hostile searches for culprits avoided, and cumulative crisis-creating processes given more attention.

2

Le management de conflits internationaux: Donnés sur des experiences sur le terrain et en laboratoire
Jean A. Laponce

L'application de données obtenues par la méthode expérimentale—de type in vivo ou expérimentale—à l'étude du controle des conflits internationaux. Deux types de données sont retenues comme valables: celles qui simulent les relations interétatiques et celles qui cherchent à isoler les mécanismes de surchauffe et d'appaisement de conflits autres qu'internationaux. Les données recueillies sont groupées sous quatre rubriques principales: la communication, la compétition, la coopération et le conflit.

Managing International Conflicts: Evidence from Field and Laboratory Experiments

An examination of in vivo and laboratory experiments relevant to the managing of international conflicts. The evidence is obtained from simulations intended to model interstate relations, as well as from games and experiments that sought to bare the mechanisms of tension building and tension reduction in fields other than that of international politics. Four main factors are considered: communication, competition, cooperation, and conflict.

3

Les structures de la pensée de crises internationales: Une analyse des milieux gouvernementaux en Allemagne, 1866-1914
Vadim B. Lukov
Victor M. Sergeev

En se basant sur des cas de crises internationales aigues du 19eme et du début de 20ème siècle (la guerre Franco-Prussienne de 1870, les crises d'avant-guerre de 1914), les auteurs analysent la structure et la dynamique de perception de situations de crises par leurs participants. Une technique d'analyse de pensée politique est suggérée, qui est une extension et un dévelopement de la méthode de "cognitive-mapping." Ils décrivent l'évolution de la pensée des protagonistes de la politique étrangère allemande: Bismarck, Bülow, Bethmann-Hollweg, et Wilhelm II. Ils suggérent une technique de simulation par ordinateur du modèle formel de pensée et quelques résultats d'une telle simulation sont discutés. Ils discutent les critères d'évaluation des modèles de pensée: niveau enthropique de l'entourage, nombres d'options possibles, probabilité d'atteindre le but. Une typologie possible de la pensée politique bourgeoise est suggérée, qui est basée sur la pensée de marionettes, d'expansionistes et de modèles de crises et de status-quo. Ils spécifient les principales particularités de chaque modèle. Ils tirent des conclusions sur: (1) la nature de l'influence des modèles de pensée politique sur le procés d'interaction de crises; et (2) l'importance et les possibilités de prendre en considération les modèles de pensée politique pour trouver une solution couronnée de succés aux crises internationales.

Patterns of Crisis Thinking: An Analysis of the Governing Circles in Germany, 1866-1914

Based on cases of acute international crises of the nineteenth and early twentieth centuries (the Franco-Prussian war of 1870, the prewar crisis of 1914), the authors analyze the structure and dynamics of perception of crisis situations by their participants. A technique of analysis of political thinking is suggested which is an extension and development of the cognitive mapping method. The evolution of thinking of German foreign policy makers is described: Bismarck, Bülow, Bethmann-Hollweg, and Wilhelm II. A technique for computer simulation of the formal models of thinking is suggested, and some results of such a simulation are discussed. Criteria for evaluating the patterns of political thinking are discussed, e.g., environment entropy level, number of possible options, and goal attainment probability. A possible typology of bourgeois political thinking is suggested based on puppet, expansionist, crisis, and status quo patterns of thinking. Principal features of each pattern are specified. Conclusions are drawn concerning: (1) the nature of the impact of political thinking patterns on the process of crisis interaction; and (2) the importance and possibilities of taking into account the patterns of political thinking for successful solutions of international crises.

4

Communications et crise: Un plan préliminaire
John Meisel

Ce chapitre explore la manière dont les médias (imprimés et électroniques) interprétent et affectent les crises internationales. La couverture des événement est déterminée par plusieurs ensembles de variables: les caractéristiques de la crise elle-même, en liaison avec la nature des conditions socio-politiques des différents pays où les nouvelles et l'information sont produites; la structure économique des organisations des médias; et enfin, les conditions technologiques et professionnelles. Le chapitre conclut en suggérant plusieurs possibilités pour les approches empiriques de l'étude des communications et des crises.

Communications and Crisis: A Preliminary Mapping

This chapter explores the way in which print and electronic media interpret and affect international crises. The coverage of events is shaped by several sets of variables: the characteristics of the crisis itself; the nature of sociopolitical conditions of various countries where news and information are produced; the economic structure of media organizations; and the technological and professional "state of the art." The chapter concludes by suggesting a number of possibilities for empirical approaches to the study of communications and crises.

5

Evénements improbables et comportement attendu
Richard L. Merritt

Les approches traditionnelles de la recherche sur les crises posent des séveres problèmes analytiques, en particulier l'absence totale de données sur la relation entre le stress organisationnel et le stress psychologique auxquels sont soumis les décideurs de l'organisation considérée. Une approche probabiliste envisage les crises dans le contexte plus large d'une recherche de solutions qui examine la probabilité que certaines classes de problèmes vont survenir. Ce point de vue a plusieurs implications. Premièrement, la plupart des problèmes internationaux auxquels sont confrontés les preneurs de décisions nationaux arrivent assez fréquemment et régulièrement de telle manière qu'ils peuvent développer des procédures d'opérations standard pour les traiter. Deuxièmement, quand des problèmes trop peu fréquents (pour que le système de décision ait développé suffisamment d'expérience et de procédures de routine pour les traiter) se produisent, la modélisation et la simulation peuvent être utiles (surtout pour l'apprentissage du comment apprendre durant une situation de crise). Troisièmement, les décideurs nationaux devraient encourager chez eux le développement de structures de comportement à long terme qui minimiseraient tout risque de déviation de la prise de décision efficace. Quatrièmement, puisque la norme internationale est la résolution pacifique des disputes, les décideurs peuvent, accroitre la portée de cette norme par des politiques qui aident à stabiliser les attentes au sujet du comportement d'acteurs nationaux dans l'arène internationale.

Improbable Events and Expectable Behavior

Traditional approaches to crisis research pose severe analytic problems, not the least important of which is the virtual absence of data on the relationship between organizational stress and psychological stress on the organization's decision-makers. A probabilistic approach views crises in a broader problem-solving framework that examines the probability that certain classes of problems will arise. This viewpoint has several implications. First, most international problems facing national decision-makers occur sufficiently frequently and regularly that they can develop standard operating procedures for dealing with them. Second, when problems arise which occur too infrequently for the decision system to have developed stores of experience and routinized procedures for dealing with them, modeling and simulation can be important (especially in learning how to learn during a crisis situation). Third, national decision-makers should encourage the development of long-term behavioral patterns at home that minimize any risk of deflecting effective decision-making. Fourth, since the international norm is peaceful resolution of disputes, decision-makers can expand the scope of that norm through policies that help stabilize expectations about the behavior of national actors in the international arena.

6
La crise du Moyen Orient: Propositions théoriques et examples
Ali E. Hillal Dessouki

Cette étude recherche l'applicabilité de quelque propositions concernant la direction des crises de 1967 et 1973 du Moyen Orient. Elle souligne la différence entre la direction des crises et la résolution des crises, et suggère que quelques états peut poursuivre "La crise comme ligne de conduite." Cette étude examine quatre dimensions de la conduite des états dans une situation de crise: moyens de traiter la perception de menace de l'adversaire, l'importance de la communication avec le superpower allié, la perception de "closure of options," et les dangers des experiences anterieures.

The Middle East Crisis: Theoretical Propositions and Examples

This chapter examines the applicability of some common propositions in the crisis management literature on the 1967 and 1973 Middle East crises. It underlines the difference between crisis management and crisis resolution and suggests that some states may pursue "crisis as a policy." The chapter investigates four dimensions of state behavior in crisis situations: ways of dealing with the adversary's perception of threat, the importance of communication with the superpower ally, the perception of "closure of options," and the dangers of past experience.

7

Evaluer le risque d'un conflit nucléaire involontaire
Daniel Frei

La course aux armements actuelle accroit le cauchemar d'une crise qui pourrait dégénérer en conflit nucléaire; même si aucun gouvernement ne désire une telle guerre ou ne projette délibérément d'en déclencher une. C'est un souci grandissant que dans des conditions de crises des accidents nucléaires et des incidents, des fautes fatales ou des difficultés d'interprétation puissent être le détonateur d'un holocauste nucléaire. Comment évaluer ce risque? En examinant toutes les informations acquises, les auteurs arrivent à la conclusion que le danger d'accident est seulement une cause mineure d'inquiétude. Des risques bien plus serieux émergent dans la tendance du système stratégique à devenir instable; car dans les conditions qui poussent à être le premier à prendre l'initiative d'utiliser les forces nucléaires, l'assaillant à l'avantage. La tendance à l'instabilité stratégique, doublée d'une crise internationale aigüe, constitue un danger réel, car en cas de crise, des incompréhensions, de mauvaises interprétations, des fautes de calculs, et autres sortes d'erreurs peuvent engendrer le procédé de prendre la décision de déclencher l'effet détonateur. Bien qu'actuellement les risques respectifs soient plutôt minimes, le danger s'accroit si la course aux armements n'est pas freinée et si la politique de force n'est pas maitrisée.

Escalation: Assessing the Risk of Unintentional Nuclear War

The current arms race has given rise to nightmares of a crisis escalating into nuclear war even though no government may want such a war or plans deliberately to unleash one. There is a growing concern that nuclear accidents and incidents, or fatal mistakes, or misunderstandings under conditions of crisis might trigger a nuclear holocaust. How is this risk to be assessed? Examining all information available, the author concludes that the danger of accidents is only a minor cause of concern. More serious risks loom in the tendency of the strategic system to become unstable, i.e., in conditions in which there are incentives to initiate the use of strategic nuclear forces because the side launching a preemptive strike gains a decisive advantage. The tendency toward strategic instability, coupled with an acute international crisis, constitutes a serious danger because in a crisis misunderstandings, misinterpretations, miscalculations, and other kinds of mistakes may occur in the process of decision-making, thus having a triggering effect. Although at the present moment the respective risks are rather small, the danger will continue to grow rapidly unless the arms race is halted and the politics of force tamed.

8

Pratiques de sécurité collective depuis 1945
Hayward R. Alker, Jr.
Frank L. Sherman

Une reconceptualisation des études empiriques Nord-américaines sur les conflits et le management de crises est nécessaire si elles doivent (1) surmonter les critiques de leurs méthodologies positivistes, (2) considérer sérieusement l'épistémologie de la recherche sur la paix marxiste, (3) traiter, d'une manière dynamique, la pertinence changeante de telles approches pour les pratiques de management de la sécurité nationale, et (4) produire des résultats de recherche véritablement cumulatifs et pertinents pratiquement. Un tel programme de recherche et proposé et illustré. Une grande correspondance conceptuelle entre les typologies de guerre et de crises de Butterworth et de Kende est démontrée empiriquement, malgré les divergences dans leurs orientations paradigmatiques et les vastes différences quantitatives dans leurs univers de crises/guerres aprés 1945. Une grande (mais en baisse) fraction des crises internationales n'est pas du tout gérée internationalement; le management de conflits tend à être plus préoccupé avec les phases d'hostilité qu'avec des fonctions préventives ou de résolution des conflits. Des nouvelles voies de réflexion au sujet des précédents de management de crises, des systèmes pour la sécurité, et leur évolution sont proposées.

Collective Security-Seeking Practices Since 1945

A reconceptualization of North American empirical studies of conflict and crisis management by international organizations is necessary if they are to (1) overcome critiques of their positivistic methodologies, (2) take seriously the epistemology of Marxist peace research, (3) dynamically handle the shifting relevance of such bodies to national security management practices, and (4) produce practically relevant, genuinely cumulative research findings. Such a research program is proposed and illustrated. Considerable conceptual correspondence between Butterworth and Kende typologies of wars and crises are empirically demonstrated despite the divergences in their paradigmatic orientations and the vast quantitative differences in their post-1945 crisis/war universes. A large but declining fraction of international crises is not internationally managed at all; conflict management tends to be preoccupied more with hostility phases than preventive or resolutional functions. New ways of thinking about management precedents, security-seeking systems, and their evolution are proposed.

9
Le système des Nations-Unies:
Transformation structurelle et crise
Kinhide Mushakoji

Dans l'actuelle situation internationale, les superpuissances commencent à perdre leur capacité à fournir un cadre assurant la stabilité et la sécurité. Le rapport présente un schéma conceptuel destiné a permettre l'étude des possibilités existant dans le système international au cas ou les grandes puissances n'exercessient pas leur fonction de gestion des crises, et notamment du rôle que pourraient alors jouer les Nations Unies. Il analyse d'autre part les aspects structurels et fonctionnels de la transformation du système international actuellement en cours. Le rapport suggère en fin de nouvelles modalités de gestion des crises répondant aux exigences institutionnelles des aspects structurels et fonctionnels de cette transformation, ainsi qu'un role nouveau pour le système des Nations Unies.

The UN System: Structural Transformation
and Crisis

In the present world setting, the superpowers are beginning to lose their capacity to provide a framework for stability and security. The present chapter proposes a conceptual scheme to study what alternatives exist in the international system in the event that the major powers fail to exercise their crisis management functions. Special attention is paid to the role the United Nations could play in such a case. The structural and functional aspects of the contemporary system transformation that is taking place are discussed. New means of crisis management meeting the institutional requirements of the structure and functional aspects of the contemporary process of transformation are suggested and a new role for the UN system is proposed.

10
Pays non-alignés dans le conflit
Radovan Vukadinović

La dynamique de l'éruption des conflits montre que pendant la période ou la tension bipolaire se relachait, et quand le mouvement non-aligné se développait, les disputes entre pays non-alignés s'accroissaient, certaines d'entre elles étant résolues par la force des armes. En essayant de trouver une typologie des causes de l'éruption des conflits, l'auteur mentionne les facteurs suivants: questions territoriales et de frontières non résolues, différences idéologiques et politiques, la présence des superpuissances. Plutôt les instruments de solution pacifique seront-ils mis sur pied, plus cela va-t-il accélérer le renforcement général des pays non-alignés ainsi que leur action commune dans les relations internationales.

Nonaligned Countries in Conflict

The dynamics of the eruption of conflicts show that during the period when bipolar tension relaxed and the nonaligned movement was developing, disputes between nonaligned countries became more frequent, with some of them being settled by force. In search of a typology of causes for the outbreak of conflict, the author includes the following factors: unsettled frontier and territorial questions, ideological and political differences, and the presence of the superpowers. The sooner that instruments are set up for a peaceful solution, the more this will accelerate a general strengthening of the nonaligned countries and their common action in international relations.

11

Crise systematique: Lessons de détente regionale
Kari Möttölä

L'auteur donne une analyse du système Est-Ouest de détente en Europe en indiquant trois variables-cadre: la bipolarité, la stabilité et la coopération. La stabilité a des dimensions à la fois politiques et militaires: l'équilibre militaire et la légitimité des deux systèmes sociaux. Il semble y avoir une absence de crises internationales dans ce système régional. Le système global est différent. Il est de plus en plus multipolaire et les suites de crises internationales sont ambigues et imprévisibles. Le système global est instable: il n'y a pas de consensus sur le *status quo* politique et la légitimité des systèmes est faible. L'équilibre militaire est plus difficile a déterminer et a maintenir. Pour ce qui concerne la coopération fonctionnelle, il n'y a pas de régle de comportement fixes ni de résultats dans la redistribution des richesses qui satisferait les attentes. Dans cette analyse comparative, le système global est dénommé détente imparfaite. En conclusion, l'auteur esquisse des réformes possibles du système international qui aideraient au management, a la prévention et a la solution de crises internationales. Il suggère aussi une division du travail possible parmi les différents niveaux d'acteurs pour ces mesures.

Systemic Crisis: Lessons of Regional Détente

The author gives an analysis of the East-West system of détente in Europe by pointing to three framework variables: bipolarity, stability, and cooperation. Stability has both political and military dimensions: military balance and the legitimacy of the two social systems. The global system is unstable; there is no consensus on the political status quo, and the legitimacy of regimes is weak. Military balance is more difficult to determine and maintain. As far as functional cooperation is concerned, there are no fixed rules of behavior nor any truly satisfying results in the redistribution of wealth. In this comparative analysis, the global system is called one of imperfect détente. In the end, the author outlines possible reforms of the international system that would help in managing, preventing, and solving international crises. He also suggests a possible division of labor of these measures among the different actor levels.

12

Suggestions pratiques pour le management de crises internationales: Un inventaire

King-Yuh Chang

Ce chapitre est un essai de faire un tour d'horizon de la littérature sur les crises internationales et leur management, l'attention principale étant portée sur les recommandations pour le comportement diplomatique en vue du management de crises internationales. A fin d'obtenir une solution pacifique aux crises, les types de comportement en politique étrangère qui suivent sont considérés désirables: maintenir les lignes de communication ouvertes et les communications spécifiques; traiter le conflit comme un conflit d'intérets et non de principes; solliciter l'intervention de parties tierces; négliger les actions provocatives; fractionner le conflit et diminuer la crise; et finalement, si la guerre est inévitable, employer la force prudemment, avec fléxibilité et controle de soi. De plus, les comportements qui suivent devraient être évités: faire des ultimatums; menacer les éléments essentiels du système de valeurs de l'opposant; mélanger des principes moraux avec le conflit d'intérets; et pousser l'autre partie au-dela de certaines limites et/ou utiliser la force.

Practical Suggestions for Managing

International Crises: An Inventory

This chapter is an attempt to survey the literature on international crises and crisis management with the primary focus on guidelines for diplomatic behavior involving international crisis management. In order to manage a crisis peacefully, the following types of foreign policy behavior are considered desirable; keeping communications channels open and communications specific; treating the dispute as a conflict of interest, not of principle; soliciting third party involvement; disregarding provocative actions; fractionating the conflict in order to diffuse the crisis; and finally, if war is unavoidable, employing force wisely, with flexibility and self-control. In addition, the following behavior should be avoided: issuing ultimatums; threatening the core of the opponent's value system; mixing moral principles with conflicts of interest; and pressuring the other party beyond certain limits and/or using force.

BIBLIOGRAPHY

ABU-LUGHOT, I. [ed.] (1970) The Arab-Israeli Confrontation of June 1967. Evanston, IL: Northwestern University Press.

ALGER, C. F. (1970) "Research on research: a decade of quantitative and field research on international organizations." International Organization 24 (Summer): 414-450.

—— (1965) "Personal contact in intergovernmental organizations," pp. 521-548 in R. C. Kelman (ed.) International Behavior. New York: Holt, Rinehart & Winston.

ALKER, H. R. Jr. (1981) "Dialectical foundations of global disparities." International Studies Quarterly 25 (March): 69-98.

—— (1979) "Logic, dialectics and politics." Presented at the IPSA World Congress, Moscow.

—— (1975) "Politometrics," pp. 139-210 in F. Greenstein and N. Polsby (eds.) Handbook of Political Science, Vol. 7. Reading, MA: Addison-Wesley.

—— and C. CHRISTENSEN (1972) "From causal modelling to artificial intelligence: the evaluation of a UN peace-making situation," pp. 177-225 in J. Laponce and P. Smoker (eds.) Experimentation and Simulation in Political Science. Toronto: The University of Toronto Press.

—— and W. J. GREENBERG (1971) "The UN Charter: alternative pasts and alternative futures," pp. 113-142 in E. H. Fedder (ed.) "The United Nations: Problems and Prospects." Saint Louis: Center of International Studies, University of Missouri.

ALKER, H. R. Jr., J. BENNET, and D. MEFFORD (1980) "Generalized disparities." International Interactions 7: 165-206.

AOI, K. [ed.] (1974) Rirou Shakaigaku (Theoretical Sociology). Tokyo.

APUNEN, O. [ed.] (1981a) "Detente—a framework for action and analysis." Research Reports 61: Institute for Political Science, University of Tampere.

—— (1981b) "Legitimation patterns of foreign military presence." Current Research on Peace and Violence 2.

—— (1977) "Non-use of force: a strategy for peace in the nuclear age." Cooperation and Conflict 3: 171-187.

ARBATOV, G. (n.d.) Détente and Problems of Conflict.

ARCHIBALD, K. [ed.] (1966) Strategic Interaction and Conflict. Berkeley: Institute of International Studies, University of California.

ARON, R. (1976) Penser la Guerre: Clausewitz, 2 vols. Paris: Gallimard.

AXELROD, R. (1980a) "Effective choice in the PD." Journal of Conflict Resolution 24: 3-25.

—— (1980b) "More effective choice in the prisoner's dilemma." Journal of Conflict Resolution 24: 379-403.

—— [ed.] (1976) Structure of Decision. Princeton, NJ: Princeton University Press.

AZAR, E. E. and S. P. COHEN (1979) "Peace as crisis and war as status-quo: the Arab-Israeli conflict environment." International Interactions 6: 159-184.

AZAR, E. E. and T. J. SLOAN (1975) Dimensions of Internation: A Sourcebook for the Study of Behavior of 31 Nations from 1948 through 1973. Pittsburgh: International Studies Association.

BACK, K. W. (1951) "Influence through social communication." Journal of Abnormal and Social Psychology 46.

BELL, C. (1971) Conventions of Crisis. London: Oxford University Press.

BERKOWITZ, L. (1957) "Effects of perceived dependency relationships upon conformity to group expectations." Journal of Abnormal and Social Psychology 56.

BISMARCK, O. von (1940/1941) Thoughts and Reminiscences. Moscow.

BLAKE, R. R. and J. S. MOUTON (1962a) "Overevaluation of own group's product in intergroup competition." Journal of Abnormal and Social Psychology 61.

————— (1962b) "Comprehension of points of community in competing solutions." Sociometry 25.

BLECHMAN, B. M. and S. KAPLAN (1978) Force Without War: U.S. Armed Forces as a Political Instrument. Washington, DC: Brookings Institution.

BLOOM, B. (1966) "Definitional aspects of the crisis concept," in H. J. Parad (ed.) Crisis Intervention. New York: Family Service Association of America.

BLOOMFIELD, L. P. and A. C. LEISS (1969) Controlling Small Wars: A Strategy for the 1970s. New York: Knopf.

BOULDING, K. (1966) "Conflict management as a learning process," in A. de Reuck (ed.) Conflict in Society. London: Churchill.

————— (1962) Conflict and Defense. New York: Harper & Row.

BOYLE, F. A. (1980) "International law in times of crisis: from the Entebbe raid to the hostages convention." Northwestern University Law Review 75 (December): 769-856.

BRECHER, M. [ed.] (1979a) Studies in Crisis Behavior. New Brunswick, NJ: Transaction Books.

————— (1979b) "State behavior in international crisis." Journal of Conflict Resolution 23 (September): 446-481.

BREMER, S. A. (1981) "The GLOBUS Project: overview and update." Discussion paper IIVG/dp 81-109 of the International Institute for Comparative Social Research, Science Center of Berlin (March), mimeograph.

BRODY, R. (1963) "Some system effects of the spread of nuclear weapons technology." Journal of Conflict Resolution 7: 663-753.

BRZEZINSKI, Z. (1982) "The failed mission." The New York Times Magazine, April 18, pp. 28-31.

BURNS, T. (1980) "Sovereignty, interests and bureaucracy in the modern state." The British Journal of Sociology 4 (December): 491-506.

BUTTERWORTH, R. L. (n.d.) "Managing interstate conflict, 1975-79." (unpublished)

————— (1978a) Moderation from Management: International Organizations and Peace. Pittsburgh: University Center for International Studies.

————— (1978b) "Do conflict managers matter?" International Studies Quarterly 22 (June): 195-214.

————— and M. E. SCRANTON (1976) Managing Interstate Conflict 1945-74: Data with Synopses. Pittsburgh: University Center for International Studies.

CAPLOW, T. (1968) Two Against One: Coalitions in Triad. Englewood Cliffs, NJ: Prentice-Hall.

————— (1959) "Further development of a theory of coalitions in a triad." American Journal of Sociology: 488-493.

——— (1956) "A theory of coalition formation." American Sociological Review 21: 489-493.

CAPPELLO, H. (1972) "International tension as a function of reduced communication," pp. 39-46 in J. A. Laponce and P. Smoker (eds.) Experimentation and Simulation in Political Science. Toronto: University of Toronto Press.

CHOUCRI, N. and R. C. NORTH (1972) "Dynamics of international conflicts: some policy implications on population, resources and technology." World Politics 24: 80-122.

CIOFFI-REVILLA, C. A. (1979) "Diplomatic communication theory: signals, channels, networks." International Interactions 6: 209-265.

CLAUDE, I. L. Jr. (1964) Swords into Ploughshares: The Problems and Progress of International Organizations, 3rd ed. New York: Random House.

CLOSE, P. M. (1979) "The principle of uncertainty as an integrative concept in international crisis research." International Interactions 5: 331-350.

COHEN, R. (1979) Threat Perception in International Crisis. Madison: The University of Wisconsin Press.

COLEMAN, J. S. (1957) Community Conflict. Glencoe, IL: Free Press.

Congressional Research Service (1981) Soviet Policy and United States Response in the Third World. Report prepared for the Committee on Foreign Affairs, U.S. House of Representatives, Washington, DC.

CUSACK, T. and W.-D. EBERWEIN (1980) A Descriptive Analysis of Serious International Disputes During the Twentieth Century. IIVG Discussion Paper 80-116. Berlin: IIVG.

DAHRENDORF, R. (1979) Life Chances. Chicago: University of Chicago Press.

DARWIN, C. R. (1936) On the Origins of Species. New York: Modern Library.

DAVIES, J. C. (1980) "Biological perspectives on human conflict," in T. R. Gurr (ed.) Handbook of Political Conflict. New York: Free Press.

DEUTSCH, K. W. (1975) "On the learning capacity of large political systems," pp. 61-83 in M. Kochen (ed.) Information for Action: From Knowledge to Wisdom. New York: Academic Press.

——— (1966) "Power and communication in international society," in A. de Reuck (ed.) Conflict in Society. London: Churchill.

——— (1963) The Nerves of Government: Models of Political Communication and Control. New York: Free Press.

——— et al. (1966) "Political community and the North Atlantic area," in A. de Reuck (ed.) Conflict in Society. London: Churchill.

DEUTSCH, K. W., S. BURRELL, et al. (1957) Political Community and the North Atlantic Area: International Organization in the Light of Historical Experience. Princeton, NJ: Princeton University Press.

DEUTSCH, M. (1973) "The effect of motivational orientation upon trust and suspicion. Human Relations 26: 123-140.

——— and R. M. KRAUSS (1962) "Studies of interpersonal bargaining." Journal of Conflict Resolution 6.

DEWAST, P. (1977) "Quelques aspects du statut des 'casques bleus.' " Revue générale de Droit international public 4: 1007-1046.

DRIVER, M. J. (1962) Conceptual Structure and Group Processes in an International Simulation. Princeton, NJ: Princeton University Press.

DROR, Y. (n.d.) "Nuclear weapons in Third World conflict." Adelphi Papers no. 161.

DUKES, P. (1970) The Emergence of the Superpowers: A Short Comparative History of the USA and the USSR. London: Macmillan.

EBERWEIN, W. -D. (1982) Militaerische Konfrontation und Eskalation zum Krieg: 1900-2000. IIVG Discussion Paper 81-112.

———— (1978) "Crisis research—the state of the art: a Western view," pp. 124-142 in D. Frei (ed.) International Crises and Crisis Management. New York: Praeger.

ECKHARDT, W. and E. AZAR (1979) "Major military conflicts, 1965-1979." Peace Research 2 (May): 201-207.

———— (1978) "Major world conflicts and interventions, 1945-1975." International Interactions 5: 75-110.

ECKSTEIN, H. (1980) "Theoretical approaches to explaining collective political violence," pp. 135-166 in T. R. Gurr (ed.) Handbook of Political Conflict. New York: Free Press.

ELSENHALS, H. (1979) "Counter-insurgency: the French war in Algeria," pp. 110-135 in M. Kaldor and A. Eide (eds.) The World Military Order: The Impact of Military Technology on the Third World. London: Macmillan.

EVRON, Y. (1973) The Middle East: Nations, Superpowers and War. New York: Program.

FALK, R. A. (1975) "Toward a new world order: modest methods and distinct wishes," in S. M. Mendlowitz (ed.) On the Creation of a Just World Model. Amsterdam: North Holland.

FARRIS, L., H. R. ALKER, K. CARLEY, and F. SHERMAN (1980) Phase/Actor Disaggregated Butterworth-Scranton Codebook. Working Paper, MIT Center for International Studies.

FERENCZ, B. (1975) Defining International Aggression: The Search for World Peace. 2 vols. Dobbs Ferry, NY: Oceana.

FISHER, R. (1969) International Conflict for Beginners. New York: Harper & Row.

FONTAINE, A. (1965/1967) Histoire de la Guerre Froide. 2 vols. Paris: Fayard.

FREI, D. (1982) The Risk of Unintentional Nuclear War. New York: United Nations Institute for Disarmament Research.

———— [ed.] (1978) International Crises and Crisis Management. New York: Praeger.

———— and D. RULOFF (1980) "Détente on record: applying social science measure techniques to East-West relations in Europe, 1957-1977." Weimar: IPSA Round Table.

GALTUNG, J. (1980) The True Worlds: A Transnational Perspective. New York: Free Press.

———— (1972) "A structural theory of imperialism." The African Review 4 (April): 93-123.

———— T. HEIESTAD, and E. RUGE (1979) On the Decline and Fall of Empires: The Roman Empire and Western Imperialism Compared. UNUP-53, UNU.

GAMSON, W. A. (1961) "A theory of coalition formation." American Sociological Review 26: 373-382.

GERARD, H. B. (1953) "The effect of different dimensions of disagreement on the communicative process in small groups." Human Relations 6: 313-325.

GILBERT, A. N. and P. G. LAUREN (1980) "Crisis management: an assessment and critique." Journal of Conflict Resolution 24: 641-664.

GOLDMANN, K. (1970) International Norms and War Between States. Stockholm: Laeromedelsforlogen.

GOTTHELF, E. (1955) "Changes in social perception contingent upon competing or cooperating." Sociometry 18: 132-137.

GROSSACK, M. (1954) "Some effects of cooperation and competition on small group behavior." Journal of Abnormal and Social Psychology 53: 341-348.

GUETZHOW, H. et al. (1963) Simulation in International Relations. Englewood Cliffs, NJ: Prentice-Hall.

GURVITCH, G. (1966) Les cadres sociaux de la connaissance. Paris: Bibliothèque de sociologie contemporaine.

———— (1955) Determinismes sociaux et liberté humaine. Paris: Bibliothèque de sociologie contemporaine.

HAAS, E. B. (1968) Collective Security and the Future Collective System. Denver: University of Denver Press.

—— (1964) Beyond the Nation State. Stanford: Stanford University Press.

—— (1962) "Dynamic environment and static system: revolutionary regimes in the United Nations," pp. 267-309 in M. A. Kaplan (ed.) The Revolution in World Politics. New York: John Wiley.

—— (1955) "Types of collective security: an explanation of operational concepts." American Political Science Review 40: 40-62.

—— R. L. BUTTERWORTH, and G. S. NYE (1972) Conflict Management by International Organizations. Morristown, NJ: General Learning Press.

HABERMAS, J. (1979) Communication and the Evolution of Society. Boston: Beacon Press.

HART, T. G. (1976) The Cognitive World of Swedish Elites. Stockholm: Esselte Studium.

HERMAN, C. F. [ed.] (1972) International Crises: Insights from Behavioral Research. New York: Free Press.

HILSMAN, R. (1967) To Move a Nation. New York: Dell.

HOCKEY, R. (1979) "Stress and the cognitive components of skilled performance," in V. Hamilton and D. F. Warburton (eds.) Human Stress and Cognition. Chichester: Wiley.

HOFFER, E. (1951) The True Believer: Thoughts on the Nature of Mass Movements. New York: Harper & Row.

HOHENZOLLERN, W. von (1923) Reminiscences. Moscow.

HOLSTI, K. J. (1977) International Politics: A Framework for Analysis. Englewood Cliffs, NJ: Prentice-Hall.

—— (1972) International Politics. Englewood Cliffs, NJ: Prentice-Hall.

—— (1966) "Resolving international conflicts: a taxonomy of behavior and some figures on procedures." Journal of Conflict Resolution 10: 272-296.

HOLSTI, O. R. (1980) "Historians, social scientists and crisis management." Journal of Conflict Resolution 24: 665-682.

—— (1979) "Theories of crisis decision-making," pp. 99-137 in P. Lauren (ed.) Diplomacy. London: Macmillan.

—— (1971) Crisis, Escalation, War. Montreal: McGills-Queen's University Press.

—— (1965) "The 1914 case." American Political Science Review 59: 365-378.

—— A. BRODY, and R. C. NORTH (1969) "The management of international crisis: Affect and action in American-Soviet relations, October 1962," pp. 62-80 in D. G. Pruitt and R. C. Snyder (ed.) Theory and Research on the Causes of War. Englewood Cliffs, NJ: Prentice-Hall.

HOROWITZ, A. D. (1973) "The competitive bargaining set for cooperative n-person games." Journal of Mathematical Psychology.

—— and A. RAPOPORT (1974) "Test of the kernel and two bargaining set models in four- and five-person games," pp. 119-161 in A. Rapoport (ed.) Game Theory, Dordrecht: Reidel.

INBAR, M. (1979) Routine Decision-Making: The Future of Bureaucracy. Beverly Hills, CA: Sage.

International Institute for Strategic Studies (1981) Strategic Survey 1980-1981. London: IISS.

International Peace Academy [ed.] (1978) Peace Keeper's Handbook.

International Studies Quarterly (1977) Special issue (March).

IPI (1980) "Assembly resolutions." IPI Report 29 (May/July): 20.

JAMES, A. (1969) The Politics of Peace-Keeping. London: Chatto-Windus.

JANIS, I. L. (1972) Victims of Groupthink. Boston: Houghton-Mifflin.

JONES, R. W. (1980) "Atomic diplomacy in developing countries." Journal of International Affairs (Spring).

KAHAN, J. P. and A. RAPOPORT (1974) "Test of the bargaining set and kernel models in three-person games," pp. 119-161 in A. Rapoport (ed.) Game Theory. Dordrecht: Reidel.

KAHLER, M. (1979) "Rumors of war: the 1914 analogy." Foreign Affairs 58: 374-396.

KAHN, H. (1965) On Escalation: Metaphors and Scenarios. New York: Praeger.

KAPLAN, M. A. (1965) System and Process in International Politics. New York: Science Editions.

KENDE, I. (1979) "Wars from 1965 to 1978." Peace Research 2: 197-200.

────── (1978) "Wars of ten years, 1967-1976." Journal of Peace Research 15: 227-241.

────── (1971) "Twenty-five years of local war." Journal of Peace Research 8: 5-22.

KENNEDY, R. F. (1969) Thirteen Days: A Memoir of the Cuban Crisis. New York: Norton.

KEOHANE, R. O. and J. S. NYE (1977) Power and Interdependence. Boston: Little, Brown.

KISSINGER, H. A. (1954) "Force and diplomacy in the nuclear age." Foreign Affairs 34: 349-366.

KLIMKIEVICZ, S. (1978) "Crisis management—the state of the art: an Eastern view," pp. 143-154 in D. Frei (ed.) International Crises and Crisis Management. New York: Praeger.

KOLODZIEJ, E. A. and R. E. HARKAVY (1980) "Developing states and the international security system." Journal of International Affairs 1: 59-89.

KOTHARI, S. (1974) Footsteps into the Future. New York: North Holland.

KUMAR-D'SOUZA, C. (1980) "Towards a new international social order." Presented to the Conference of Asian Peace Research in the Global Context, Yokohama.

LAGOS, G. (1963) International Stratification and Atimia. Chapel Hill: University of North Carolina Press.

LAPONCE, J. A. (1981) "The use of in vivo and laboratory experiments in the study of elections." International Political Science Review 2.

────── (1966) "An experimental method to measure the tendency to equibalance in a political system." American Political Science Review 60: 982-993.

────── and P. SMOKER [eds.] (1972) Experimentation and Simulation in Political Science. Toronto: University of Toronto Press.

LAQUER, W. (1968) The Road to Jerusalem. New York: Macmillan.

LATHAM, A.J.H. (1978) The International Economy and the Underdeveloped World. London: Croom Helm.

LAVE, L. B. (1965) "Factors affecting cooperation in the prisoner's dilemma." Behavioral Sciences 1: 26-38.

LEVIN, N. C. Jr. (1970) Woodrow Wilson and World Politics: America's Response to War and Revolution. New York: Oxford University Press.

LEVY, M. (1951) The Structure of Society. Princeton: Princeton University Press.

LOURAU, R. (1970) L'analyse institutionelle. Paris: Editions de Minuit.

LUARD, E. (1968) Conflict and Peace in the Modern International System. Boston: Little, Brown.

LUCKHAM, R. (1979) "Militarism: force, class and international conflict," pp. 232-256 in M. Kaldor and A. Eide (eds.) The Military World Order: The Impact of Military Technology on the Third World. London.

LUKES, S. (1974) Power: A Radical View. London: Macmillan.

LUKOV, V. B. and V. M. SERGEEV (n.d.) Experience of Modelling the Thinking of Historical Decision-makers. Moscow (mimeo).

MADSEN, M. and D. LANCY (1980) "Cooperative and conflictive behavior as related to ethnic identity and urbanization in Papua, New Guinea." Presented at the Shambough Conference, University of Iowa.

MAHONEY, R. B. and R. B. CLAYBERG (1979) Analysis of the Soviet Crisis Management Experiences: Technical Report. Arlington, VA: CACI.

MAZRUI, A. (1976) A World Federation of Cultures. London: Heinemann Education.

McCLELLAND, C. A. and G. D. HOGGART (1969) "Conflict patterns in the interactions among nations," pp. 771-824 in J. N. Rosenau (ed.) International Politics and Foreign Policy. New York: Free Press.

McGRATH, J. E. (1976) "Stress and behavior in organizations," pp. M. Dunnette (ed.) Handbook of Industrial and Organizational Behavior. Chicago: Rand McNally.

MEFFORD, D. (1982) "The Soviet use of force, 1945-1980." Ph.D. Thesis, MIT.

MINTZ, A. (1951) "Non-adaptive group behavior." Journal of Abnormal and Social Psychology 46: 150-159.

MITCHELL, C. R. (1976) "Peace keeping: the police function." The Yearbook of World Affairs 30: 150-173.

MIZUHARA, T. and S. TAMAI (1952) "Experimental studies of cooperation and competition." Japanese Journal of Psychology.

MONTBRIAL, T. de (n.d.) "Perceptions of strategic balance and the Third World conflicts." Adelphi Papers no. 161.

MOROSOW, G. I. (1976) "The United Nations in the light of tendencies of the future," in UNITAR (ed.) The United Nations and the Future. Moscow.

MORSE, E. L. (1976) Modernization and the Transformation of International Relations. New York: Free Press.

——— (1972) "Crisis diplomacy, interdependence and the politics of international economic relations." World Politics 24 (Spring): 123-150.

MÖTTÖLÄ, K. (1979) "Norms and conflict in détente." Presented to the 16th IPSA World Congress, Moscow.

MOVIKOW, J. (1893) Les luttes entre les sociétés humaines et leurs phases successives. Paris: Alcan.

MULLER, E. N. (1980) "The psychology of political violence and protest," pp. 69-99 in T. R. Gurr (ed.) Handbook of Political Conflict. New York: Free Press.

MUSHAKOJI, K. (1980) "From the deference system to a new international order: an extra-Euratlantic point of view," pp. 32-48 in the National Association of Political Science of the GDR (ed.) Detente: Reason—Demands—Obstacles, Vol. 2. Weimar.

——— (1978) "Peace research as an international learning process: a new meta-paradigm." International Studies Quarterly 22 (June): 173-194.

——— (1977) Kokusai Seiji wo Miru Me (An Approach to International Politics). Tokyo.

——— (1971) "The strategies of negotiation: an American-Japanese Comparison," pp. 109-132 in J. A. Laponce and P. Smoker (eds.) Experimentation and Simulation in the Political Sciences. Toronto: University of Toronto Press.

——— (1968) "Negotiation between the West and the non-West: cultural problems in conflict resolution," in Proceedings, Second International Peace Research Association General Congress, Vol. 1.

——— (1960) Gendai France no Seiji Ishiki (Political Consciousness in Modern France). Tokyo.

NEUHOLD, H. P. and C. F. HERMAN (1978) "Principles and implementations of crisis management," pp. 4-19 in D. Frei (ed.) International Crises and Crisis Management.

New York: Praeger.

NICK, S. (1981) "Peaceful resolution of disputes." International Affairs 743.

NOMIKOS, E. V. and R. C. NORTH (1976) International Crisis. Montreal: McGill Queen's University Press.

NORDIN, T. (1980) "Theory and practice in conflict research," in T. R. Gurr (ed.) Handbook of Political Conflict. New York: Free Press.

OSGOOD, C. E. (1962) An Alternative to War or Surrender. Urbana: University of Illinois Press.

PARSONS, T. (1951) The Social System. New York: Free Press.

PERROUX, F. (1954) L'Europe sans rivage. Paris.

PETTMAN, R. (1979) State and Class: A Sociology of International Affairs. London: Croom Helm.

PHILLIPPS, W. R., P. T. CALLAHAN, and R. C. CRAIN (1977) "Simulated foreign policy exchanges: a formal theory of foreign policy interaction." International Relations 3: 345-368.

——— (1974) "Simulated foreign policy exchanges: the rationale underlying a theory of foreign policy interaction." International Interactions 1: 237-254.

PIRAGES, D. C. (1980) "Political stability and conflict management," pp. 425-460 in T. R. Gurr (ed.) Handbook of Political Conflict. New York: Free Press.

POSPELOV, D. A. (1980) "Otto von Bismarck, 1868-1878," in T. R. Gurr (ed.) Handbook of Political Conflict. New York: Free Press.

RAPOPORT, A. (1974a) Conflict in Man-Made Environments. Harmondsworth, Eng.: Penguin.

——— (1974b) Game Theory as a Theory of Conflict Resolution. Boston: Reidel.

——— (1966) "Models of conflict: cataclysmic and strategic," in A. de Reuck (ed.) Conflict in Society. London: Churchill.

——— (1960) Fights, Games and Debates. Ann Arbor: University of Michigan Press.

——— and A. CHAMMAH (1965) Prisoner's Dilemma: A Study in Conflict and Cooperation. Ann Arbor: University of Michigan Press.

RAVEN, B. H. and H. T. EACHUS (1963) "Cooperation and competition in means-interdependent triads." Journal of Abnormal and Social Psychology 62: 307-316.

RESAI, M. (1980) "Theory and research in the study of revolutionary personnel," pp. 100-131 in T. R. Gurr (ed.) Handbook of Political Conflict. New York: Free Press.

REYCHLER, L. (1979) "The effectiveness of a pacifist strategy in conflict resolution: an experimental study." Journal of Conflict Resolution 23: 228-260.

RICHELIEU, Cardinal de (1929) "Testament politique," in Oeuvres du Cardinal de Richelieu. Paris: Tallandier.

RIKER, W. (1967) "Bargaining in a three-person game." American Political Science Review 61: 642-656.

RIKHYE, I. J. et al. (1974) The Thin Blue Lines. New Haven, CT: Yale University Press.

RIVERA, D. (1973) "Toward a theory of political aggression." Presented to the 9th IPSA World Congress, Montreal.

ROBINSON, S. A. (1962) Congress and Foreign Policy Making. Homewood, IL: Dorsey Press.

ROETHLISBERGER, F. J. and W. J. DICKSON (1939) Management and the Worker. Cambridge, MA: Harvard University Press.

ROTH, B. M. (1979) "Competing norms of distribution in coalition games." Journal of Conflict Resolution 23: 513-537.

RUBIN, J., J. BROCKNER, S. SMALL, and S. NATHANSON (1980) "Factors affecting entry into psychological traps." Journal of Conflict Resolution 24: 405-426.

RUGGIE, J. G. (1974) "Contingencies, constraints and collective security: perspectives on UN involvement in international disputes." International Organizations 28: 493-520.

RUSSETT, B. (1981) "Security and the resource scramble: will 1984 be like 1914?" International Affairs 1.

SAFRAN, N. (1979) From War to War: The Arab-Israeli Confrontation, 1948-1967. New York: Pegasus.

SAMIR, A. (1976) Impérialisme et sous-developpement en Afrique. Paris.

SCHANK, R. C. and K. M. COLBY [eds.] (1973) Computer Simulations of Thought and Language. San Francisco: Jossey-Bass.

SCHELLING, T. C. (1971) "The diplomacy of violence," pp. 76-99 in R. J. Art et al. (eds.) The Use of Force: International Politics and Foreign Policy. Boston: Little, Brown.
——— (1960) The Strategy of Conflict. Cambridge, MA: Harvard University Press.

SCHLESINGER, A. (1965) A Thousand Days: J. F. Kennedy in the White House. Boston: Little, Brown.

SCHROEDER, H. M., M. J. DRIVER, and S. STRENFERT (1967) Human Information Processing. New York: Holt & Rinehart.

SCHWARTZ, D. (1967) "Decision making in historical and simulated crises," in C. F. Herman (ed.) International Crisis. Insights from Behavioral Research. New York: Free Press.

SCOTT, A. M. (1977) "The logic of international interaction." International Studies Quarterly 21 (September).

SEIBOLD, D. and T. STEINFAST (1979) "The creative alternative game: exploring interpersonal influence processes." Simulation and Games 10: 429-457.

SHARABI, M. (1970) Palestine: The Lethal Conflict. New York: Pegasus.

SHERIF, M. et al. (1961) Intergroup Conflict and Cooperation: The Robber's Case Experiment. Oklahoma City: The University of Oklahoma Press.

SHURE, G. H., R. J. MEEKER, and E. A. HANSFORD (1963) "The effectiveness of pacifist strategies in bargaining games." Journal of Conflict Resolution 7: 106-117.

SIGAL, L. V. (1979) "Rethinking the unthinkable." Foreign Policy 34: 35-51.

SIMMEL, G. (1908/1955) Conflict. K. Wolff, trans. Glencoe, IL: Free Press.

SINGER, D. J. and M. SMALL (1974) The Wages of War, 1816-1965. Ann Arbor, MI: Inter-University Consortium for Political Research.

SIPRI Yearbook (1980) World Armament and Disarmament. London: Taylor & Francis.

SMOKE, R. (1977) War: Controlling Escalation. Cambridge, MA: Harvard University Press.

SNYDER, G. and P. DIESING (1977) Conflict Among Nations. Princeton, NJ: Princeton University Press.

Der SPIEGEL (1980) Title story, no. 17.

SUEDFELD, P. and P. TETLOCK (1977) "Integrative complexity of communications in international crises." Journal of Conflict Resolution 21 (March): 169-184.
——— and R. CARMENZA (1977) "War, peace and integrative complexity: UN speeches on the Middle East problem, 1947-1966." Journal of Conflict Resolution 21 (March): 427-443.

Sunday Times (1974) The Insight Team. London: Andrew Dutch.

TANAKA, A. (1980) China, China-Watching and China-Watchers. Cambridge, MA: Harvard University Press.

TANTER, R. (1978) "International crisis behavior." Jerusalem Journal of International Relations 3: 340-374.
——— (1975) "Crisis management: a critical review of academic literature." Jerusalem Journal of International Relations 1: 71-107.

THOMAS, E. J. (1957) "Effects of facultative role interdependence on group function-ing." Human Relations 10: 347-366.

TUNSTALL, J. (1977) The Media Are American. London: Constable.

United Nations (1980) Report of the Secretary-General on the World of the Organiza-tions. General Assembly, Official Record: A/35/1, New York.

VIDICH, A. J. (1979) "Legitimation of world regimes in world perspective," in A. J. Vidich and R. M. Glass (eds.) Conflict and Control. Beverly Hills, CA: Sage.

VRIVOHLAVY, J. von (1976) "Psychologie der Kooperation und die Anwendung der Methoden der experimentellen Konflikte." Zeitschrift fuer Psychologie 90: 141-155.

VUKADINOVIĆ, R. (1979) Nonaligned Countries and Detente. Belgrade.

WALLERSTEIN, I. (1980) Capitalisme et economic—du monde: 1540-1640. Paris.

WALTZ, K. (1981) "The spread of nuclear weapons: more may be better." Adelphi Papers no. 175.

——— (1959) Man, the State and War: A Theoretical Analysis. New York: Free Press.

WASKOW, A. I. (1964) "Nonlethal equivalents of war," in R. Fisher (ed.) International Conflict and Behavioral Sciences. New York: Harper & Row.

WELTMAN, J. J. (1981) "Managing nuclear multipolarity." International Security 3.

WHITING, A. R. (1960) China Crosses the Yalu: The Decision to Enter the Korean War. New York: Macmillan.

WIEGELE, T. C. (1978) "The psychophysiology of elite stress in five international crises: a preliminary test of a voice measurement technique." International Studies 22 (Decem-ber): 467-511.

WILLIAMS, F. (1976) Crisis Management. New York: John Wiley.

WORKIE, A. (1967) "The effect of cooperation and competition on productivity." Ph.D. dissertation, Columbia University.

YERKES, A. M. and J. D. DODSON (1980) "The relation of strength and stimulus to rapidity of habit formation." Journal of Comparative and Neurological Psychology 18.

YOUNG, O. R. (1967) The Intermediaries: Third Parties in International Crises. Prince-ton, NJ: Princeton University Press.

ZACHER, M. W. (1979) International Conflicts and Collective Security, 1946-1977. New York: Praeger.

ZHURKIN, V. C. (1975) SSA i medzdunarodno-politiceskie krizisi. Moscow.

ZIMMERMAN, E. (1980) "Macro-comparative research on political protest," pp. 167-237 in T. R. Gurr (ed.) Handbook of Political Conflict. New York: Free Press.

ZINNES, D. A. (1966) "A comparison of hostile behavior of decision-makers in simulated and historical data." World Politics 18: 474-502.

ABOUT THE
CONTRIBUTORS

HAYWARD R. ALKER, Jr. is Professor and Director of Graduate Studies in the Department of Political Science at the Massachusetts Institute of Technology. For six years he was the Convenor of the IPSA Research Committee on Quantitative and Mathematical Approaches to Politics. In addition to having authored, co-authored, or edited numerous books and articles in the field of international organization studies, he has recently edited a special issue of *Poznan Studies on Dialectical Logics for the Political Sciences*. He is currently writing a book on *The Dialectics of World Order*.

ROBERTO DE OLIVEIRA CAMPOS is Brazilian Ambassador to the Court of St. James (i.e., to Great Britain). Before entering the foreign service he was Professor of Money and Banking and Business Cycles at the School of Economics, University of Brazil. From 1964-1967 he served as Minister of State for Planning and Coordination. In addition to having authored many reports for GATT, the World Bank, and other international institutions, he has published nine books on various problems of economic development and related topics.

KING-YUH CHANG is Professor of International Relations and Director of the Institute of International Relations (IIR), Taipei, Taiwan, Republic of China. He received his Ph.D. from Columbia University. In 1974 he assumed the chairmanship of the Department of Diplomacy of National Chengchi University. He was also an American Council of Learned Societies Fellowship grantee, spending a year at the School of Advanced International Studies, Johns Hopkins University, as a visiting fellow. He then served as Deputy Director of the IIR and Professor at the Department of Diplomacy, National Chengchi

University. His articles and essays on international relations and China studies have appeared in various scholarly periodicals around the world.

ALI E. HILLAL DESSOUKI is Professor at the Faculty of Economics and Political Science, Cairo University (Egypt). During his academic career, he has taught at McGill University, the American University in Cairo, The University of California—Los Angeles, and Princeton University. He has written extensively in Arabic and English on Arab politics. In English he has been editor of and contributor to: *Democracy in Egypt, Islam and Power, The Iraq-Iran War*, and *Islamic Resurgence in the Arab World*; and co-author of *The Political Economy of Income Distribution in Egypt* and *The New Arab Order*. He is currently writing a book on Egypt.

KARL W. DEUTSCH is Stanfield Professor of International Peace at Harvard University and Director of the International Institute for Comparative Social Research at the Science Center in Berlin. He received a JUDr. from Charles University, Prague, and a Ph.D. from Harvard University, and in addition holds six honorary degrees. From 1969-1970 and 1976-1979, respectively, he was President of the American Political Science Association (APSA) and of the International Political Science Association (IPSA). His books, many of which have been translated into other languages, are: *Nationalism and Social Communication, Political Community at the International Level, Nerves of Government, Analysis of International Relations, Politics and Government, Tides Among Nations*, and *Comparative Government*.

DANIEL FREI is Professor of Political Science at the University of Zurich (Switzerland). He received his education at the University of Zurich, the London School of Economics and Political Science, the Graduate Institute of International Studies, Geneva, and the University of Michigan. He is the author, co-author, or editor of the following books in English: *International Crises and Crisis Management, Evolving a Conceptual Framework for Inter-Systems Relations, Definitions and Measurement of Détente, East-West Relations in Europe: A Systematic Survey*, and *The Risk of Unintentional Nuclear War*.

NIELS HANSEN, before his present appointment as Ambassador of the Federal Republic of Germany to Israel, served as Head of the

Planning Staff of the Foreign Office, Bonn. His previous assignments include the directorship of the sections for European Integration and the Mediterranean in the Foreign Office, Bonn.

JEAN A. LAPONCE is Professor of Political Science at the University of British Columbia, Vancouver, Canada. His main interests are the study of political perceptions, ethnic conflicts, and experimentation on small groups. His main works include: *The Protection of Minorities; The Government of France under the Fifth Republic; People vs. Politics;* and *Left and Right: The Topology of Political Perceptions.* Those of his publications directly relevant to this volume are: *Experimentation and Simulation in Political Science*; "An experimental method to measure the tendency to equibalance in a political system" (*American Political Science Review*, 1966); "Voting for x" (*Social Science Information*, 1980); and "Experimentation and Elections" (*The International Political Science Review*, 1981).

VADIM B. LUKOV is a senior research fellow of the Laboratory of Systems Analysis of International Relations, Moscow State Institute of International Relations. He graduated from the same institute in 1975 as a Candidate of science (history). His current research sphere includes systems analysis of European security and cooperation problematique. He is co-author of *World Socialism and Problems of Developing Countries* (Moscow, 1979) and *Definitions and Measurement of Détente* (Cambridge, Massachusetts, 1981) and has authored a number of articles on problems of European security and cooperation and on the methodology of political negotiations analysis.

JOHN MEISEL was Hardy Professor of Political Science at Queen's University (Canada) until 1980 when he became Chairman of the Canadian Radio-Television and Telecommunications Commission. He is general editor of the *International Political Science Review*.

RICHARD L. MERRITT is Professor (and Head of the Department) of Political Science and Research Professor in Communications, University of Illinois at Urbana-Champaign. His research has focused on politics in the Federal Republic of Germany and on quantitative approaches to international communications. He has been Vice-President of the International Political Science Association and the International Studies Association.

KARI MÖTTÖLÄ is Director of the Finnish Institute of International Affairs and editor in chief of *Ulkopolitikka* and *Yearbook of Finnish*

Foreign Policy. He has done research on security policy issues in Northern Europe and Europe, East-West economic relations, and nuclear arms control. Presently involved in a study on the nonproliferation regime, he worked formerly as a journalist before joining the Institute in 1978 and has acted as its Director since 1978.

KINHIDE MUSHAKOJI is Vice-Rector for Regional and Global Studies at the United Nations University, Tokyo, Japan. He previously worked as Director of the Institute of International Relations, Sophia University, and Professor of Political Science, Gakushuin University. He has published various articles in scholarly journals and is the author of *Behavioral Science and International Politics* and *Scientific Revolution and Multi-Paradigmatic Dialogue.*

VICTOR M. SERGEEV is a senior research fellow at the Laboratory of Systems Analysis of International Relations, Moscow State Institute of International Relations. He graduated from the Moscow Power Engineering Institute in 1967 and from the Moscow University in 1970 as a Candidate of science (physics and mathematics). His current research involves the modeling of the human thinking process. He is the co-author of *Definitions and Measurement of Détente* (Cambridge, Massachusetts, 1981) and has written a number of articles on political thinking and on the methodology of political negotiations analysis.

FRANK L. SHERMAN is a graduate student in the Political Science Department at Pennsylvania State University. He has been a research consultant at the Center for International Studies at the Massachusetts Institute of Technology. His thesis research is focused on the politics of recognizing and responding to international disputes.

RADOVAN VUKADINOVIĆ is Dean of the Faculty of Political Sciences, Director of the Post-Graduate Program in International Affairs, and editor in chief of the Yugoslav political quarterly, *Politicka misao.* He is the author of numerous books and articles published in Yugoslavia and abroad, among them *Relations among Socialist States: CMEA-WTO, International Relations, European Security and Cooperation, Theories of International Relations,* and *Theory of Foreign Policy.*